The Right Corporate Governance

Fredmund Malik

The Right Corporate Governance

Effective Top Management for
Mastering Complexity

Translated from German by Jutta Scherer,
JS textworks (Munich, Germany)

Campus Verlag
Frankfurt/New York

The original edition was published in 2008 by Campus Verlag with the title *Die richtige Corporate Governance. Mit wirksamer Unternehmensaufsicht Komplexität meistern.* All rights reserved.

The chapters Introduction to the English Edition, Preface to the English Edition and Terminology Aspects are
reproduced from Fredmund Malik: *Effective Top Management. Beyond the Failure of Corporate Governance and Shareholder Value,* page 9–22, 2006. Copyright Wiley-VCH Verlag GmbH & Co. KGaA. Reproduced with permission.

ISBN 978-3-593-39695-8

Copyright © 2012 Campus Verlag GmbH, Frankfurt am Main.
All rights reserved.
Cover design: Hißmann, Heilmann, Hamburg
Typesetting: Fotosatz L. Huhn, Linsengericht
Printing: Beltz Bad Langensalza
Printed in Germany

This book is also available as an E-Book.
www.campus.de

Contents

Part I

Introduction to the English Edition

Rarely before has a greater doctrine been spread in so short a time as the American doctrine of shareholder value and stock-market-related value creation as the central factors of corporate governance. Rarely before was anything also proclaimed with so much smugness and self-righteousness as this false doctrine. It is wrong and damaging for the management of a company.

It would have been possible to leave the question unanswered for a while as to whether the shareholder value doctrine is suitable as a management philosophy, at least for the USA itself. But the scandals and corporate collapses indicate the opposite, and so far it is also not possible to see that the correct steps for corporate management are being taken.

The damage that has already been done all over the world is immense; but even more is probably yet to come. The financial losses are not even the most important thing, although these, too, are larger than at any other time. It is the immaterial damage that counts. Much more significant than the money are top management's loss of credibility and the loss of trust in the senior management of large corporations. Added to this is the far-reaching miseducation of two generations of managers, who have learned nothing apart from the doctrine of shareholder value and who are incapable of imagining that it is false and that there are alternatives to it. They are so miseducated that the necessary retraining is difficult or impossible.

In the meantime, doubts about the magic recipes have spread. Lack of orientation and perplexity have arisen; the result is helplessness. According to temperament, what follows may be either lethargy or activism. It is time to stop imitating American management methods, in particular those for corporate governance.

Two errors in reasoning have led to the naïve imitation of seemingly superior US management methods. The first is that the US economy is strong. In fact, it is merely large. The second error is to believe that the reason for this strength is that the management of US companies is good and superior to management all over the world. In fact, American management can only be used where it has to deal with simple conditions. For complex, multicultural, or even global tasks it is unsuitable and damaging.

The US economy is in a desperate state, which is disguised by wrong figures, tendentious media reporting, and a dubious economic theory. Neither the growth rates for the economy nor the employment figures are correct; the profit figures for companies are not right and the economic recovery is not worth mentioning when it is compared with the six recessions since the Second World War. The theory of economics dominant in the USA, that of the "asset-based, wealth-driven economy", is one of economics history's ironies.

America has large companies that impress managers around the world and stimulate imitation. The USA does not owe the size of its companies to the quality of their management. US companies are large because they have something that has never otherwise existed in a developed country, namely, a big and largely homogeneous domestic market. It is no wonder that large companies arise where there are about 290 million consumers who all speak the same language, who pay in the same currency, and who, to a large extend, have a mentality which makes the consumers receptive to uniform advertising and promotion and which makes uniform product design possible. Management is simple when there are no customs frontiers to be overcome and where regulations and tax laws are all the same. None of this existed in Europe until a short time ago. We can only envy the Americans for their comfortable situation; we shouldn't imitate them.

The export quota of the typical US company is small or nonexistent; that of the typical European company is large. America is an importing nation; Europe lives from export. Where English is not spoken, the USA is by no means, as people like to believe, the center of global thought and business activity. On the contrary, the center lies where more than five hundred years ago business relations existed with China and Japan, without E-mail, cell phones, and jet planes, and where hardly any fuss is being made about globalization because it has long been nothing particularly new. That center is Europe.

For the reasons mentioned, it is much easier to manage a large company in the USA than in Europe. There is therefore no cause to look at America in order to learn about management for complex situations. American management is like doing the standard compulsory figures in ice-skating; managing a large company in Europe is like doing the more demanding freestyle.

As a result of the shareholder value doctrine, a type of manager has reached the very top of major companies who previously would hardly have had a chance: the money-driven manager, who is unable to distinguish the logic of the real, nonfinancial economy from that of the financial economy, because for him the only thing that exists is what can be quantified in money. This type of manager could be described as the *monetarist manager.* This has little or absolutely nothing to do with good corporate management. Genuine management begins in any case where quantification, especially quantification in money, is no longer possible but where nevertheless decisions and action have to be taken.

Consistent in his error, the monetarist manager believes that the supreme goal of a company is profit, because he is not able to see that in a market economy there are essentially no profits but only costs: the costs of current business and the costs necessary to stay in business. This type of manager is also not capable of distinguishing between dealmakers and genuine entrepreneurs or between the company as the object of crafty financial moves and the company as a productive social system.

The shareholder value doctrine has failed and what is thought to be its salvation, the stakeholder approach, is a step backwards. The americanized managers with their MBAs will now have to change their ideas quickly and fundamentally. They will have to construct a completely different notion of the company which does not focus on interest groups, either shareholders or stakeholders, but on the company itself. The company itself, its health, and its viability have to form the criterion for corporate governance.

Those managers holding an MBA will also have to learn that managing a company does not consist in solving case studies but in exactly the opposite, namely recognizing where what case could be brewing. If everything can be put down in writing nice and neatly in a case study, a case is no longer a problem but merely the carrying out of work. If a business plan à la business schools can be drawn up, others have long done the work, because they reacted to the faint signals instead of waiting for the ten-year cashflow analysis. Business administration is what the name says it is: *administration* and not anticipatory, entrepreneurial, or even strategic action.

This generation will find that the orienting factors propagated around the world as ultimate truths – shareholders, stakeholders, value creation – are in fact the opposite, namely disorienting factors. For this reason, lack of orientation and perplexity are already to be seen in top management; they are less and less easily concealed, even if still glossed over with posturing and showing off.

Preface to the English Edition

In this book I take a view of corporate governance that is fundamentally different from the more or less prevalent view taken in the second half of the nineties. To a major degree, it is diametrically opposed to this latter view. Right from the very beginning, and unlike virtually everybody else, I have taken as my point of departure not wealth for the shareholders but the ability of the company to perform. My thoughts have been focused on the strong, healthy, and viable company and on the question of how it should be managed and supervised.

There have been comments on the subject suggesting that there are no real but only apparent differences between the two ideas – shareholder value on the one hand, and the high-performing company on the other. It has been said that in fact they are the same thing or are very closely related. Above all, it has been claimed that an orientation to shareholder value necessarily and automatically produces a healthy company. I have always had a different opinion and, for logical and empirical reasons, have never accepted this latter view.

It is now being shown, in a fairly dramatic way, that this view is in fact utterly wrong; that not only is it not correct, but that actually the opposite has happened: the shareholders have become poor and the companies weak, and some of them are in a desperate state.

The inspiration for this book came from Germany. However, I did not want to confine myself to the situation in Germany but wished instead to consider the topic of corporate governance on a broader basis. The legal context in different countries certainly varies, but the management issues are the same everywhere, and to a large extent the answers are also the same. Management forms and styles may differ, but in the end there is only one kind of management; namely, good and effective management. In my view, that can be achieved everywhere regardless of the differing legal contexts.

I have thus chosen a general terminology and use the expressions *governing body* or *corporate governance* for the German or Austrian supervisory board and also for what, in my view, the Swiss administrative board has in common with it – and for what they should both be doing. The term *executive body* relates to the role of the board of German or Austrian joint-stock companies, the management of companies with limited liability, and Swiss businesses, which are normally joint-stock companies. *Top management* and *corporate management* almost always mean both of these bodies unless it is clear form the context that is not the case.

This book necessarily deals with the corporate management of a business, for the governing body cannot be understood nor logically controlled without the executive body, and vice versa. It is however written primarily from the perspective of and with regard to the governing body. For this reason, important topics relating solely to the executive body are not considered here. Executive top management alone would of course justify a book in itself, and thus the aspects examined here are primarily those regarding the *interaction* of these corporate bodies.

The basic premise of this book is that corporate governance *can* and *should* manage – in a quite specific sense of course and while upholding the executive body's integrity and ability to function. In countries with a one-tier corporate management structure, this is self-evident. What is not always quite so clear, however, is how this should be done in practice. In countries with a two-tier system, this topic may initially prompt certain skepticism or even be perceived as provocative. Nonetheless, I consider it essential to strive for this solution for reasons that I hope will be made clear in this book.

My intention is not to produce another scientific treatise to add to the scores already in existence. This book is instead intended as a practical guide to the effective design of corporate management and in particular corporate governance. Hence, special cases and exceptional situations are not discussed.

Since the heart of the trouble as I see it is not the advisory bodies as such but the errors of corporate governance, I have changed the original title of this book by making what was previously the subtitle into the title. In that can also be found the starting points for the required reorientation and for the restoration of the economy to a healthy state. However, the key to right and good governance is, of course, the top management, its executive body, and its supervisory body. It is the supervisory body that has the final responsibility; it is there that the expert knowledge is needed; it is there that the courage has to be shown to take a stand against the trends of the day and the idiocies of fashion and, something that is seldom appreciated, it is the supervisory body that is the correcting mechanism that operates in advance of the market. The market does work, but there are important ways in which it works too late. The market does not prevent mistakes, it simply punishes them. They have to be prevented by the top management and, in the final analysis by the supervisory body.

The first edition of this book appeared in German at the beginning if the period when a whole system of errors and misunderstandings relating to the term corporate governance, at the center of which was shareholder value, was being generally propagated.

For the second edition, which appeared (also in German) at the end of 1998 or, in other words, in the middle of the great stock exchange boom, I wrote in the preface that the growth in the American economy appeared to be an exception to the general stagnation, but that in fact the potential there for an implosion or for instability had become not smaller but greater. Those were the days when people still believed that in the "New Economy" there would never again be any cyclical ups and downs, and one well-known economist took the view that "this expansion will run forever".

The third edition, which is here translated into English, appeared at the beginning of the phase of disillusionment and doubt about the correctness of shareholder value as a guiding principle for sustainable corporate management. My view is that that really does mark the beginning of the end for this economic and management paradigm. I mentioned the short life that could be conjectured for it in chapter 4 of this first edition of this book. There are more and more indications that its decline could be accompanied by a collapse of those economies that believed this approach should be followed with particular exactness. There have already been some initial cases of this.

I saw no reason to make any amendments to the text of the book. The Great Transformation of business and society that is described in chapter 3 is in full swing. Neither at the time nor now was there any reason to interpret this as any sort of "New Economy", even though, by the time it comes to an end, we shall probably have a New Society. And the errors of management described in this book are continuing to be made, though in some cases under different names. As I mentioned in the preface to the second edition, they have also been joined by a few more.

Rather than making amendments to the text, I have written a detailed new introduction, in which I start by giving a summary of the position I adopt and relate it to the developments since the book first appeared.

I have also added two appendices, in which I discuss two particular subjects in detail. The first of these subjects is the fact that the much-lauded American economic miracle was not a genuine miracle but a phony one. This is an important point because the American economy, which appeared to be booming in contrast to the stagnating economies in Europe, was the strongest argument in favor of the claimed superiority, and hence the spread of the shareholder value theory, as well as the sort of corporate governance that was based on it.

The second appendix is a discussion of the other "miracle" that the advocates of the wrong sort of corporate governance appeal to for support, that of the "New Economy". Both these miracles have proved to be deceptive mirages; unfortunately though only after the false management doctrines based on them had had their effect.

The book is divided into two parts. The first part considers the direction in which corporate governance should develop and why. Chapter 1 raises the question whether corporate governance should manage. Chapter 2 looks at how the governing body functions today and where its functional shortcomings are. The third chapter considers the question of whether corporate governance is equipped for the future, even if one feels it has been so in the past and is in the present. It also looks at whether corporate governance is properly prepared and effective enough for the radical changes currently experienced by economy and society in almost very country, for what I call the Great Transformation. Chapter 4 is devoted to the question of the standards by which an enterprise should be managed and in whose interest an enterprise should be run, regardless of industry and business area. It is in my view essential that the governing body should be involved in clarifying these issues and have the last word in answering them. Following this, the fifth chapter discusses the variables and benchmarks for assessing a business, in particular in the light of the question of what a healthy business is and how its health can be assessed.

The second part looks at the "what" and "how" of corporate management. Chapter 6 provides a brief overview of the elements of the company constitution (also known as corporate bylaws). Chapters 7 and 8 consider the issues surrounding the formation of supervisory and executive bodies, their roles, how they function, and the principles for their effectiveness.

Chapter 9 takes a view on the differences between management and leadership, the latter of which is threatening to become a fashion trend. It is precisely the top corporate bodies that need to look very closely at this difference, for it is from the top of a business, if anywhere, that leadership stems. Chapter 10 goes to the very heart of the problems of power, responsibility, and liability. And chapter 11 examines the key issues of personnel selection and recruitment to the most senior positions.

The book is thus intended first and foremost for top managers and for all owners of company shares. It should further be of interest to anyone who has to work with senior managers or those on the higher managerial echelons. And finally, it may well be of use to anyone with a broad interest in general business management or who has to take an interest in it for professional reasons – for anyone who has any interest in a well-functioning economy and society.

The economy is unmistakably in a phase of experimentation. Solutions need to be found for new problems, and seldom before has it been possible to study attempts to do so and the effects of them so well. The basic tasks of corporate governance I describe in this book are therefore still highly topical.

A brief word about individuals' and company names: descriptions of actual cases and examples would perhaps have been useful illustrations in the book, and may also have pandered to the public's taste for sensation. However, I have exercised extreme restraint in this regard. Although I am quite familiar with a few real-life examples of dramatic failure by supervisory and executive bodies, I do not think it is right to detail dates, facts, and names. It is my opinion that name-dropping does not provide any useful information; furthermore, it could wrongly implicate people whose involvement was not causal, and in many cases even the person actually responsible may previously have produced excellent performances in other domains. As I will establish, success and failure do not depend solely on people but also and to a considerable extent on the situation in which they are placed – a situation that they all too often did not seek out. In the final analysis, this is no excuse; the consequences of failure cannot be ignored. However, people and situations must be considered in close relationship with each other.

That is precisely what why I make no attempt to improve the effectiveness of corporate governance primarily by *people-driven* proposals, but instead by *constitutional* controls. This thinking pervades the whole book and is, as I am often able to see at first-hand, largely a new concept for business managers with a technical of scientific background. Lawyers in contrast have no problem in accepting it. They know from their own discipline that if anything will work, a constitutional solution will.

Where I do name people in this book, I have abided by the following principles: first, the people are no longer alive – in fact in most cases they died quite some time ago. I know there is huge interest in examples of today, but in my view a certain chronological detachment is needed to be able to come to a relatively reliable assessment of someone's performance. In the media world of today, judgments – and prejudices – are, it seems to me, made too hastily and without proper thought. Second, other than a few exceptions, which seem well justified, I have only mentioned people in positive terms. Third, I only use the names of people where I believe I have studied their lives in sufficient depth to be able to form an opinion. I have no truck with the popular game of "name dropping". Based on these principles, I hope I have dealt fairly and honestly with a topic that is discussed almost exclusively in terms of personal categories.

The views expressed in this book come from a number of sources. They stem from experience I have gathered in my professional activity with top management bodies as a consultant and as an active member. A further source is the numerous talks with managers who are on governing bodies or who work with governing bodies as executive managers. Furthermore, the content of all the chapters in this book have formed the material of countless lectures and above all seminars I have held for thousands of managers over the past twenty years. I have been able to learn a great deal from the ensuing discussions, and in this perspective, the views expressed here and the suggestions proffered have most certainly been put to the test. Without any false modesty, I would also say that a large number of current managers and entrepreneurs have told me that these seminars have helped them gain a new and better perspective.

I would like to thank the many managers with whom it has been possible for me to discuss the problems of corporate governance in seminars and at lectures and whose critical attitude demonstrated that they had quickly and rightly become concerned about the direction in which things were developing. They became so because their experience told them there was something about this loudly trumpeted new type of corporate management that could not be right.

Although they were also obliged to pay lip service to what the stock-exchange analysts were saying, they managed their companies from totally different and correct points of view. They kept quiet for a time for tactical reasons, because they needed to spend their time on something more important, namely on managing their companies well. And perhaps they did not always have their counterarguments ready to hand, neatly grouped and organized, particularly when the "experts" tried to make a big impression with complicated formulars for calculating things. What they had instead, though, was a great sense of what is right and what is not, which is perhaps the most important ability that competent managers can have. Also influential in writing this book was the outcome of discussions stretching over one and a half years in a focus group initiated by Dr Dana Schuppert and run by Mr Hans-Wolfgang Pfeifer on the functioning of the German supervisory board. The following people belonged to this focus group: † Dr Dr hc Reinhard Goerdeler, accountant and solicitor, Dusseldorf; Dr Wolf R. Klinz, deputy chairman of the board of Lurgi AG, Frankfurt am Main; Dr Heiko Lange, member of the board of Deutsche Lufthansa AG, Frankfurt am Main; Dr Frank Niethammer, president of the Chamber of Trade and Industry, Frankfurt am Main; Dipl.-Ing. Dr-Ing. Eh Hermann Franz, chairman of the supervisory board, Siemens AG, Munich; Dr Guido Sandler, personally liable shareholder Dr A. Oetker, Bielefeld; Dr Horst Teltschik, member of the board of BMW AG, Munich; Rüdiger von Tresckow, Palm & Partner, Frankfurt am Main; Dr Udo N. Wagner, member of the board of ABB AG, Mannheim.

I would also like to thank Professor Dr Hans Siegwart for reading the manuscript with the critical eye of the business manager and experienced administrative board member, and for his valuable suggestions. My thanks also go to Ms Ruth Blumer for her typing, and to Mr Hans-Wolfgang Pfeifer for his patience. He could not believe the number of manuscripts passed to him. I would also like to express my special gratitude to Dr Dana Schuppert, who ensured with such kindness and determination that I actually started and finished this book. She performed her task of coach judiciously and efficiently.

Terminological Aspects

The discussion about corporate governance over the past ten years has been strongly influenced by the juridical perspective. At the time when corporate law in most of the highly developed countries came into existence, one actually knew little about corporate management. This fact dominates the legal standards and how to deal with them until today. Particularly the latest reforms, which have been implemented under the influence of the corporate governance debate – and above all under the pressure of corporate governance scandals – show how little modern knowledge about management has been incorporated into legal reforms.

I wrote this book accordingly from another standpoint, namely, from the perspective of management. Only when the question of what is effective and good business leadership is answered can a comprehensive body of legislative norms within the framework of the general legal system be created. One of the many results of this book has been hereby proved: that effective management is possible under all current legal systems as they developed, as different as they may be, especially when one compares the Anglo-Saxon and the German laws.

Proper management does not depend on the technical terminology within the individual legal systems. I have therefore not paid special attention to the question of terminology and intentionally use general concepts, based on German usage, throughout. Nevertheless, the English-speaking reader may find the following definitions helpful:

Top management: The highest leadership organ or body, including both the executive and supervisory bodies together, independent of any particular juridical conceptualization.

Corporate governance: The institution that oversees the managing executive body of a corporation to ensure that the latter is fulfilling its mission and running effectively vis-à-vis internal and external factors.

This term is used interchangeably with *governing body* and *supervisory body*.

Executive body: In the German joint-stock company (AG), the board of managers (*Vorstand*) in its entirety; in the company with limited liability, the top managers (president, chief executive officer, etc.) as a whole. In other legal systems there are other combinations between the executives and the advisory board.

Supervisory body: In the German joint-stock company, this is the advisory board (*Aufsichtsrat*), also referred to here as the *governing body*. It is comparable to the Anglo-Saxon board of directors. In other legal systems there are combinations between executives and the advisory board.

Chairman of the governing body: In German, the chairman of the supervisory board (*Vorsitzender des Aufsichtsrats*), comparable to the chairman of the board in English. Under German law there is no connection between the chairs of the executive and supervisory bodies, as there is between the chairman of the board and the CEO.

Board of managers: In German this is the *Vorstand*, or executive board. These managers fulfill their duties as a collective, and their liability is collective as well, regardless of their internal organization.

Chairman of the board of managers: There is no comparable position in the Anglo-Saxon community; the best parallel would be the CEO. The German *Vorsitzender des Vorstands*, however, is not at all related to the CEO, even though that is often claimed on business cards and other documents. The realm of powers of the CEO are large, nearly limitless; those of the chairman of the board of managers are very small. He leads the meetings of the board of managers and coordinates the domain of the *Vorstand*; he is however not the superior of its members and has no supervisory authority over them. The members are appointed and recalled by the so-called governing body (*Aufsichtsrat*). Disciplinary questions are handled by the supervisory board, in most cases in a committee.

Preface

This book was written for *practitioners*, in particular those in charge of the overall governance of organizations, who are determined to carry out their task with diligence and to manage correctly and well. These can be practitioners in any function: members of administrative and supervisory boards or executive officers and their shareholders. It is intended, above all, for those who will not content themselves with fulfilling legal diligence duties, but who strive for entrepreneurial success, nothing less.

Current corporate governance practices are far from achieving that. In my view, virtually all business failures since the mid-1990s have been caused in one way or another by the kind of corporate governance that emerged at that time. Owing to the current corporate governance theory, *wrong* corporate management has been legitimized as "best practice" and disseminated through negligent consulting practices, executive searches, governance ratings, as well as through Wall Street marketing, MBA programs, and a host of business media. I use the term "negligent" because, contrary to widespread opinion, it is very well possible to define what *right* corporate management is. My understanding of it is laid out in this as well as my other books.

Successful companies are successful because in essential points – and without violating any rules – the way they are managed is altogether at odds to what today's corporate governance standards suggest. Therefore, a right and sustainable way of doing business requires radical reforms: the present corporate governance theory needs to be turned around by 180 degrees, specifically when the interests of real shareholders – not those of investor-type shareholders – are to be protected and high returns are to be achieved.

I would not venture such statements were I not able to base them on many years of personal experience as a member and chairman of several top management and governance bodies, where I have been able to see what right approaches and what wrong ones are, what is feasible and what is not. From an outsider's point of view, it is impossible to make a reasonable judgment of the professionalism and effectiveness of such panels; much less is it possible to form an accurate opinion based on the numbers in published accounts. External ratings are therefore presumptuous. But even supposedly scientific surveys, though they may be based on interviews with experienced individuals, do not permit an objective, fact-based judgment.

It is my contention that, in the absence of any personal experience, it is impossible to acquire a sound knowledge of how top management bodies and corporate governance function and that, consequently, it is just as impossible to judge them or make workable suggestions for improvement. The information required in order to do so – not to mention the necessary theoretical knowledge – can only be gained in many years of active participation in such bodies in a responsible function, preferably not only in good times but also in periods of crisis. I have repeatedly experienced such crises, and there have even been cases where the problems were beyond solution because earlier mistakes and failures had done too much damage.

It is only in situations like those that one will truly experience the reality of corporate governance, and that the true nature of those in charge, their skills, character traits and personalities will be revealed. This is where courage and cowardice, competence and failure come to light – and where it is made very clear what *true* leadership is, as opposed to the naïve and deluded theories that have become fashionable; for it takes a crisis to prove true leadership. It will become evident what works and what doesn't when there is maximum complexity, dynamics, and risk. In circumstances like these, people learn to appreciate the value of knowing the laws of science, which reliably help us to master complexity and to find solutions even where others have long given up trying. With existing corporate governance and the constraints it imposes on management bodies, it is possible neither to master a crisis nor to take advantage of entrepreneurial opportunities – which is just as important.

This book was written at the time when the general corporate governance debate was beginning to intensify. Back then I already had plenty of hands-on top management experience, which I had gained by closely working with companies and corporate leaders, actively participating in top-level management boards, and pursuing my own entrepreneurial activities. Its substance is still valid today.

Some of my key suggestions have been taken up by practitioners, for instance with regard to the size and composition, workings, and management of supervisory boards. Another thing that has largely been implemented is the much-needed two-tier structure of corporate governance, which has been fully established in the UK but not in the United States. In other crucial points, such as the substance of right and good management, current corporate governance practice is still off the track or has not found the courage to formulate clear statements.

I have added a new introduction to this book in chapter 1. It should help readers to get an overview of the major developments that have taken place since the book was first published, and what developments have been missed.

Apart from this book's practical relevance, the reason it remains valid and relevant is that the issues it deals with differ greatly from those generally addressed in the general corporate governance debate. The central question here is: what is right and good corporate governance? In other words, this book is about what top managers need to do to ensure proper corporate governance.

That is in stark contrast to the prevalent view of governance, which chiefly focuses on legal and financial aspects. My aim is not to remind readers of the formal rules of the Stock Corporation Act; rather, I am getting deep into the question of how companies, and thus the business world as a whole, can function properly in a society and a world that are increasingly complex.

Needless to say, good corporate governance will always occur within the boundaries of the relevant legal framework, and will always have to involve financial considerations. Both, however, must be derived from a concept of right governance, not the other way round. After all, the success of corporations is a result of their standing the test of the world market – with globalized business, science, and technology changing at an unprecedented pace, combined with the realities of a radically transforming society. Business success is never a result of a company's abiding by the law, the basic principles of which (despite numerous amendments) go back to as far as the early 20th and even the 19th century.

In other words: the provisions of the law and the corporate governance codes will have to be adapted to the functional principles of institutions that form parts of highly complex global systems, not vice versa. The functional principles of mastering complexity are governed by the laws of nature, just like the functional principles of technology. And the laws of nature cannot be changed with legal provisions and codes.

Wherever this simple fact is not accepted, there will soon be no business sector at all, nor a functioning society, because other countries are able to shape their rules with a view to the future and to align their institutions with the complex circumstances of the 21st century, not with the past.

This book, and my entire work for right and good management, have been influenced by my day-to-day work with practitioners – top managers, entrepreneurs, and those working with them most closely – as well as by my own activities as an entrepreneur and as the owner of the largest and leading Swiss firm in the field of top management consulting and education.

In over 30 years I have probably met more executives than most other people ever will, working with them, giving them advice, and training them in all matters of corporate general management, corporate policy and strategy, structural and organizational issues, corporate culture, and in building top management teams as well as functioning governance bodies. The positions I espouse in this book have proven their worth in hundreds of cases, having been applied in cooperation with managers and entrepreneurs. As for the scientific basis for these views, I provided them in my 1976 professorial thesis entitled *Strategie des Managements komplexer Systeme* ("Strategy of the Management of Complex Systems"). In the same thesis, I also explained and provided my reasoning for why cybernetics, as a science of control, regulation and steering, is the only valid foundation for functioning management and why the economic sciences fail to provide that foundation.

Ever since then, building on the foundations laid in my thesis, I have developed and tested a comprehensive, universal, and modular general management system, published it in several books, and created the organization required for its implementation, with the world's largest staff of general management experts operating from an international office network.

The rapidly increasing complexity of all societal systems calls for professionalism in the management profession, applying technical and conceptual standards of the kind that has long been known for all sophisticated professions. There should be no room for wrong theories, for fashions, and for rotten compromises. Functioning reliably under the conditions of high and increasing complexity should be the maxim for the 21st century:

this is how we can prevent evolution from being destroyed by stagnation or revolution.

June 2008   Fredmund Malik

Chapter 1

New Introduction 2008: A Drastic Cure to Ensure a Functioning Corporate Governance

Corporate Governance Must Transform Into Functioning Management

Corporate governance, and the corporate governance codes suitable for it, need to be aligned with the established principles of right and good corporate management – that is to say, with functioning management rather than the kind of formal rules that can be filled with virtually any content you like.

Corporate governance, as it is currently understood, is a much-discussed but, for the most part, very misguided step in the history of modern corporate management. It is correct in that it attributes great significance to top management, in particular the supervisory function, as compared to the way things used to be before. It is wrong in three respects: with regard to the content of corporate governance, with regard to the actual tasks of the top management bodies, and, consequently, with regard to their design and modus operandi.

An argument frequently put forward is that it is impossible to say what right corporate governance is. I think this view stems from a lack of knowledge about management, for much of what constitutes right and good corporate governance can be sufficiently well defined for practical purposes. There is no reason to neglect it, let alone exclude it systematically from the corporate governance codes.

Today's corporate governance must therefore be realigned, profoundly and radically reformed in its most essential points, so that it will not only effectively ensure right management being practiced, but also contribute to effectively functioning institutions, a productive business sector, and a viable society under the conditions of the 21st century.

For the purpose of right corporate governance, the first thing that needs to be accomplished is a 180 degree turnaround in the objective of corporate governance. Instead of shareholder value, the main reference variable should be customer value. Instead of value creation or increase, the overriding goal should be competitiveness. The logic of doing business does not leave any room for compromise.[1]

The purpose of a business is to create satisfied customers. Although everyone is basically free to define the purpose of economically productive institutions as they please, even wrongly, this can only be done in a responsible manner if the consequences are taken into account – specifically, the serious misdevelopments that would result from any other definition with an inner logic.

This definition of purpose, which is oriented towards the customer, covers both customer value and competitiveness. Only by fulfilling this purpose can a company satisfy its shareholders and achieve a value increase for them. It can also satisfy its stakeholders, as best it can, as a result of pursuing the right goals. It does not work the other way round.

The current understanding of corporate governance has its origin in the Wall Street excesses of the 1990s and early 2000s. These led to partly irreparable damage to listed companies and their shareholders, as well as to the reputation and credibility of their management.

Moreover, they were in danger of bringing the business sector as such into disrepute, and in the context of neoliberalism they provoked a new hostility in society toward those doing business.

Hence, the current state of corporate governance as reflected in different corporate governance codes is not the result of a systematic analysis and consideration of pertinent questions, but a consequence of disruptive and critical events – which, as is commonly known, rarely leads to lasting solutions.

---

1 Contrary to popular opinion, customer value can be determined and measured very precisely. An overview can be found in my book series "Management: Mastering Complexity", Volume 1: *Management. The Essence of the Craft.* Frankfurt/New York, 2009. See also: Chussil, Mark/Roberts, Keith: The meaning and value of customer value; Online Sheet 02/2007; Malik Management Zentrum St. Gallen, www.mzsg.ch.
Very exhaustive, with rationales and scientific foundations: Buzzell, Robert D./ Gale, Bradley T.: *The PIMS Principles. Linking Strategy to Performance*, New York, 1987, as well as Gale, Bradley T.: Managing Customer Value, New York, 1994.

As a consequence of the orientation towards crisis management, corporate governance in its current form is unbalanced and biased in favor of legal and financial considerations because the scandals occurred in exactly those categories. Legal and financial disciplinary means were the only way to curb the excesses.

What remained largely unnoticed was the fact that there were and still are many well-functioning companies in all countries, both listed and unlisted. Instead of learning proper management from them, new rules were invented to prevent wrong practices.

Preventing mistakes, however, does not necessarily mean doing the right thing. In addition, the debate about corporate governance rather uncritically adopted the positions of the prevailing zeitgeist – neoliberalism and the stock exchange and finance euphoria – as basic principles. Many of these positions are demonstrably wrong, systematically misleading for management, and harmful for companies.

Previous efforts to correct this situation do not suffice to ensure right and good corporate management. The following twelve propositions summarize the necessary reforms which I will expand upon in this book.

Twelve Propositions for Reforming Corporate Governance

1. Corporate governance that works can only and exclusively be derived from the requirements related to right management and the functionality of complex systems. Anything else is harmful to companies in the long run. Therefore, with regard to its content, corporate governance must be formulated from the perspective of control and management. It emerges neither from legal nor from financial formal rules, which nowadays dominate the corporate governance codes. Such rules are necessary but not sufficient. They can only fulfill their purpose if applied to the content of right corporate management.
2. Corporate governance must form a unity with corporate policy and corporate strategy. Together, they form the constitutive basis for proper action of the top-level management bodies of a company.
3. Corporate governance must uncompromisingly be geared towards the company itself and its performance in the market. Corporate gover-

nance must not be oriented towards interest groups, neither shareholders nor stakeholders. Orientation towards interest groups systematically leads to wrong decisions on the part of top management, and thus to an undesirable development of the company.

4. "Best practice" and "good corporate governance", two key concepts in today's understanding, are not useful criteria. Even if applied to perfection, they cannot prevent a company from getting into difficulty, nor can they generate success and a smooth functioning of the company. Some regulations of today's corporate governance, particularly financial considerations, even increase the risk of failure systematically because they dictate or recommend misleading parameters such as shareholder value and value increase.

5. It is evident that strict fiscal discipline is essential for proper corporate management. It is the foundation for the success of the company, but it is not its cause. The reasons for entrepreneurial success lie in other parameters, such as market position, innovation performance, productivity, as well as in the professionalism of management.

6. The only suitable indicators of top management taking the right kind of action are customer value and competitiveness. These alone bring success, and they are the only parameters that cannot be manipulated. While shareholder value, the value increase doctrine and, in general, all the criteria oriented towards the financial markets certainly do have to be respected in managing a company, they are not suitable for guiding the strategic actions of the top team.

7. In its current form, corporate governance essentially results in the misallocation of resources at the macroeconomic level. It is therefore hostile to investment and innovation, and it harms businesses' current and future potential for success. It undermines crucial performance areas, weakens competitiveness, and thus achieves the opposite of what it aims for: improving long-term profitability. In fact, it is detrimental to it.

8. Because of the damage done to long-term earning power, corporate governance ultimately also harms the interests of its declared target group, the shareholders – in part because it assumes all shareholders to share the same interests. Today's understanding of corporate governance cannot meet the requirements of the socio-economic structure of shareholders. It damages the interests of those who currently form the most important shareholder group: the future pensioners. They

are presently the main providers of capital, in the form of pension funds. Under current corporate governance standards, the managers of these funds are compelled to counteract the interests of their investors.

9. Today's corporate governance encourages and systematically justifies bad choices in filling top management positions. It creates the conditions in which a certain type of manager – the greedy, exclusively money-driven type – is allowed to move into key positions. Under different conditions, this type of manager would not stand a chance, because heading a company is radically different from managing money. Combined with the practice of tying managers' income solely to financial variables, such as stock prices, which is common, this creates a vicious circle which will quickly and automatically lead the company into trouble.

10. Today's corporate governance leads to an inadequate training of junior managers. Due to its appearing very plausible on the surface, simplistically reducing management to a handful of money factors, corporate governance is taught in MBA programs worldwide. The result is a whole generation of inadequately trained potential leaders who are not even aware of the alternatives that exist. They will need to retrain from scratch.

11. Corporate governance today is based on misconceptions regarding the nature and purpose of a functioning economic system, of the market, and of enterprise. This is reflected, firstly, in the wrong ideologies of neoliberalism and the "asset-driven economy", secondly, in the misconception of the company as a profit maximization system, and thirdly, in the idea of management being based on power and control.

12. The thinking and conceptual categories of today's corporate governance derive from the 20th century and are thus oriented towards the past. With the fundamental economic and social change going on, these ways of thinking are rapidly becoming irrelevant. In the 21st century, the crucial capital is not money but information and knowledge, as both are necessary to master the complexity of global business.

Capable managers are aware of the weaknesses of corporate governance codes, and able to compensate for them with experience, courage, and personal credibility. For managers with less competence and weaker personalities, the rules of corporate governance codes constitute an open invitation and justification for yielding to the temptations of short-sighted and poor management. Corporate governance codes present a danger when in inexpert hands.

One of the best CEOs of the past twenty years, the head of a global enterprise with about 100 billion Euros in annual sales, described this very impressively in an interview he gave in late 1998, shortly before the bull market peaked and the stock market hype set in. He essentially said that at the moment he was being forced to perform a huge balancing act, and that he did not know how long he would be able to go on like this. In the morning he was expected to tell the financial community what they wanted to hear; in the afternoon he had to make his people do the opposite, without anyone outside the organization noticing.

There is probably no better way to describe the dilemma between wrong corporate governance and right management. This man was lucky because, starting mid-May 2000, significant doubts arose as to the landmarks of the financial world, and as stock prices declined, so did the pressure from the analysts.

Why Today's Corporate Governance Cannot Meet its Purpose

The development of complex problems and systems depends on the course of history. Hence, my considerations regarding corporate governance ought to begin with a historical overview. In order to be able to shape the future in a sensible way, it is necessary to have a sound understanding of the history of corporate governance.

Intensive Care in a Field Hospital

The form of corporate governance currently practiced is an American invention to protect shareholders from getting robbed by corrupt managers. The idea was triggered by the unprecedented occurrence of mismanagement and self-enrichment in the top echelons of US listed companies since the mid-1990s.

The anonymous shareholders of American public corporations were defenseless victims of a legislation which, in effect, made it easy to undermine any effective control of management. In the euphoria surrounding the booming stock markets, the shareholders themselves contributed to the mismanagement of their companies because, being misled by the shareholder value theory, they were under the illusion that everything was happening in their best interest. Academia, the financial services industry, accounting and consulting companies strongly encouraged this belief and, in doing so, incidentally developed profitable business areas for themselves.

As legal reforms progressed very slowly in the Anglo-Saxon countries – even after huge bankruptcies with total losses for shareholders – a tool for voluntary self-commitment was created as a kind of first aid: the corporate governance code. It then spread outside the Anglo-Saxon world; not so much out of necessity but out of the media-induced fear that investors would stay away, and because it was fashionable to view American practices as progress even if they were lagging behind.

Systematic and broad-based "US-type" self-enrichment and mismanagement mainly occurred in countries with Anglo-Saxon legal traditions. In Germany, which has a totally different stock corporation law, such cases were few and far between. The reason is simple: under Anglo-Saxon law, as well as under Swiss law, managers can supervise themselves. Notwithstanding all the scandals, these countries still have the single-tier system in place. German stock corporation law, however, stipulates the two-tier system which effectively excludes self-supervision.

The principle which is crucial for effective corporate governance – the strict personal separation between the executive and the supervisory board – has long been implemented in Germany, essentially as a consequence of the painful experiences from the world economic crisis in the 1930s. Of course, neither of the two systems can provide effective protection against deliberate attempts to evade supervision or against fraudulent practices.

Lately, the two-tier model has started spreading in the English-speaking world as well, despite some fierce opposition. After years of hesitation, people have come to realize that German legislation is superior when it comes to the crucial subject of corporate supervision. The change in thinking is most advanced in England; the United States are dramatically behind.

The first step in the development of corporate governance was taken under an unlucky star, as several events coincided: the explosion of financial markets and the mass psychological stock exchange hype, the overwhelming prevalence of financial thinking as a result of neoliberalism with its money-drivenness across all business activities, the naïve New Economy illusions, the reduction of business management to a mere management of shareholder value, as the supposedly only relevant control factor, and the resulting financial excesses and even criminal doings in many boardrooms.

Neoliberalism is rooted in remarkable misconceptions regarding the functioning of the market and society, and in grotesque misunderstandings regarding true liberalism. It is naïve in its primal trust in the efficiency of the markets, and it underestimates the possibilities we have today for navigating organizations based on advanced strategic skills and information technology.

For several centuries, profits and relative prices were the only points of reference for entrepreneurial decisions, market theory had to work with these parameters because there was nothing better. As a result, advances in the availability and usage of information and knowledge were apparently overlooked. Empirical strategy research alone has made such enormous progress since the 1970s that prices, costs, and profits now only play a key role in operative corporate management. For *strategic* management, they have largely become meaningless because novel orientation parameters and control variables have been discovered and made available.[2]

In view of the fact that corporate governance has to account for future-oriented decisions, neoliberal nostalgia is of little use here. Metaphorically speaking, basing corporate governance on these principles is like practicing 18th century maritime navigation using a sextant, when modern satellite navigation is actually state-of-the-art. The requirements of modern corpo-

---

2   Relevant sources include the results of the world's largest research program on the relationship between profit potential and corporate strategy. Buzzell, Robert D./Gale, Bradley T.: *The PIMS Principles. Linking Strategy to Performance*, New York, 1987. Also, the research results obtained by Cesare Marchetti at IIASA, Institute for Applied Systems Analysis, and certainly the advances made in cybernetics-based corporate management. These topics are described extensively in: Malik, Fredmund: *Corporate Policy and Governance. How Organizations Self-Organize*, Frankfurt/New York (Volume 2 of the series "Management: Mastering Complexity").

rate management in the complex world of global business cannot be met with this kind of backward-oriented approach to corporate governance.

So the corporate governance that is practiced today is the outcome of past emergency measures. The present corporate governance codes, which go back to the early 2000s, were needed to respond to an acute crisis of corporate management. Rapid relief would not have been possible without improvisation. Under the given circumstances there was no time for dealing with the details of right and good corporate management, of professional top management, and of the configuration that organizations need in order to function. Metaphorically speaking, our present corporate governance is equipped like a modest field hospital, providing first aid treatment for the worst wounds. The patient is yet to be transferred to a fully equipped trauma hospital, permitting his restoration to perfect health and vitality as well as his rehabilitation.

Some of the pioneers of the first corporate governance codes were fully aware of these circumstances and their significance. Their work was also affected by the pressure from financial analysts, the media, and the fund managers. In this situation, corporate governance was bound to get stuck mid-way, or even partly go in the wrong direction. The road to the hospital, as it were, was blocked by time pressure and the mass-psychological distortion of economic thinking; also, there were acute problems which had to be solved on the spot. All in all, the prerequisites for thoroughly working through the subject matter were lacking.

Superficially, the problems were of a financial and legal nature and they demanded immediate solutions. For this reason, it was mostly lawyers and financial experts that were involved in the corporate governance debate. Business management experts were hardly involved. As a result, the discussion was based on management models from the 1980s and 1990s, which were already outdated. Other theories uncritically adopted included those of neoliberalism, efficient financial markets and shareholder value. They were among the immediate causes of said corporate scandals, as I will show later.

Clear-sighted executives knew that a thorough approach to the solution of the corporate governance problem would have proceeded from the symptoms to the underlying causes: to the question what proper corporate management *can and must be*. The answers would have led far beyond the purely legal and financial regulations that today's corporate governance focuses on.

This is evident from the fact that in the context of all the excesses and bankruptcies of the 1990s, which were caused by bad management, actual *laws* were rarely broken. This is why only few cases of poor corporate management were taken to court and only a minority of these led to convictions. The problem was not that current legal provisions had not been respected – the problem was that the law permitted excesses which were not prevented by corporate governance. In other words, wrong behavior was not prohibited, but it would have been the responsibility of right corporate management and specifically of corporate supervision to prevent such behavior, even if it was formally permissible. In the course of the stock exchange hype, procedures that were demonstrably harmful to businesses were even proclaimed to be new standards of particularly progressive management – predominantly by people lacking personal management experience, such as financial analysts, journalists and consultants, who represented the prevailing zeitgeist.

"Best Practice" – The Road to Bankruptcy?

Corporate governance according to the "best practice" standards defined in the corporate governance code can lead straight into bankruptcy. Actually, the probability is relatively high – why, is explained in this section and other chapters of the book.

As long as there are no clear concepts about right and good corporate governance, "best practice" is defined by the zeitgeist: by the current economic situation, by the financial markets, and by what the media propagate to be "best" – and by how, according to these values, they judge or condemn managers.

As long as it has not been made very clear what right corporate management means, today's best practice may well be tomorrow's worst. As long as there are no binding criteria, "best practice" is nothing but fads and mainstream thinking. It is what the majority does, and that is hardly a recipe for sustainable business success.

Formal rules are important, but they are not enough. If corporate governance is not geared to the content of management it will inevitably end up in formal clichés, as there is no other way to shape it.

As mentioned before, it is perfectly possible to define what right and good corporate management includes. In fact, it can be defined for all relevant fields: corporate policy, corporate strategy, corporate structure, and corporate culture. Moreover, it is equally possible to define what right and good people management is and how it is implemented technically and professionally. In my other books, I have dealt with these issues at length.[3]

The tragedy of the kind of corporate governance that emerged under the pressures described is that it inadvertently leads to bad and sometimes even wrong management. The corporate governance we have today has permitted and encouraged the worst aberration of recent economic history: the shareholder value focus. It has enabled totally unfit individuals to move up to the corporate top: the money-driven manager type who perceives and judges the world, himself, and his actions in monetary terms only. It also legitimizes the "performance-related turnover" of CEOs, which has increased by several hundred percent since the mid-1990s, with performance almost exclusively being understood to mean financial performance. In view of the returns expected these days, this practice regularly harms companies' innovativeness and power to invest – a fact that goes largely unnoticed, for there is nothing in the corporate governance codes to monitor and control it.

Under the given circumstances, "best practice" is assuming an extremely precarious meaning – that is, doing the wrong thing but doing it as best one can, for *best* practice is not the same as *right* practice. Business lawyers know that even the most meticulous compliance with all legal provisions cannot prevent a company's bankruptcy; in some cases it will even lead straight into it, and it can definitely accelerate the process. Why? Because the law calls for the "diligence of the prudent businessman" but not for *entrepreneurial success*. That, however, is exactly what it is all about. Fulfilling the legal duty of diligence is a *necessary* condition, but by no means a sufficient one for the effective management of a company.

In short, the notion of "best practice" is not only devoid of meaning, it may actually create the opposite of what is intended. So what is this

---

3   Malik, Fredmund: *Managing, Performing, Living. Effective Management for a New Era.* Frankfurt/New York, 2009. *Management. The Essence of the Craft* (Volume 1 of my series "Management: Mastering Complexity"), Frankfurt/New York, 2010. *Uncluttered Management Thinking. 46 Concepts for Masterful Management.* Frankfurt/New York, 2011.

yardstick of "best practice" in corporate government all about? From a legal-logical perspective, it is an interesting trick. It creates a blank space, the content of which is to be newly defined, over and over again, by reality itself – a reality that, at any given time, happens to result from the corporate governance codes.

The definition of best practice is self-referential. It tells us more about those who define best practice than it does about the issue of corporate governance, or about sound corporate management under reliable criteria. According to current understanding, a company's performance is judged based on stock market and financial parameters. Why should this be right? What can these parameters tell about the company's situation tomorrow and the day after? Why should the current zeitgeist, of all things, define what best practice is? What does it tell us about the future?[4]

Both the business sector and society as a whole need companies that are managed *rightly*. Most relevant benchmarks are inherently oriented towards the future and not the past because current success is not a guarantee for success in the future.

In anticipation of my further discourse, I will just mention the example of financial planning, which is strongly emphasized in the corporate governance codes, and the extensive stipulations for annual reports. Both are important, no doubt, but only if they are pursued in the context of proper company management. A wrong strategy results in financial planning, just as a right strategy does. Financial planning, however, cannot help distinguish one from the other, because the validity of a strategy does not reveal itself in financial terms. It was not without reason that the financial plans of New Economy companies were just a particularly quick, though much-acclaimed, way into bankruptcy. The annual audit is important, but it only serves the purpose of *ascertaining* the success of the business. It is meaningless for its cause and origin.

Wrong content inevitably leads to misdirection. Even the closest compliance with corporate governance codes cannot prevent a business from getting into trouble – conversely, a business can be very successful indeed without either having or following a corporate governance code.

The famous Military Order of Maria Theresia, the Austrian empress, was awarded to commissioned officers who achieved a military success

---

4   To give a far-fetched but illustrative example: in astronomy, Copernican "best practice" was the exact opposite of what was standard at the time.

by contravening an order. In other words, it rewarded military personnel who acted based on immediate necessity rather than legal requirements. Managers of listed companies are in a similar situation at present. Many businesses function only because they have enough managers acting *"contre ordre"*, doing the opposite of what corporate governance codes say they should be doing. Supervisory bodies are nevertheless satisfied because good results are achieved – precisely because people have done the opposite of what corporate governance codes stipulate.

It can often be observed that top managers and supervisory boards pay lip service to the corporate governance codes, yet their actual actions are justifiably different. In this context, the CEO of a very successful company once said that, fortunately, his key managers were competent and courageous enough to do the right thing even when regulations suggested something else.

When Corporate Governance Is Confused With Good Management

Some examples from the contemporary business scene should help to illustrate the dilemma of current corporate governance.

The US automotive industry can surely not be accused of disregarding the rules of corporate governance; yet its companies have not been blessed with much success lately. Their board members fail because they have been neglecting fundamental laws of right and effective corporate management for decades.

Who but the supervisory body – in this case the board of directors – could and should have enforced decisions to ensure that the right cars would be built, customer requirements would be met, and the European and particularly the Japanese competition would effectively be countered? Where else but in the corporate governance codes should the respective obligations have been defined, clearly and unmistakably, in substance and not only formally?

The next recession, not to mention the continuation of the bear markets in the stock exchanges, will drastically reveal the deficiencies of many companies in which corporate governance is confused with good management.

Here is another example: The often elaborate recommendations in corporate governance codes regarding the committees of supervisory bodies are of no consequence to customers, shareholders, and employees, as long as these committees decide on misguided investments, inappropriate organizations, and excessive management salaries. Setting up committees is no guarantee for right decisions; often it is quite the contrary. The well-intended clause in one of the German corporate governance codes, demanding that the members of supervisory bodies undergo advanced training, strikes me as being a mere commonplace, devoid of content and commitment.

And yet another example: It may be useful to repeat in a corporate governance code what is already stipulated in the German Stock Corporation Act – for instance, that the executive board is to determine the company's goals and strategy – but it says nothing about what their content should be. The emphasis that the former DaimlerChrysler CEO placed on the corporate governance code increased with the amount of capital he lost. The codes were complied with perfectly, there was also a strategy – but there was no one to correct the company's ruinous strategy in time. We may safely assume that there was no shortage of financial planning. Proper corporate management, by contrast, is about having the right strategy, the right investments, and a top-quality market performance for the customer. The judges of good corporate management are satisfied customers, not the stock markets or financial analysts. The best capital comes from the customers, not from financial markets.

Further indispensable elements of proper corporate management are professional innovation management, a functioning corporate structure, and a robust corporate culture. All of these elements are hardly ever mentioned in corporate governance codes. Further absolutely critical factors are the staffing requirements for key positions, the criteria according to which these positions are to be filled, and the procedure for the selection of suitable candidates. It is not enough simply to call for qualification profiles, as some corporate governance codes do, for even failed managers have met requirement profiles before they were appointed, and the decisions to appoint them were also made by committees.

The broadest space is usually dedicated to supervisory tasks which are actually a glance in the rear-view mirror: the questions of *financial reporting*. Annual reports and the publishing of business results are certainly important but they *focus on the past*. One of the important recent contributions to improving corporate governance was provided by the long-time CEO of Porsche AG, Wendelin Wiedeking, who refused to publish quarterly financial statements. Sometimes it takes courage instead of a code, even courage *against* a code. What Wiedeking did was certainly not perceived as "best practice"; no one else had done it before and he risked having his shares eliminated from the index. It was not "best practice" but it was "right practice" in the sense of right corporate management.

The widespread opinion that "unfortunately" it is impossible to say what a healthy company and proper corporate management are, or what could be a suitable measure of managerial performance, other than financial parameters and stock prices – this opinion may have been acceptable twenty years ago. Today, it is certainly possible to define right and wrong corporate management and governance and to define it precisely enough to serve as a target, even a *specification* for the activities of corporate managers. It would be helpful if the essence of it could also be found in the corporate governance codes, and it would certainly help to increase their usage and acceptance. A sensible business and management concept will always include corporate governance. Anyone studying truly well-managed companies will quickly find this fact confirmed.

What Is a Shareholder, Anyway?

The corporate governance codes ignored changes in the shareholder structure. The image of the shareholder whose interests are protected by the Swiss corporate governance code, for example, has little to do with today's investor-shareholder. What is an "investor" nowadays? Due to the development of the financial markets and of the funds industry, the concept has almost lost its meaning. It takes careful analysis to determine what is meant by it in each individual case. Although investors and shareholders are both owners of company shares, and thus almost identical in form, this does not mean that they share the same interests.

It is one of the universally adopted dogmas of neoliberalism that shareholders are a *homogeneous* stakeholder group; a dogma which has never been verified. This way, the demand for shareholder value is bound to lead nowhere. Moreover, the shareholder structure has changed fundamentally over time. Let me give you some facts:

In 1959, approximately 90 percent of all US shares were held by private households; today they account for a mere 30 percent. Institutional investors, by contrast, are now holding almost 70 percent of shares, up from a mere 9 percent in 1950. The 100 largest money managers in the United States manage roughly 60 percent of US shares. Needless to say, the interests of both groups are radically different.

Among other things, this is evident in the turnover rate – the percentage of shares that change hands each year. From 20 percent in the 1950s and 1960s, this rate had risen to 90 percent by the early 1990s.

What is generally called a "shareholder" today – whose rights are to be protected by corporate governance codes – has actually become a "share turner". And although even a temporary holder of shares is an *owner* formally and by law, he is not an owner with an entrepreneurial interest, nor even a true interest *in* the company or business. He is not interested in the prosperity of "his" company, the business he owns shares in.

This is absolutely legitimate and fulfills an economic function. I am not criticizing it as such. It does, however, raise a crucial question with regard to corporate governance, concerning investors' right to influence the management and the management bodies of a business. Why should this type of shareholder enjoy particular protection and the special attention of corporate governance bodies? Only few months after having purchased his "property" he will be gone.

It is true that every shareholder has the right to do what he pleases with his shares. However, if his interests are short-term and purely financial in nature, he should not be entitled to have a part in constitutive decisions on the company and its governing bodies. He can simply buy the shares wherever he can expect to get the highest immediate returns. However, since he is not really interested in the fate of the company, as the turnover rates reveal – otherwise, he would hold his securities for a longer term – he should not be permitted to interfere with entrepreneurial matters. This is easy to accomplish: *Anyone involved in the appointment of the supervisory board, and thus in a business's corporate governance, should be obliged to observe a certain holding period. Anyone failing or refusing to do so should not be given a vote at the annual shareholders' meeting, and thus have no influence on decisions regarding corporate governance, for he will not be held accountable for the consequences of said decisions.*

So if the purpose of a company is determined from the perspective of the management's control function, there is an elegant way to eliminate all discrepancies resulting from a purely finance-oriented corporate governance.

Logic and Rhetoric of the Market

There is yet another aspect to what I pointed out above. The finance sector, with its power and media presence, is the main cause of the misdirection of management and its bias towards shareholder value.

The underlying logic is correct. In the finance industry, shareholder value is identical to customer value because the industry's customers – in particular fund managers – want exactly that: shareholder value and value increase. For the real economy, it is a very different story. Only in very rare cases is the customer of an automobile manufacturer also its shareholder, nor do shareholders always buy their cars from the company whose shares they own.

In zeitgeist-driven mass psychology, however, and pressured by analysts and the media, business organizations are misled or even forced to behave like the financial industry. It causes them to divert their gaze away from their customers toward the very different interests of their shareholders.

However, while the financial sector's rhetoric changes the *outward appearance* of the market, it does not change its *logic*. In the logic of the market, the company needs to get its bearings from the constituency that actually pays its bills: none other than the customers. When people claim that ultimately the shareholders "pay the bills" it is just a slogan, and a misleading one. It may be true that shareholders will have to record a loss, in particular when a company no longer attracts customers to pay the real bills. The shareholder carries the ownership risk, but he does not foot the bills.

So if owners are truly interested in the value and value increase of their shares, they must do everything in their power to enable the company to create customer value, and they must put management in a position to be able to focus on nothing else.

Strictly speaking, shareholders should reverse their logic by 180 degrees. Instead of asking what the company can and should do for them, they should ask what they can do for the company and how they can ensure that it fares well. In other words, shareholder *interest* is not the same as shareholder value. Precisely when the goal is to serve shareholders well, customer value must be the top priority.

This is particularly important for pension fund investors, or the future retirees. They depend on receiving their retirement pay in 20 or 30 years' time. Consequently, their vital interest must be the *long-term* performance of a company, not the short-term stock price. The art is in *generating* economic output first, only then can it be distributed. When it does get to the point of being distributed, shareholders may be the first to be served. But where nothing is earned, there will be nothing to distribute.

The Best Companies Are Overlooked

One of the reasons for deficient, lacking, or wrong content in corporate governance and its codes is that, quite unnecessarily, the focus is restricted to just a part of all businesses: those listed at the stock exchange. They may be important, but not as much as their media presence would have us believe. Superbly managed corporations no doubt exist. But contrary to popular belief, large corporations are anything but typical examples of good business practice and right corporate management. Quite a few of them are the very opposite, and we are all too familiar with their notorious problems: bureaucracy, hierarchy, and often inefficiency.

Ever since the seemingly endless upward trend of the financial markets has entered society's mindset, and the naïve idea of a New Economy has emerged, media reports have been dominated by two segments of the business sector: listed companies and dot.coms.

Since all attention is on them, the best companies have simply been overlooked. As far as the media take notice of them at all, they usually refer to them somewhat condescendingly as "small and medium-sized businesses" – a term that further adds to limiting public awareness, thus causing systematic blindness for the most successful and important part of the business sector.

This is where the true gems of business performance may be found. I call them "entrepreneurially managed enterprises", or *EMEs*, to distinguish them from the SMEs – the small and medium-sized enterprises[5] – for it is not their *size* that matters but their *strength*. These are the sustainably prosperous businesses. Many of them are market leaders in their fields; many have been in business for decades, some for a century or more; and

---

5 See Malik, Fredmund: *Corporate Policy and Governance. How Organizations Self-Organize.* Frankfurt/New York, 2010 (Volume 2 of the series "Management: Mastering Complexity").

they have weathered all the crises and changes and carried their success through many generations. Most of them went global long before the term "globalization" even existed. The terms "New Economy" and "Old Economy", which have almost vanished by now, never fitted these companies because they represent the *Right and Effective Economy.*

These companies do not need a stock exchange because they have their capital flowing in from satisfied customers. They do not allow the financial markets to limit their entrepreneurial freedom. They get their bearings from their customers, not from financial analysts or the media. They seek publicity with their customers, no one else. They compete for customers based on their market performance, not for investors based on stock prices. Their managers focus on their tasks, not their media presence.

In Germany, this segment includes names such as Boehringer Ingelheim, Würth, Stihl, Bertelsmann, Otto Hamburg, Bosch, Braun Melsungen, Haniel, and Aldi. Austria has the Raiffeisen group, the Plansee group, Spar, Swarowski, and Blum. For Switzerland, I can name Spuhler, SFS, the Arbonia group, the Migros and Coop retail groups, Logitech, Kaba, and a series of others which keep a low public profile. This group of excellent companies also includes listed corporations such as Nestlé, Porsche and BMW, which, although they have to take account of the financial markets in their decisions, consider this to be a basic condition and not an overriding goal. Hence, the EME category cuts across all other categories used, which are largely meaningless for judging the quality and professionalism of corporate management.

The logical consequence from this is that entrepreneurial, or right and good management is *always* possible – irrespective of the size, type of business, legal form, or industry of a company, and irrespective of its being listed at the stock exchange or not. It also shows that it is not ownership that matters, but the degree of professionalism in management. Salaried managers can practice it just like owner-entrepreneurs can, and both can lack it. Ownership is important in another context. Corporate management is a profession, and like any other profession it requires a kind of professionalism that is not tied to ownership as such.

The best-managed and therefore best-functioning organizations are easily overlooked because the media consider them and their management boring. After all, what should a journalist write about companies that simply do a good job, businesses where there are no such things as scandals and executive compensation excesses, egomaniacs and personality cults, spectacular appearances, showing off, and grand statements by people whose names – as opposed to their products – everyone knows? The top-end business media may feature an occasional report about them, but they will rarely hit the front-page headlines.

In well-managed businesses there has been no reason to specifically deal with corporate governance. First off, there were no corporate governance problems; second, the things stipulated in the corporate governance codes had long been a natural part of proper corporate management. This is why these businesses were immune to the misconduct that led to the corporate governance debate, and immune to the lure of the zeitgeist.

When at the times of the greatest corporate governance hype I would outline my perception of right and good management in my seminars and speeches, people in the audience would often object that this kind of management was outdated. This reveals a remarkable lack of knowledge about the realities of business, and an alarmingly careless over-adoption of mainstream thinking.

Missed Opportunities

Actually, the term *corporate governance* would have been the proper name for the entirety of top executive functions in corporate management, as it contains the crucial root of the word *cybernetics.* The latter derives from the Greek *kybernetes,* meaning *helmsman,* which in English was transformed into *governor* and *governance.* The Cadbury Commission's original definition of corporate governance, dated 1992, is in precise accordance with my considerations: *Corporate governance is the system by which companies are run.* This definition does not specify what corporate governance should focus on, and so it is left to us to discuss and decide it.

However, the current perception of corporate governance has diverged so much from this line that it would create more confusion than clarity if the term was used as a synonym for corporate management and corporate policy. With both other definitions prevailing today, misunderstandings are inevitable. The definition by Böckli places shareholder interests above everything else; in Witt's definition the stakeholder approach is set in stone.[6] Both definitions are wrong in that they define purposes and goals wrongly, thus facilitating misdirected control and systematically leading to the wrong top management decisions.

In the German code, the executive board is rightfully committed to serve the organization's interests; in the same sentence, however, it is also committed to the sustainable increase of the enterprise's value, which is a contradiction, as I will show at a later point. By contrast, the supervisory board is unrestrictedly committed to the company's best interests, which, in turn, means that managing a corporation solely based on shareholder value is essentially against the law, or the Code.[7] It all goes to show that the confusion could not be greater.

Today, the name *corporate governance* is given to a travesty of corporate management which – as has been pointed out before – is characterized by the scandals and white-collar crime of the past 15 years, rather than by a comprehensive understanding of complex systems. The fact of the matter is that this has created an alarming practice of misguided corporate management. The massive drop in share prices between early 2000 and late 2002 had already made those false doctrines quite visible. They will become even more obvious in the current economic downturn, and chances are that this or the next will also mark the end of conventional corporate governance.

To this date, the development of the concept of corporate governance has, in several respects, been a pathetic succession of missed opportuni-

---

6   "Corporate Governance is the sum of all guidelines oriented by *shareholder interest*, aimed at achieving transparency and a sound balance of leadership and control at a company's top management level while preserving the ability to make decisions and maintaining efficiency" (Böckli, 2002, and thus adopted in the *Swiss Code of Best Practice*; economie-suisse, version of 2007, translated from German with emphasis added. Prof. Peter Böckli is the author of the Swiss Code). However, Article 15 of the Code then stipulates that the president of the board of directors has to perform the board's chairmanship *in the company's best interest*. Either shareholder interests and company interests are viewed as being identical, which would be extremely unfortunate, or we have a contradiction here. The other widespread definition is: "The term 'corporate governance' refers to the organization of leadership and control of a company with the objective of *balancing interests between the different stakeholder groups*." (Witt, 2001), translated with emphasis added.

7   German Corporate Governance Code, version of 2007, sections 4.1.1 and 5.5.1.

ties. What is more, it is exemplary of circumstances in which something fundamental is lacking: the consideration of how complex systems function and operate. It is a history of an enormous confusion of terms and of a massive mismanagement of companies, resulting from fundamental misperceptions of the nature and purpose of companies as complex systems.

Corporate governance, as it is understood today, has little to do with corporate management's basic task – corporate policy. It does fulfill this basic function with regard to financial markets, financial analysts, and financial media. However, when looking at it from the management perspective in the proper sense of the word, and in particular when management is oriented by complexity, then today's concept of corporate governance is slanted towards the financial side of things and places excessive emphasis on legal aspects; also, it is directed towards the wrong purpose – shareholder value – and altogether overregulated.

The *corporate governance codes* being used today regulate *too much* and *too little* at the same time. They give *too many wrong recommendations* and *not enough right ones*. The perspective of managing a company, the actual issue of controlling and directing, is largely overlooked or blocked out. Quite to the contrary: the way the *corporate governance codes* are handled increasingly leads to the strangulation of the top-level management bodies which, as a logical consequence, are shifting further and further away from their entrepreneurial task. Members of management bodies nowadays have less and less time to look after the company's welfare, as they have to take care to comply with legal provisions, pamper the financial media, serve the short-term interests of investors (which are often harmful to the business) and shield themselves against liability claims. In the real economy there is a clear tendency towards formal governance rules, at the expense of such crucial things as entrepreneurial vision, courage, willingness to take on risks, and imagination.

Recent half-hearted attempts at reform once again lurch in the wrong direction, in that they seek to revive the so-called stakeholder approach. Apparently the "reformers" are not aware that it was the *failure* of the stakeholder approach that led to the emergence of the shareholder concept, which does not work either. Once again, the company is made a prey to the varying balance of power between various stakeholder groups.

The issues being addressed by attempted reforms are very legitimate since they are neglected, even systematically violated, by the shareholder approach. The solutions proposed, however, are wrong. The stakeholder approach, and in this context this also applies to corporate social responsibility and corporate citizenship, will do nothing to solve the problems predictably caused by the shareholder principle. It is time to adopt a new approach, which I will outline in this and other books.

Two Functions and Two Management Bodies

A well-functioning corporate top management requires *two* functions and thus a *minimum* of two management bodies. A single body will never be able to perform the task, for fundamental reasons and ultimately by law of nature. Both functions are *true* management functions at the level of the overall organization, which need to collaborate in a division of responsibilities to ensure that the overriding purpose – a well-functioning enterprise – is fulfilled.

For this book, I have chosen the terms "supervisory" and "executive" function and, corresponding to these, "supervisory" and "executive body". Contrary to the German two-tier model, which reflects a very narrow and rigid perception of supervision, both of these bodies need to perform *management tasks*. However, contrary to the Anglo-Saxon single-tier model, *two different* bodies have to perform these tasks.

These distinctions alone can help eliminate much of the confusion currently affecting the corporate governance debate and leading it in the wrong direction. A further distinction may help eliminate another type of confusion that originated in the term "corporate governance" itself.

Why do we need the term in the first place, and why did it appear? It is simply superfluous because we have had a much better one all along: the much more comprehensive term *"corporate management"*, which originated at least as far back as in 1946, when Peter F. Drucker published his book *The Concept of the Corporation*. Hans Ulrich and Walter Krieg based their approach on Drucker's concept when in the 1960s they created the *St. Gallen System-Oriented Management Approach* – the first comprehensive management theory ever in the German-speaking world – and after that the *St. Gallen Management Model*, which has been developed further ever since, and made into the MMS® ("Malik General Management Systems"), at what is today Malik Management. To this date there is nothing comparable in the Anglo-Saxon world.[8]

It goes without saying that corporate management has always been understood to mean the comprehensive, wholistic management of the company including all management functions, or in other words: corporate *top general* management as opposed to *divisional general management*.

The creators of the term "corporate governance", which emerged much later, seem to have been unaware of this. Also, it appears they have not realized that the term *management* has always comprised *three* different *dimensions* which are easily distinguished by experts: the *functional*, the *institutional*, and the *personal* dimension. It is quite simple and straightforward. The first stands for the *work* to be done, the second for the management *bodies* required for that purpose, and the third for the *persons* who, by virtue of their seats on these bodies, perform that work.

The neologism "corporate governance" is not only inherently superfluous; it also denotes only one of several facets of wholistic corporate management, and one that, incidentally, has always been observed in well-managed corporations. As has been mentioned before, the term "corporate governance" originated from a lack of knowledge about the state of development that management theory had reached at the time. It has brought us nothing in the way of new insights but plenty of new confusion, and in addition, the term has displaced almost every perception of right and good corporate management, reducing it to an admittedly important, but rather small share of corporate top management.

---

8   One example of the continuance of the comprehensive corporate management approach is the book by Martin Hilb, *The New Corporate Governance*, 3rd edition, New York 2008 (German original edition published in 2006). It offers new and useful proposals for solving a number of questions.

Chapter 2

Fundamental Reorientation[9]

Businesses and management – and with them, all of society – are in a phase of fundamental reorientation. At its heart is the question of what right corporate governance is and, more broadly speaking, what constitutes right institutional governance.

The necessity to rethink results from two widespread misconceptions: first, shareholder value is believed to be the supreme and only reference variable for businesses, especially for large corporations; second, it is based on a fundamental misconception of liberalism which would not have passed muster with any of the great liberal thinkers. Both are irreconcilable with successful corporate management, sustainable business approaches, and a well-functioning society. I believe that in this book I have laid down some of the essential foundations for the correction of mistakes, for the proper management of organizations, and thus for the necessary reorientation of business.

In other words, I am building a case for all those who consider many of the recent business developments and much of the related way of thinking to be wrong and dangerous – as I have from the very beginning. I am not referring to the youth revolts against globalization, which is not the core of the problem at all. From countless seminars and speeches I have held on the subject and the discussions that followed, I know that there are a remarkable number of top-level executives from business and politics who have been worrying about this development for quite some time. It is not as if the so-called prevailing doctrine – actually more of a zeitgeist fad

---

9   This chapter contains the new introduction to the 3rd edition of the German book (dated 2002) for which the title has been changed to *Die Neue Corporate Governance* (formerly *Effective Top Management*). Although some basic statements overlap with the first chapter, I have left the text unchanged.

propagated by the media – is uncritically accepted by a majority of those who deal with the realities of managing large corporations every day, and who bear the responsibility that comes with it. They just happen rarely to have the time for lengthy discussions; often they also lack the theoretical foundations and are thus at a loss for persuasive arguments.

I do not deny or ignore that there are many top managers who have unhesitatingly adopted, spread, and followed the new creed. Otherwise it could not have been established. More than a few of them and their businesses, including numerous banks, now face major difficulties – quite predictably so, because this was bound to happen. Just as inevitably, the damage they have done by far exceeds their immediate field of action. The number of those affected is by far larger than that of the originators. The fact that the German version of this book is now in its third edition might just be an indicator that the group of those who ponder and critically reflect is growing larger.

The time is right for a new debate. And not only that: it is also a good time because there are obvious signs that the same views that have been believed to be new and in part even ultimate truths since the mid-1990s now turn out to be highly questionable or downright wrong – that is to say, they have become false doctrines. Now that the recent, unexpectedly negative realities of business and the financial markets can no longer be ignored, the positions that have been defended with so much zeal are beginning to erode. The financial analysts have fallen silent; the terror they could so arrogantly exert for years – based on their supposed infallibility – no longer has an effect. The realization is spreading that the world of finance and the real economy were fatally confused. The illusion of never-ending bull markets and the New Economy euphoria prove to be what they have always been: a lack of economic expertise, even though nicely wrapped in the glamour of the zeitgeist, a lack of knowledge about economic history, youthful inexperience, often sheer economic stupidity, a casino mentality, imposture, and occasionally nothing less than white-collar crime.

A fundamental debate on the reorientation of entrepreneurial and managerial thinking and action – in particular with regard to large corporations – will be unavoidable. It should be actively sought by those interested in a free society, a free enterprise system, and a business sector driven by the markets wherever possible. The discussion must be sought and actively shaped by those advocating the establishment of a true rather than a false liberalism, and who refuse to make way for ideologues – be it from the left or the right wing, or of a whole new kind. It will take the votes of those who are able to recognize the real danger of a new anti-business attitude and hostility originating from disappointments and frustrated expectations, and who know how important it is especially for business leaders to be credible. In my view, the trust placed in them, their power of conviction and their personal integrity seem even more important than the trust placed in politicians – the more so as reports of scandalous failures in business abound; be it organizational or individual failures, be it insider trading, balance-sheet fraud, or self-enrichment excesses.

If – as can be expected – the highly controversial opinion becomes fashionable again that business is "too important to be left to entrepreneurs and managers", it will be time for all those relying on powerful arguments instead of misconceived peer loyalty to actively participate in the discussion. They will need the courage of their superior expertise to make it very clear to the world that business must not be left to *bad* managers or *incapable* entrepreneurs.

What Is Corporate Governance? Consequences of a Question Wrongly Posed

When the first German-language edition of this book was published, corporate governance was not a run-of-the-mill topic. It was yet to be affected by the lopsided view which later emerged and was broadly and uncritically adopted, and which regards the business enterprise and its purpose exclusively from the perspective of finance and the stock exchange, analysts, fund managers, and stock market participants.

In lieu of numerous similar cases, I will mention just one typical example of this lopsidedness: a heap of figures, referred to as a study, compiled by a consulting firm on behalf of a leading German magazine. In it, the shares of Euro Stoxx 50 companies were evaluated by 200 fund managers and analysts based on the following criteria: *shareholder rights, quality of the supervisory board, takeover barriers, transparency,* and *commitment to shareholder value*. As in every comparison with the US, the findings of this study were devastating for European companies. Except for the criterion "quality of the supervisory board", these evaluation criteria have nothing to do with the *performance* and *competitiveness* of the companies in question. Owing to its one-sided blindness, this perception of corporate governance obviously loses sight of the actual object of "analysis": everything is analyzed – except for the company itself.

The root cause of this development is a question *wrongly* posed. It is: *"In whose interests should a company be managed?"* From that point, a seemingly logical and plausible path leads to the shareholder. But appearances are deceptive. This answer is neither logically compelling, nor is it the only possible answer – much less the best one. As a matter of fact, it can only appear plausible under certain, rather unusual conditions.

These conditions prevailed in the United States by the end of the 1980s, whereas in most other countries they did not exist at all or only in rudimentary forms, and have only been implemented artificially and temporarily to date. Prime examples include Japan and certain "Tiger Countries" which, having been said to represent the economic future per se for quite a while, collapsed precisely because of these artificially created conditions – a financial bubble based on excessive borrowing – and not because the conditions were lacking.

Another example of rare special conditions, which was not visible for a long time but is all the more significant now, is the fact that the shareholder theory can only appear reasonable, indeed even the only theory possible, in times of rising stock prices – which was also the case in the US, specifically since 1982. This date seems unknown to most of the people who started investing at the stock exchange during the 1990s, claiming that stock market developments were closely linked to economic prosperity and business performance – some of them citing grotesque theories about the rationality of capital markets and their superior wisdom in questions of business valuation.

Along with the New Economy illusion, this ultimately led to a temporary speculative mass mania, as has regularly happened in economic history at longer time intervals – long enough to forget the bitter experiences of the past, and to shrug off any lessons learned by saying *"this time things are different"*. What in the first two decades of the 20th century was referred to as the "New Era" was now the "New Economy" of the century's last two decades. Lazy journalists could simply copy their headlines from old copies of the *Wall Street Journal* or the *New York Times*.

It is, of course, absurd to assume that stock markets will keep going up – yet this absurdity has determined all thoughts and actions. It is even more absurd to base corporate governance on it. Although this view has always been wrong, the extent of its pointlessness will become increasingly clear as the bear market continues.

The shareholder concept appears most plausible in the context of large corporations with international activities, *if and as long as their stock is growing up*. However, apart from the fact that it is only the appearance of plausibility rather than real logic, the major corporations are not representative of the business sector. They only attract the greatest media interest. Large corporations account for a relatively small share of economic power in all countries. Only rarely do they account for more than one-third of economic value-added, or one-third of employment. Major corporations play an important role, but they are not typical for what happens in the business sector.

The same applies to another segment which, ten years after the invention of shareholder value, almost hypnotically attracted the attention of the masses: the start-up businesses in the internet and e-business sector. They, too, are not representative of the economy – not even of a New Economy, the hype for which grew in inverse proportion to people's understanding of economics. In all countries, around two-thirds of the economic output is produced by small and medium-sized businesses, and they account for the same share of employment. For these businesses shareholder value is not only useless, even with lots of well-intentioned adaptations; it also produces its misleading and detrimental effects quickly or even immediately.

So, as we can see, there would be several possible answers even to the wrongly posed question, and it was only due to a very specific circumstance that the shareholder theory could be received well enough to even appear the only theory possible. It is an irony of history that now, in the light of recent occurrences, the first of many previously dogmatic proponents of the shareholder theory – realizing that their doctrine has its deficiencies – are getting ready for a major "reform". In fact, what they do is mutate the shareholder into the *stakeholder theory* – while overlooking the fact that it is just another flawed variation of the interest group theory. Obviously they also do not know that it was the practical failure of this very theory that accidentally led to shareholder value being viewed as plausible, and to be received so well.

Whichever way you look at it: There are no right answers to questions wrongly posed. Questions should begin at an earlier stage, and at another logical point: not at the *distribution* of business profits but at their *cre-*

ation. Consequently, the first question must be: *"What is proper corporate management?"* Proceeding from there, the next question is: *"What is a strong, healthy, viable business? What has to be done by the executive top management and by the supervisory body to ensure that such a business is built and maintained?"*

Only thus, by ensuring proper management of the businesses in question, will there be an appropriate result in terms of productive potential, be it "bricks" or "bytes", goods or services, national income or national product, wages, taxes, interest rates, or profits.

Only after the financial result has been generated can it be distributed. Only then can the key question of the shareholder theory – how much to give to whom – make any sense at all. Only then can there be a meaningful discussion about which of the different stakeholder groups, whatever their legitimization, should get what part of the profit. At that point there may be legitimate reasons to give shareholders preferential treatment.

Grave Management Misunderstandings and Their Consequences

As the key question of corporate governance, I therefore suggest something very different from what the shareholder theory focuses on: a question aimed at the *generation* rather than the *distribution* of business results. Generating performance is the *difficult* part of doing business – distributing the results is *easy*.

Instead of basing everything on the interests of different constituencies, thus placing the business at the mercy of the shifting political and social balances of power, and in effect destabilizing it, the very different and much more comprehensive corporate governance questions I am proposing here view the company *itself* as a productive unit which creates prosperity and a standard of living. The more it creates, the better it functions, independently of the specific interests any stakeholder group may have. Shareholders, too, can only benefit from the company's welfare. Rather than *"the best balanced interest of interest groups"*, the key criterion for the activities of top management bodies must be *"the best interest of the company"*. A solution along these lines was never considered by *Alfred Rappaport*, the creator of the shareholder value concept.

This perspective focuses on the *real-economic* side of doing business, not – as shareholder value thinking does – on the *financial* side. In conjunction with the stock market upturn, the shareholder value theory led to a confusion of both: the real economy and the financial economy. The inevitable consequence was that entrepreneurs and entrepreneurial tasks were confused with investors and investment tasks.

Both are necessary, both serve important functions in a modern economy, but they follow an entirely different logic. Years ago, the real economy and the financial economy were clearly related: the financial economy served the purpose of financing the real economy. Up until the late 1980s, financial volumes were therefore a stable proportion of global trade flows and global investments. Over time, both types of economy developed in such different directions that we now have to speak of two different economic systems. They each have their own, entirely different laws, logic, time horizons, and motives for action.

In fact, they are so different that time and again their representatives fail to understand each other because they talk about two different worlds. As I explain in this book, this is one of the reasons why I recommend restraint in putting bankers on the supervisory boards of non-financial businesses. They may be excellent finance experts, but their understanding of the real economy is limited. *Peter Drucker* once said, perhaps exaggeratedly, that *bankers understand everything about money, but not much about the economy* – or words to that effect.

There have hardly been any cases where bank managers were successful managing the operations of an industrial company (and vice versa). Companies have regularly run into trouble when finance people, balance-sheet experts, accountants, treasurers, or controllers took the top seats. Examples include Daimler-Benz during the Reuter era, or Swissair in the days of Bruggisser.

It might be more than coincidence that Alfred Rappaport is an accounting expert, and that accounting firms were the first to be fascinated with his theory, propagating it through their consulting branches. Also, it should be kept in mind that the reason why accounting firms expanded into general management consulting was not their extensive expertise in the field but their simple economic survival. The problems that resulted were not only the inevitable collisions of interests – one example being Enron – but also the questionable competence they brought to matters of strategy and management.

This could turn out to be further proof of what *Aloys Gälweiler*[10], one of the top experts on corporate strategy, has claimed: that a company cannot be managed with accounting variables. That, however, is precisely the illusion upheld by the "bookkeepers", and they keep trying to substantiate their belief with impressive, complex formulae. Any improvement to accounting is welcome, of course, and I do agree with Rappaport when right at the beginning of his book he criticizes the shortcomings of conventional accounting. However, his further-reaching reflections do not go beyond the limits of accounting, least of all do they lead us into the realm of corporate strategy.[11] There is one thing the accounting tricks can accomplish better than anything, and it is not in the best interest of proper corporate management: they lull insecure managers into an illusionary sense of security. The fact that a part of academia in economics and business administration has done its bit to provide this wrong thinking with "scientific" sustenance may be due to a lack of practical experience. It would not have been necessary, however, to show quite the amount of servility that could be observed being shown to the media and analysts.

A major factor in the swift spread of the shareholder value concept was probably the belief that it was possible to resolve issues through calculation, when in fact judgment and experience would have been required. Strategic management and corporate governance start where accounting, even of the most sophisticated kind, reaches its limit – because there is no way of quantifying the really crucial questions of corporate management in monetary terms.

Historically, whenever money was confused with business, and every time the financial economy and its logic (mostly due to circumstance) assumed a dominant position and influenced people's thinking and actions for a period of time, the result has been the opposite of what is used to build a case for finance-centered thinking: not a flourishing economy marked by rugged expansion and a steady value increase, but financial markets careering out of control due to excessive debt, followed by col-

---

10 See Gälweiler, Aloys: *Strategische Unternehmensführung*, 3rd edition, Frankfurt/New York, 2005.

11 Incidentally, Rappaport's deliberations do not go beyond the level that business administration in German-speaking countries had already reached with its theory on business valuation, as Horst Albach has conclusively demonstrated. See Albach, Horst: "Shareholder Value und Unternehmenswert"; in: *Zeitschrift für Betriebswirtschaft*; Volume 71 (2001), pp. 643 – 674.

lapse and a phase of economic contraction and deflationary destruction of value. In each case, the result has been not prosperity for all but poverty for many – which in the worst cases, due to widespread loss of confidence in the ruling institutions, gave rise to a period of political radicalization and totalitarianism.

I am explicitly referring to *deflationary* destruction of value, not the danger of inflation so often cited particularly by the central banks. It is not the destruction of the value of money, measured by a basket of commodities, that results from collapses of this kind in the financial economy, but the destruction of real values – falling share prices, declining real estate prices, drops in the prices of products and services. Companies' sales revenues and people's incomes shrink, a kind of economic despair spreads, and a deflationary spiral starts pulling everything down, with no central bank policy being able to help the economy get out of it.

For a society to function properly, it takes companies that prosper. It is the maximization of the *real* productive power of companies which creates real value, as opposed to financial value, and which provides the things that improve peoples' lives in real terms: more and better food, clothing, and living space, more and better education and training, more mobility and communication, more and better leisure, more and better art and culture. That is what the terms "standard of living" and "prosperity" mean. Contrary to widespread opinion, financial values cannot help to achieve these things; let alone speculative bubbles which divert economic resources away from true wealth creation and channel them into the stock markets. For a time, it may look as though more and better values are created there; the fact of the matter, however, is that this also creates the conditions for their permanent destruction.

Corporate Governance in the Best Interest of the Company

From the point of view of the *management* of a company, of the creation and increase of its productive performance and its success in the marketplace, my suggestion is not to focus attention on either interest group, neither the shareholders nor any other so-called stakeholders, but on the *company itself.* The corresponding term used in this book is *corporate capitalism*, as opposed to *shareholder capitalism* or *stakeholder capitalism*.

Looked at in this way, the company is not the object of a cluster of interest groups but an institutional unit in its own right, namely the archetypical productive entity in a developed society. To the legal mind this is a familiar concept; it was not for nothing that the corporation was constituted as a legal entity in its own right. What is good for the company will always lead to necessary adjustment, and for some interest groups – temporarily even all of them – to sacrifices. My suggestion, however, is to assume that a company's purpose is not to satisfy interest groups but to produce an output for the market.

This is not a law of nature, of course, and no one can be compelled to adopt my suggestion. Whatever approach is considered – a decision has to be made, and it should be the one that is most likely to ensure the proper management of the company.

Seen from this perspective, the purpose of the company is not to make shareholders rich, nor – as is often claimed by the opposing party – to create jobs. In other words, the goal cannot be to introduce some diffuse notion of social responsibility, as is often attempted by other critics of the shareholder value concept. This line of argument has been refuted by the experiences made with the social welfare state. A prospering company, however, will always be able to satisfy the interests of its stakeholders – above all, its shareholders. As was mentioned in the beginning, in particular anyone interested in a well-functioning free enterprise system and a permanently functional market economy ought to accept the arguments supporting this logic.

This rationale turns the spotlight onto the key question: *When does a company prosper, and how should it be managed in order for it to prosper?* The answers can be found in this book, and they are confirmed by the way in which the global economy has been developing. A company does not prosper, in terms of either operations or strategy, if it is geared towards shareholders and the stock markets; it prospers if it has *customers* paying for its services. It should therefore be considered the *purpose* of a company to create and satisfy customers. If the creation of value is to have any significance (which does not necessarily have to be the case) it must be customer value, not shareholder value, which should be the consistent and continuous guiding parameter for corporate management.

This alone will maximize the *chances* of making decisions that will be right in the long run, that is, market decisions, but it is not a *guarantee* for making the right decisions. There is no such thing. As I will show in this book, there are *several* factors – at least six of them – to be taken into account *simultaneously*. This seems to be one of the notions that managers find most difficult to accept, and apparently the consequence is that they keep searching for the *one*, the only and ultimate guiding parameter. Corporate management is not as simple as that. But anyone who has customers will always be able to find providers of capital, and ultimately have satisfied shareholders and stakeholders, too – not as the aim but as a consequence of doing business successfully. The top management bodies, both executive and supervisory, should be set up and committed accordingly, and they should be appointed, assessed, and compensated according to this premise.

Some may object that this is just another way of advocating the stakeholder approach, customers being one of several possible stakeholder groups. Seeing customers as stakeholders or as an interest group would be completely wrong, however, and would ignore the fact that customers and stakeholder groups follow an entirely different logic. Rappaport himself makes that mistake.[12] Customers do not have an *interest* in the company but they pay for its *product or service*. If a company fails to provide them with that service they will take their business elsewhere. They do not depend in the least on their interests being defended or asserted. Customers only become interest groups when there is no competition – that is, when companies have monopolies and, as a consequence, those buying from them lack the key attribute of a customer: the ability to choose, the ability to say no. The logic by which customers operate is determined not by their interests but by the benefits they gain, by the price-performance ratio the particular company offers, compared to its competitors.

This also shows that the *fundamental question* of corporate strategy has been misunderstood, due to the shareholder value theory. Its logical consequence were the so-called value creation or value enhancement strategies – which were focused on creating or enhancing value for the shareholder, not the customer. Their aim is to increase the company's value in the market – that is, the stock exchange.

It is, however, not a purpose of the *company* to be valuable. It cannot

---

12 Rappaport, Alfred: *Creating Shareholder Value*, revised version, New York, 1998, chapter 1.

even be a purpose for *shareholders* except when at bottom they are not interested in the company as such, but in the securities confirming ownership in the company – that is, the shares – and thus confuse one with the other. This is why companies' articles of association never contain a sentence along the lines of "a stock corporation established to serve the purpose of being valuable". The purposes usually given in the articles of association are very different, such as "trading in goods of all kinds" or "conducting banking business" or "manufacturing computer software", or automobiles, or machine tools.

The overriding aim of the company must be to be *competitive* in its field. That is something entirely different from being valuable. A company is competitive when it can do whatever customers pay for better than other companies. For this very reason, the logical equivalent is to say that a company's purpose is to create *satisfied* customers. Let me repeat this once more: neither the creation of jobs nor the increase of shareholder value can be a purpose of the company.

Its purpose must be directed at creating customer value. And contrary to occasional objections, this of course does not mean that products and services have to be "given away". Logically speaking, in business the term "satisfied" can only ever mean "relatively satisfied"; that is, satisfying the customer better than the competition can.

The view Rappaport and his followers take is very similar in part,[13] but his counterarguments in this context and the examples he uses are not conclusive; but actually lead to the wrong solution here because his thinking is based on the wrong central question. Of course, no one would ever demand that customers be subsidized until the company is bankrupt. Rappaport is quite right when he says that customer value does not automatically turn into shareholder value. And nobody has ever claimed that it does. There is no such automatism; nor is there any that works the opposite way, from shareholder value to any other kind of value.[14]

There is no causal relationship between the value of a company – however it may be defined or determined – and its competitiveness. As the

---

13 For instance, when he writes: "Even the most persistent advocate of shareholder value understands that without customer value there can be no shareholder value. The source of a company's long-term cash flow is its satisfied customers." Rappaport, Alfred: Creating Shareholder Value, revised version, New York, 1998.

14 See appendix on customer value.

stock markets made very clear even to the most unperceptive, once the hype had died down, there is simply no way of inferring a company's competitiveness from its share price. At no point in economic history has this ever been possible. The only thing to be inferred from stock prices is the naiveté, greed, and anxiety of investors. There *may* be a causal relationship the other way round, but there doesn't *have* to be one. The causal relationship between competitiveness and share prices is in no way absolute, as the recent valuation excesses have clearly shown.

For customers do not pay for the value of the *company*, as shareholders do, but for the value of its *products* or *services*. That is a value neither *of* nor *to* the company. It is a value to the *customer*. It is what is valuable in his eyes – and only his – and the only reason why he makes the purchase. Whether it will add to the value of the company is totally immaterial to him.

The value of the company is important only to those who have no intention of managing it, but want to buy or sell the company or parts of it. In other words, the question of the company's value does not even arise with regard to its entrepreneurial activity – its *business*. Here, the urgent and unrelenting question that arises day in, day out is that of performance and competitiveness.

One point to be kept in mind here is that shareholder value is primarily applied and arithmetically determined not by those acting *for* companies (that is, their top management) but by those trading *in* companies – a trend that came up in the late 1980s when the wave of mergers and acquisitions gained momentum. So what we are dealing with here, clear for all to see, is *shareholder* purpose being confused with *company* purpose, and being equated with it in a highly questionable manner. A further point I have mentioned before, and which is now becoming obvious from yet another perspective, is that there is a dangerous confusion between what is nowadays referred to as "investor" and what the term "entrepreneur" signifies (with the entrepreneurial manager being included). The interests of investors and entrepreneurs are as different as the logic of their situation, which can easily be recognized from the fact that every entrepreneur is an *investor* but very few investors are *entrepreneurs*.

My suggestion to focus corporate management on the company itself and its prosperity is not directed against profits. Quite the opposite is true: as we will see in chapter 5, this approach is more likely to lead to higher profit requirements compared to the shareholder value approach. Above all, these profits are to result from the operation of the company, not from shareholders' arbitrary acts – or, as has often been the case, from downright greed additionally spurred on by analysts. What is even more important, the company-centered approach leads to *real* profits, as opposed to the phantom profits generated by creative accounting and balance-sheet management – another phenomenon inherently resulting from the shareholder value approach, particularly in times of stock market booms. We have seen plenty of those over the past years.

It goes without saying that a company needs to cover its capital costs and generate profits. This does not mean, however, that this is its purpose – much less its only purpose. No one would deny that people have to eat. That does not mean that eating is their main purpose, and anyone centering his life around it will hardly be satisfied with the outcome.

Illusions Instead of Practical Management

In the minds of a generation of young managers, journalists, analysts, consultants, management trainers, and scientists, the shareholder value theory and the value creation strategies based upon it have been established as the supposedly only way to manage companies and do business. It is natural for these people – because they have not experienced anything else – to interpret everything in the context of the bull market, apparently unaware that they know only *half* of the stock exchange reality: the *pleasant* half. Most of them have never experienced a bear market; they do not know how brutal it can be, how long it can take, how deep prices can plunge, and that historically, every upturn – *without exception* – has been followed by a downturn pushing prices back to where they were before, if not lower. They have not learnt anything else but shareholder value and the stock market boom. They do not know any alternatives. They do not know why this theory emerged in the first place, in the late 1980s, or from what situation or historical development it resulted. Hence they consider this theory to be the only conceivable truth – and they defend it with dogmatic persistence, as half-truths have always been in history.

As has been outlined above, however, the shareholder value theory is by no means the *only* theory. It was simply the *newest* one for this generation – and it is probably the *worst* one ever developed. Peter F. Drucker expressed his doubts back in the early 1990s, and has repeated them several times since. I explain my own skepticism in this book, and have outlined it in numerous other publications. I consider the shareholder value theory to be wrong and misleading, in some essential points even dangerous, since strict abidance by it has serious negative consequences for business and society. A frequent argument in related discussions is that shareholder value was merely *misunderstood*. That is not the problem. The concept is not misunderstood – it is *wrong*. That is, it is wrong as a reference for sustainable entrepreneurial and managerial action. The shareholder value approach is hostile to investments and innovation, and it leads to a misallocation of resources.

As I have pointed out before, this alone does not have to be a *compelling* reason for managers and supervisory bodies to dismiss shareholder value altogether. In a free society, everyone is free to choose one or the other theory, even a wrong one. It would be wise, however, to make one's choice while being aware of the implications of a theory, and in the light of available alternatives and their consequences.

One of the inevitable and dangerous consequences of the shareholder orientation is the temptation it holds for managers to do anything to make the company look profitable, even when it's not. This includes pampering the public with profit expectations, reporting pro-forma profits in the absence of real ones, sugarcoating balance sheets, and channeling one's last reserves to the stock market to avoid disappointing the expectations so laboriously nurtured.

Shareholder value thinking could only take root only under certain, accidental circumstances, as explained above. In conjunction with the greatest stock market upturn in history and with severe, illusion-driven misinterpretations of business and economics, it led to a mix of beliefs which for many people turned into something of a cult, and frequently it was defended with aggression rather than arguments if any doubts were raised about it.

The most flagrant case I experienced myself was that of a top manager at a German electronics company which was making one of the most talked about and apparently most successful public offerings at the height of the boom. A particularly keen follower of the shareholder philosophy, not only was the man unable to get anything out of the thoughts I expressed; he absolutely failed to understand what I was talking about. He openly expressed his rejection of my arguments in front of a large audience, making no attempt to conceal his aggressiveness – which in the eyes of most of the people present was not exactly a credit to his upbringing. Basically, though, he was just a pathetic case. Not only are his stock options worthless today, which means he put in several years of work for nothing; in addition, he is now mired in insoluble financial difficulties for having taken out credit to purchase great quantities of shares in his own company and, out of blind trust in the zeitgeist, in other high-tech and "high-potential" companies as well.

Some of the most unfortunate developments in economic history were a result of this cult, and they led to the obvious structural weaknesses of the American economy and, due to unthinking imitation, of many other economies as well. It is quite possible that the 1990s and 2000s will go down in economic history as a period of collective errors and of mass delusion.

How could these cult-like phenomena come about? They were not only caused by the shareholder value theory with its superficial logic and plausibility; it also coincided with some other factors in a combination which, though not unique, is certainly rare. The *first* of these factors was the supposedly spectacular economic miracle in the United States after a serious, but comparatively short recession in the early 1990s. It was believed to have been brought on by the clever economic policy of the US authorities, specifically the Federal Reserve, and by the powerful effects of Corporate America's shareholder-value-based management philosophy. The *second* factor, which appeared to be a consequence of the first, was the longest bull market in the history of the stock exchanges, in which every fall in share prices was nothing but a good buying opportunity. The *third* factor was the belief in a globalization that would suffer no setbacks and would ultimately be to everyone's benefit. The *fourth* was the theory that digitalization and the internet were creating a business world that was not only new but sheer *paradise* in every way. These four are topped by a *fifth* factor – perhaps the most effective in quickly spreading such beliefs: an unprecedented level of media propaganda for all these seemingly so new and desirable phenomena.

Entertainment Instead of Information

One important aspect of the boom was – and still is – the *wide gap* between economic realities and what the media report about business and economic matters. The two have almost nothing in common. As I have repeatedly pointed out in my publications, particularly my monthly management newsletter, there has always been a certain discrepancy between business in reality and in depiction. But never before, except maybe for the 1920s, has this discrepancy been greater than in the past fifteen years, and never before has it been nurtured with such professionalism and thus so effectively.

The reason for this is not a decline in quality of the classic business media, such as the *Financial Times,* the *Economist,* or – for the German-speaking world – the *Frankfurter Allgemeine Zeitung.* These media are just as good today as they have always been. They are also just as dry and "boring" to many people. The public therefore do not derive their information from them, but prefer the new business *tabloids,* as we might call them.

These have turned the business sector into an *entertainment* arena. Their aim is not information but sentiment. Above all, this new business showbiz is meant to be a *business,* and that can only work out if reports are optimistic. The old media wisdom that *only bad news are good news* is reversed. No one wants to hear bad news about business or the economy, least of all about the stock markets.

The result is an unholy alliance with the sales interests of the Wall Street industry, for which the new media are a superb vehicle for presenting itself in the best light. This is true of many print media, but it is most obvious with television. One example of many in the genre is the US television network CNBC. As far as professionalism – and thus effectiveness – are concerned, this broadcaster could hardly be surpassed. The tendentious nature of its reports is quite blatant – bullish, bullish, bullish; sheer optimism and forced euphoria... It is "impressive" to see how artfully even the most negative facts and occurrences, such as major bankruptcies, Wall Street crime, collapsing business profits, are turned into something positive – far removed from reality (apart from the psychology of greed), but excellently crafted.

Many economies, however, and above all that of the US, are still suffering from the consequences of the misguided economic theories of the 1990s and the resulting misallocation of resources. Their current state is such that a swift and sustainable recovery appears highly unlikely. In all probability, the almost universal belief that this is only a short-term – a "V-shaped" – recession will be painfully dispelled, the reasons being of a structural nature.

The first and perhaps most important of them is what one could justifiably refer to as the profit implosion at US corporations. There has
never been anything like it in the history of American business. Its cause
is simple. Financial figures were groomed to the point of balance-sheet
fraud – all in the service of the cult of shareholder value, and in deference
to the analysts. Another reason lies in the excessive level of debt in both
the business and the private sector. The third reason is a striking lack of
investment, another thing that had never reached comparable dimensions
before.

Many refuse to face the truth, just as they once were unwilling to admit
that there could be a recession at all – even when it had already begun,
as the US authorities have meanwhile admitted. There was a widespread
belief that business cycle fluctuations were no longer possible. To illustrate
the opinion generally held at the time, I cite a *Wall Street Journal* article
dated June 1998, in which R. Dornbusch, Professor of Economics at MIT,
is quoted as saying: *"The US economy likely will not see a recession for
years to come. We don't want one, we don't need one, and, as we have
the tools to keep the current expansion going, we won't have one. This
expansion will run forever."*

Similar things happened to the economies of other countries: after having been indiscriminately praised and euphorically celebrated for years,
and portrayed as new paradises, they are now in a desperate state. Above
all, this is true of Japan, certain "Tiger States" and many Latin-American
countries. There is no way of telling what the situation is really like in
India and China, as the figures published are notoriously unreliable.

The Delusion of a Superior US Economy

Anyone making a sober analysis of economic developments, in particular in the US, where the recent aberrations originated, would soon come
to the following conclusions, whose validity became more apparent with
each month that passed:[15]

The much-lauded, and naively admired, American economic miracle
never actually took place. It was a *media event* – nothing else. First and

---

15 See also the appendix to this book.

foremost, the US growth rates – even as officially published – were no higher than those in earlier periods, as a comparison of the years since the Second World War will reveal. They were also massively inflated by the statistical effect of the so-called *hedonic price indexing*. Meanwhile, the authorities in charge have begun to correct their figures in retrospect, which, however, largely goes unnoticed by the public.

There never was a *productivity miracle*, except for the small segment of computer manufacturing. Professor Robert Gordon of Northwestern University in Chicago is one of the few clear-sighted analysts of the productivity figures published. He managed to demonstrate that there was and is no quantitative evidence to support the claims made for increasing productivity.

The *profits* of US firms were largely owed to creative accounting and the sugarcoating of balance-sheets – not to real economic output. They resulted, *first,* from the incorrect accounting of stock options and associated tax benefits; *second,* from software expenses being carried as assets rather than written off immediately; *third,* from salaries being kept artificially low in conjunction with stock options; and *fourth,* from financial market maneuvers such as share buyback programs.

The bull market was not based on true value creation, but on the exorbitant level of debt of all sectors of the US economy. The much-lauded American *budget miracle* is another phenomenon that never existed. The United States' public debt continues to increase, and is now at a higher level than it has ever been.

Most figures on the US economy of the past five years are either *incorrect* or they have been *misinterpreted* and *propagandized* through the media. People's activities have thus been guided in a wrong direction, which, in turn, led to a massive *misallocation* of resources. Now that the illusion of a never-ending upturn has been shattered, ample corrections are called for which will take some time to implement.

The widely held belief that the success of US corporations is *owed to* their exceptionally good management and sophisticated corporate governance, is *wrong*. The current business failures and their results are evidence of the fact that this kind of corporate governance does not guarantee effective control of management, neither in the best interest of the company itself nor – ironically – in the best interest of the shareholders. Despite the supposed sophistication and superiority of US-type corporate governance, with the high level of transparency, the shareholder rights and other security rules it stipulates, there are still dramatic business failures, with Enron probably being the first of many more to come. And despite Europe's supposedly backward state of development, we have superbly managed companies here, with Nestlé being just one of many examples.

The truth is that there are poorly managed and well managed companies all over the world, irrespective of any corporate governance rules. Note that I am not averse to setting basic rules for the management of companies, as long as they are reasonably defined. But laws and provisions cannot really ensure or prevent good corporate governance – at least not to the extent frequently alleged by their proponents. More than anything, the key is the competence of top management – both the executive and the supervisory board – and the way they work and collaborate.

It is therefore just as naïve to believe in a basic and universal superiority of US management practices, as it was naïve from the mid-1980s to the early 1990s to believe in Japanese superiority. The US economy certainly has many strengths that European and Asian economies do not have, but it also has its deficiencies. It should be emulated in those areas where it is strong. Contrary to popular opinion, management, and specifically corporate governance, is not among those areas.

Entrepreneurs and managers will have to face the fact that a profound reorientation is called for. It requires rigorously abandoning the high-flying ideas of the 1990s and 2000s, and being prepared for rough times. A robust, customer-focused business strategy; uncompromising productivity increases; professional innovation management; letting go of all the illusions, the bragging and the big-talking heard in all parts of the company; a sober analysis of what is really behind all the "e"-bravado; responsibility and performance at all levels – these are the crucial points of orientation for the next years. Bluffers and phonies should not be given the chance to climb the corporate ladder. They had their chances – and plenty of them – in the 1990s. It is time to demand real substance once again.

Capable managers are immune to fads, their thinking is not influenced by the zeitgeist. They are masters of their managerial craft. They set benchmarks for modesty and sobriety, which are much more effective in inspiring people's motivation and commitment – which will doubtlessly be necessary for the required reorientation – than any vision or illusion can ever be. The latter only encourage false hopes and expectations.

Part I

Chapter 1

Should Supervisory Bodies Manage?

Though we have every reason to be wary of the cult of the great leader, no modern society and no economy can survive, let alone thrive, without leadership. By *leadership* I mean the function responsible for the big tasks at hand, such as being ahead of change and leading the "Great Transformation". But what should it look like, and how should it work? Who should exercise it? How should the responsibility be handled?

As sensitive as the subject may be, leadership beyond even the best management will continue to be important – the more so, as both society and business are undergoing one of the greatest transformations in history. In 10 to 15 years – and maybe we will not even have that much time – nothing will be like it is now. Transformation processes of this kind have never been smooth. They put societies to the toughest of all tests. In ordinary times, management leadership may not be necessary, nor is poor leadership likely to do too much damage. It is necessary in *difficult* times – and when times are difficult, bad or even incompetent leadership can do irreparable damage. Leadership is needed – and may even be needed more over the next ten years than it has ever been in the last and this century. But *who* should lead?

In modern society, with its multitude of organizations and institutions, any conceivable answer to this question must be in the *plural* form. I am not going to try to answer the question. Just this much: from the perspective laid out in this book, one institution which over the past two decades was not involved in the kind of *leadership* in *business* management any more, or involved in a wrong way – as I will explain at a later point – ought to have a powerful voice in the orchestra of management: the *supervisory body*. I am *not* saying that it should be the *only* corporate body in charge of management. That would be neither feasible nor desirable. In this regard, I find the one-tier management system that some countries have to be rather inexpedient. For instance, the Swiss stock corporation law clearly goes too far in my view, and as recent reforms show, its deficiencies can only be compensated by laying an *extreme* amount of responsibility on the board of directors, which is more of a hindrance than a help in increasing management effectiveness. On the other hand, the supervisory body's restriction to a mere (and narrowly interpreted) monitoring function, as it is *permitted* (though not *mandatory*) under German law, is definitely not enough.

Rather, top management bodies need to *collaborate* in a well-thought-out and balanced manner, allowing them to complement and also to monitor each other. Recent efforts by the regulators to strengthen the supervisory body's leadership role are headed in the right *direction*: above all, they are aimed at extending the scope of liability and accountability, and we can expect this tendency to increase. So far, however, most efforts at reform have been half-hearted and indecisive. They fail to add clarity in vital matters. Where reforms of corporate supervision are bolder (and perhaps even too bold), as in the case of Switzerland, they are lopsided and practical implementation is lagging behind.

So the supervisory body should have a leadership function. Why? As I hope to make sufficiently clear in the next chapters, there have never been such enormous and difficult tasks to be solved by society and business as will result from the profound changes currently going on. Therefore, although it would be desirable for *all* societal institutions to work well, it will be of central importance that *business* institutions fulfill their tasks. Of course they will never be able to solve all the problems of a society in transformation. As a matter of fact, business can only fulfill a limited number of tasks – and it should restrict itself to those. These few tasks, however, are an essential prerequisite for all other problems to be solved.

Business enterprises need to fulfill a narrowly defined set of tasks: those of which this – and only this – type of societal institution has proved itself capable. They must, however, fulfill these narrowly limited tasks in a *much broader context,* also taking into account the many inconsistent demands being made – all of which is not only in the best interest of society but also in their *own*, well-understood best interest.

The work to be done cannot be left to one entity alone, least of all to the executive body which under German law has a dominant role. In addition, a strong and effective supervisory body is needed. To fulfill its – executive – tasks, which in themselves demand full commitment and undivided attention, the executive body works *within* the system, so to speak. The supervisory body, on the other hand, has to work *on* the system. Its task is to ensure that the executive body can and does meet its obligations, that appropriate conditions are created for its effectiveness, and that its perception and attention are directed at the right categories.

Metaphorically speaking, the supervisory body must be a teacher, a mentor, and a judge, all in one. To this end, it needs to deal with numerous questions which seem to be unrelated to economics as such. In truth, they are questions concerning the essentials of management and doing business. They are dealt with more extensively here than what might be called the "technical" details of the top management organization and its mode of operation. As important as those may be, they can only be determined in consideration of certain purposes and tasks, which therefore need to be clarified first.

In this connection, the supervisory body will have to eliminate a series of misunderstandings, errors, and false doctrines about business management which have emerged over the past 20 to 25 years, and to make sure there will be nothing more of the sort. This requires leadership both in the mental-conceptual sense and in terms of personal relationships. It is up to the supervisory body to define what purpose a company has to fulfill, what it should and should not do, what constitutes performance and results, what basic conditions have to be met, and by what criteria the company's business activities should be judged and accounted for. The answers to these questions cannot be left to either the market or to politics. These questions – not all, but most of them – must be subject to the autonomy of the business sector, and answered by it, as otherwise it will not be able to fulfill its task. Finding convincing, credible, and correct answers to questions of this kind requires a considerable degree of leadership.

But there are more arguments in favor of a strong supervisory body. In the past few years, the first effects of the fundamental change outlined above have become quite obvious. Proper response requires drastic, harsh decisions, forcing people to make dire sacrifices and even give up some of their vested rights and achievements. Above all, it requires another, new perspective on business. Both of these – the new perspective and the drastic decisions – can only originate in the supervisory body. It has to make sure that the right perspective is taken, and it also has to bring about the necessary decisions. Political institutions are no longer able to do that with the kind of democracy and the media society we have today. I have made this point in the preface to this book, and will elaborate on it later. Politics has largely become ineffective, and virtually unable to make and implement unpopular decisions, even when they have been recognized as being urgently required.

So the supervisory body *should* manage – but *can* it manage? The answer is: yes and no. It is *yes* to the extent that in *all* legal systems, even the German one with its rather tight restrictions, effective management by the supervisory body is quite *possible*, and to a much greater extent than is generally admitted in public debate. It is *not* for large parts of real-life practice, where the management impact of supervisory bodies is clearly underdeveloped. In many cases, the kind of structure that the supervisory body has given itself, exercising its right to self-organization, as well as the tasks it has given itself and its working approach are not suitable for achieving real impact. For the same reasons, it does not provide the best example for the executive body. The resulting leadership vacuum will not remain unfilled. Either the executive body takes advantage of it, or third parties use it to promote their ideas, which are frequently business-adverse or evidence of business illiteracy.

It is up to the supervisory body to decide *whether* it *wishes* to manage. Occasionally there may be valid reasons for delegating all management to other organs (or for simply *de facto* leaving it to others) except for those tasks legally reserved for the supervisory body. But if the supervisory body wishes to manage actively, it most definitely *can*. In my opinion it *should*.

The central question of this book is: what has to be done, and what can be done, if the supervisory body is to actively contribute to the management of a company – and to do so under the present legal conditions?

For the purposes of this book, I assume the conditions provided by the current legal systems as given. Although one or the other amendment to certain legal provisions could facilitate quite a few things, and enforce some others, my suggestions are not addressed to the legislators. Although appeals and recommendations to the legislative power might occasionally be justified, it would be impractical to wait for legal reforms to tackle concrete situations. It is not necessary either, because there are more possibilities for supervisory bodies to exercise management and have a practical impact than is currently believed and taken advantage of. All that is needed is the will. And that will should be there – the free will, as otherwise there will soon be legislative action because no nation in the world can afford to have poorly managed businesses. Legal regulations, however, cannot automatically be assumed to be favorable. It is therefore a better solution to autonomously define and fulfill sensible requirements, thus giving government no reason for additional regulations.

This book was written with major corporations in mind. The vast majority of its content, however, equally applies to small and medium-sized businesses which – depending on their size and legal form – may not be obliged by law to install the respective corporate bodies, but *de facto* have or need them. In the final analysis, every company needs the same management functions, for the tasks to be fulfilled are the same. The functions may be organized differently and the tasks may be carried out by varying numbers of people. In the worst case, everything will be concentrated in one person. It is, however, a cardinal error to believe that large corporations *as a matter of principle* have to be managed differently from small or medium-sized ones. This view, which I consider to be altogether wrong, is held by many managers – both in large corporations and in medium-sized companies, but for different reasons. Unquestionably, the size of a company has an influence on the How of management, but never on the What.

These considerations are even important for *family-run enterprises*, which are always exposed to the temptation of giving family matters priority over the interests of the business. Their fate and success, more than anything else, depend on a well-thought-out and timely drafted regulation of overall management.

In this book, I largely refrain from discussing the legal aspects of problems. They are dealt with exhaustively in the relevant literature on legal and business administration issues. The central question here is aimed at good, proper, effective, and practical management. Even if, for example, under German law the members of the supervisory board can be denied certain things by the executive board – such as the right to directly talk to the managers of subsidiaries – a competent and persuasive chairman will get his way if he feels it is important, simply by virtue of this natural authority, and based on constructive collaboration with the management board. He can "request" this conversation, and any CEO will know how this "request" is to be understood.

One obstacle to effective overall management is the widespread habit of misperceiving management issues as being mostly matters of personal power. I do not deny that power – even personal power – does or should play a role in business. However, management problems can only be discussed sensibly, and perhaps solved, if the discussion is not dominated by aspects of power but by the *tasks* to be fulfilled, and the *responsibility* resulting from them. They have to mark the starting point of these considerations, while the questions of power should be shifted to the very end.

My suggestions to strengthen the supervisory function do not result from the intention to limit executive bodies' room to maneuver. Quite to the contrary: an effective supervisory function makes it *possible* to provide executive bodies with the greatest possible liberties and powers. Besides, it will become obvious that a supervision that is not restricted to control in the narrower sense, but exercises management – or co-management, to be more precise – does not primarily depend on hierarchical superiority to work well. In fact, the view put forward here enables top-level management bodies to collaborate as partners, with the supervisory board growing beyond a mere control and monitoring function to include something equally important: a *helping* and *supporting* function, a sounding board and an advisor to the executive body, which is generally well appreciated by experienced executive managers. This, in turn, makes it possible to turn power into legitimate power, power that is accountable, without limiting the performance and competitiveness of the company.

Chapter 2

Functional Deficiencies of Current Systems

Corporate Supervision – A Fiction?

The names and legal forms of supervisory bodies differ greatly by country. Regardless of variety, however, they all have one thing in common: With few exceptions they do not work, or at least not well. As a general rule, they perform just the minimum of tasks required by law, irrespective of whether that law gives them a more restricted role – as in Germany – or a rather strong one, as is the case in Switzerland. At least this is how it has been.

Wherever there are exceptions, one will usually find a particularly fortunate constellation of people performing their tasks with special, extraordinary care, diligence, and thoroughness, as well as with a particular sense of responsibility. Or the firm has retained the constellation under which it was originally established – and for which corporate supervision was originally designed: a strong presence of company owners in the supervisory body. In a considerable number of cases – a number that is much too big – the supervisory body's actions does not extend beyond a set of irrelevant rituals, compulsory exercises, and the completion of formalities.

Another case where supervision *seems* to work is when, over extended periods of time, the general economic development is particularly favorable, marked by *prosperity* and *stability*, so that supervisory bodies have not really had to face major challenges.

With nearly all major corporate collapses or what seemed to be sudden threats to companies' existence, the supervisory bodies were usually the last to be informed about the actual situation. In most cases, employees and executives, customers and suppliers, the media and the public were privy to more and better information earlier on.

Every time a "scandal" was brought to light, the same accusations and could be heard and the same "reasons" were given: the failure of supervisory bodies, ignorance, negligence, and incompetence or, alternatively, the executive body's failure to inform the supervisory body exhaustively and in due time.

In the majority of cases, the problem smolders somewhere and remains unnoticed by most. Only those directly involved are able to see it, with most failing to realize what is happening. When asked, "how does your supervisory board or board of directors work?", in two-thirds of all cases the answer is a polite smile and eloquent silence, irrespective of whether the question is addressed to supervisory or executive bodies.

Deficiencies in overall management only become dramatically *visible* in very spectacular cases where problems can no longer be hidden. In numerous other cases which attracted less or no publicity at all, the supervisory body probably did not function too well either. How else could one explain the numerous structural problems in key industries, which – apparently surprisingly – surfaced in the 1990s, in what turned out to be the first genuine recession after the Second World War? In part they may have been due to political circumstances, but many other causes lay in the companies' *management:* from a considerable backlog in productivity, technology, and innovation they ranged to serious restructuring needs in manufacturing, to the bloated, in part grotesquely overstaffed middle management and central staff departments, to highly questionable acquisitions and diversification efforts. Even the corporate raiding that originated in the US and all associated excesses were ultimately a consequence of a failure of the board, which either did not pay enough attention to corporate governance or had a misguided perception of corporate performance.

And while the counter- and corrective measures which have since been introduced are quite encouraging, the fact remains that *originally* all these developments were *allowed* to happen, in that the respective decisions were *made* and approved at some point or that decisions which could have prevented them were *not* made. The adjustments belatedly made in the business sector were not made based on *proactive* management – otherwise, the developments in question could not have happened – but *subsequently* as a response to market and competitive pressure.

When a problem manifests itself so frequently and irrespective of individual legal arrangements and designs, its reasons cannot lie in the failure of individual people; rather, there must be underlying causes not necessarily of a legal but of a *constitutive* nature. The constitution of a corporation has always been a difficult issue, as is evident from the various reforms of current and previous stock corporation laws. Incidentally, these reforms were never undertaken with a proactive focus on the basic questions of corporate management, but always as a response to failures, bankruptcies, or questionable practices.

In the times of Georg von Siemens, however, or of John P. Morgan, the supervisory body obviously worked, and its performance and functional effectiveness could be considered a given. So what has changed since then, and what are the reasons for current problems? The following seven points are essential:[16]

1. One major reason lies in the *emergence and basic success of large public companies*. In its original design, the *owner-entrepreneur* was supposed to be represented in their top decision-making bodies, which used to be the case in the major corporations of the 19th and early 20th century. Shareholders were a limited number of individuals, each of whom held a sizeable share in the company. Their interests were clear and unambiguous to anyone – and they were of an entrepreneurial nature. They devoted their full attention to the company, as well as a major share of their time, and if they held seats in more than one supervisory body their commitment was limited to very *few* of them.

   Today, only very few supervisory bodies have real owners among them, people who represent a genuine *entrepreneurial* interest, are liable with their personal assets, and have plenty of relevant industry knowledge and business expertise. The members of today's supervisory bodies may have a *general* knowledge about economic processes, and they may know *their* industry and *their* business (e. g., banking representatives), but very often they are far from knowing enough about the specifics of the company supervised, one major reason lying in the immense complexity modern companies usually have.

2. Another reason is that the tasks of the supervisory body actually require *full-time commitment*, or at least a major share of a person's time, whereas in most cases the function is performed as a part-time activity, and is often afforded a very *small* share of people's time.

---

16 See also Drucker, Peter F.: *Management*, London 1973, pp. 627 et seq.

One exception could be made for supervisory functions under German law, or under provisions emulating German law: here, contrary to other countries, the supervisory body (restrictively interpreted) exercises control functions *only*. But even these, and the rights and obligations of approval and the responsibility associated with it, require a multiple of the time usually dedicated to it, if the tasks are to be performed in a diligent and responsible manner.

3. Another reason for functional deficiencies is the unquestionable fact that strong executive managers often do not *want* a capable supervisory body. At the very least, many of them share an *ambivalent* – though unspoken – attitude towards corporate supervision. Under German law, they have plenty of possibilities to keep the supervisory board "out of the loop", and they often do so.

The reasons for the ambivalence are obvious. An effective top-level body requires top performance from executive boards; it asks many unpleasant questions; it demands to know details and asks for reasons – and it does so before decisions are made or approved. Effective supervisory bodies insist on discussing alternatives before requests are approved, and whenever key personnel decisions are due they ask to get to see several candidates before one of them gets their approval.

Many executive boards understand these things to mean that their rights are being restricted, their ability to respond quickly to events is being curtailed, boundaries are being overstepped, their expertise questioned, and they are being distrusted; occasionally they also feel that their position of power is being threatened.

4. The fourth reason for functional deficiencies lies in the *information base* to which supervisory bodies usually have access. *Competent* supervisory board members will occasionally demand to know how the *key systems* in a company work (such as strategy, planning, and control), whether executive boards really deal with the *essential problems*, whether the *right* things are being monitored and measured (e. g., productivity) and they will occasionally want to keep an eye on *corporate culture*. Off and on, they will want to talk to the managers of subsidiaries and divisions, and they will personally want to verify the situation in the markets, the sales organizations and channels.

Without ever dealing with these things, it is *impossible* to exercise competent top-level control, except, as mentioned before, in periods of favorable and stable economic development.

5. There is a fifth reason explaining the ambivalence of executive bodies towards supervisory bodies, as well as the functional deficiencies of the latter. It happens quite often that supervisory board members have *a lack of management know-how*. A deficiency, by the way, which is also encountered in many executive boards – much more often so than would be desirable.

   How else could one explain the grave errors regularly occurring in acquisitions, diversification efforts, and the building of conglomerates, all the misguided growth strategies (mostly based on product line expansions), all the poorly handled key innovations, all the hopelessly inadequate organization structures, all the disastrous human resources policies in place?

   Supervisory bodies can and must know what the elements of a good and right corporate policy and strategy are; that acquisitions, diversifications and conglomerates have rarely worked well, and if so, only under certain conditions; how ill-advised growth strategies can be distinguished form *healthy* growth; and what the criteria and "measuring instruments" are for assessing and determining a company's "health".

6. Another reason, related to what was said under point 5, is that to this date there is no consensus on how a company should be managed *in the first place*. What is commonly referred to as corporate governance is a disaster zone in terms of theory, lacking both substance and consistency. Part of the reason may be that it is an intersection of several academic disciplines: the law, business administration, economics, management, psychology, and, to a certain degree, also political science. Cross-sectoral issues do not fit in academic categories. They would require interdisciplinary work.

   Only very few, particularly capable business leaders have adequate knowledge about corporate governance. When the *basics* are not even clear, it is no wonder that the functionality of corporate supervision is deficient. Years ago, these basics may have played a minor role. A fair amount of pragmatism may have offset the fact that they were lacking. Today, the very significance of major corporations makes clarity on this point an indispensable requirement.

7. One last reason is the *immediate leadership* exercised in a supervisory body by its chairman. As trivial as it may sound, poorly prepared, managed, and reviewed meetings are much more frequent, even on this level (let alone the levels below) than one would think.

In many cases, the discussion leaves much to be desired in terms of breadth and depth, open-mindedness and persistence, decision-making processes, and so on. Group-dynamic and group-think phenomena play a much greater role than people would care to admit.

As I mentioned in the preface to this book, it is impossible to discuss the function of corporate supervisory bodies without expressing some criticism. Potential objections to my critical remarks may be that a majority of companies are doing okay, and that a few problematic cases, crises, and scandals should not be perceived to be symptomatic of the totality of businesses.

With regard to the *first* point, I concede that there are also cases where corporate supervision works well. We should learn from them. As far as the *second* point is concerned, my criticism does not relate to the *companies* as such, but to the overall management *bodies*, in particular the supervisory function and, to some extent, also to the executive board. Companies *can* function even when their supervisory bodies are weak and ineffective. A capable executive board *can* do excellent work. In that case it will be despite the supervisory body – not because of it. I will even go one step further. A company can function even when its supervisory board *and* its executive board are weak, at least for a certain period of time and in economic circumstances that do not require any major and far-reaching decisions.

It is not that rare for a capable, experienced middle management tier to compensate for deficiencies at the top. The real work is often done at the levels below top management. In my consulting practice, I have encountered quite a few situations where executive boards did not get much going, but still the company produced relatively good *operational* results. In most cases, however, I also realized that the *strategic* position had been eroding. That, however, did not really bother those executives, or it was drowned in the sometimes Kafkaesque power structures, as long as it did not show on the balance sheets. We know the phenomenon from politics: it is not rare for teams of excellent officials to prevent incapable ministers from causing real damage. So the fact that a *company* works well should *not* lead anyone to assume the same for all of its managerial bodies.

In many countries, the provisions of corporate law governing corporate supervision have undergone reforms over the past years; mostly – as mentioned before – not because someone had the good sense to take precautions or adjust to changes in the business environment, but from painful experience in concrete instances. Most reforms pointed in two directions: *first,* they enhanced the supervisory body's accountability and streamlined the procedures for claiming this accountability if and as needed; *second,* they expanded the supervisory body's competencies, in some cases – as in Switzerland – to the point where the overall management of the company is assigned exclusively, and indelegably, to the board of directors.

These reforms, which in part went too far or at least approached the limits of what can be considered to be reasonable, have failed to achieve any improvements in the way supervisory bodies function. Well-managed companies do not need any changes, and poorly managed ones have yet to see any. First of all, what emerged from these reforms was confusion and uncertainty, as they have made the extent and scope of functional deficiencies clearly visible. The question which now arises is how the regulators' new, higher demands can be met *in practice.* That, in turn, is not a legal problem but a *management issue* – not in the trivial sense of the word "management" but in the sense of comprehensive design, guidance, and control for the company, for the only institution that creates wealth for a society. Now it becomes evident how little there is in terms of foundations and clarity for "corporate governance" – a concept for which we do not even have a fitting term in German.

Is Criticism Justified?

The question is whether the business sector in the German-speaking world – but also in other countries – is as good as it can and should be. It *used to be* good over extended periods of *favorable economic cycles* and in a period characterized by *sellers' markets.* But what about *getting prepared for the future?*

In every country there are superbly managed and functioning businesses. There are, however, lots of industries where pronounced deficiencies have developed over the past years, where recession has painfully revealed existing inadequacies and the need for countermeasures, which could have been avoided if the executive board had exercised a *forward-looking* kind of management and if capable supervisory bodies had been in place.

Here are some examples:

- Programs to *cut costs* in the double-digit percentage range only become necessary when cost control has failed over many years, having been neither executed by executives nor enforced by supervisory bodies.
- *Capacity cuts and mass redundancies* can only become necessary if at some point before there were decisions – taken by somebody and approved by somebody else – which led to overcapacities and created overstaffed organizational entities.
- *Productivity backlogs* in the order of magnitude that could be observed do not happen overnight. It takes years for them to build up, and they have to be regarded as an indicator of the failure of executive and supervisory boards.
- *Lack of market orientation*, *quality backlogs*, the failure to set up operations that provide *customer value*, the failure to notice the emergence of innovative sales channels, and many (not all) of the *failures to adopt new technologies* can only be explained by inadequate management and supervision.
- *Proliferating bureaucracy* and *bloated central staff departments* can only be prevented or eliminated from the top. If it does not happen there, it will not happen anywhere else.
- *Power struggles* between executive board members, going on for months on end, right under the eyes of a very amused public and shocked employees, are only possible when corporate supervision fails.

The emergence of *these* problems, at the very least, is down to top management, entirely irrespective of economic cycles and economic policy. With the exception of overcapacities, these problems have nothing to do with an *erroneous* assessment of the situation – they are owed much more to a *lack* of assessment.

Erroneous assessments of a situation will always have to be reckoned with. In my view, they do *not* pertain to the failures of top management but to the unavoidable risks of doing business. However, from my contacts with executives at all organizational levels I can conclude that the art and methodology of assessment are often underdeveloped. Too many managers, including those at the top, uncritically believe in the merits of growth; too many extrapolate past developments into the future; too many trust in economic cycles to help them out, and are generally not thorough, diligent, and careful enough in *thinking through* and *challenging* the foundations and conditions of their businesses, as well as not observing emerging trends and, above all, the disruption and reversal of trends. Only very few are mentally prepared for a potential recession. So it is another one of the supervisory body's tasks to ensure a precise assessment of the business situation.

Classic yet Avoidable Management Mistakes

In recent years, some *classic* management mistakes occurred – too often – reflecting poorly on the capabilities of top-level management bodies.

When *small* companies run into trouble the general public usually does not notice. It is a different story when the same happens to *major*, renowned corporations. Major corporations are highly *visible* and believed to set *standards* for the quality of management actions. They are perceived to be representative of business *in general*.

When major corporations face financial distress, the dimensions involved are of interest to everybody. Thousands of jobs in a labor market that is already difficult; losses running into the billions, which have to be faced all of a sudden – and to the apparent surprise of everyone – although shortly before there had been talk of a balanced or even good economic result; the fate of entire regions and industries being at stake. Management celebrities who were considered role models of foresightedness and entrepreneurship are suddenly forced to resign, give up, plunge into the entrepreneurial abyss. Monuments of business are toppled from their pedestals, and quite often it is the same journalists that praised these companies and individuals to the sky shortly before who suddenly turn into their harshest critics.

Were these journalists mistaken? Was it really impossible to see it all coming? Was the disaster caused by "the circumstances" – the general economic situation, the economic and industrial policies – or did the managers commit mistakes?

Usually, it is a combination of *several* factors. But as much as "circumstances" such as the economic situation, economic policy, currency fluctuations, labor costs, and tax burdens may play a role in this – in most recent cases some *classic* and *severe* management mistakes were evident. At the very least they could have been avoided.

They illustrate, in part quite dramatically, how important capable, good, and right management can be. They also make vividly clear how *zeitgeist trends* and *fads* can contaminate people's thinking. This may have to be tolerated for the bulk of the population. It is not tolerable for *top-level executives* in business and society.

The critical comments I am making here are not a case of 20/20 hindsight; in fact, I have openly expressed my views on these things for many years, both verbally and in writing, clearly stating the names of those responsible. It is not the first time in economic history that mistakes like these have occurred. Quite to the contrary – they keep repeating themselves with alarming regularity. The lessons learnt, however, are quickly forgotten each time, or people simply find it unnecessary to learn a lesson in the first place. History is not one of the key strengths of managers. It would be worthwhile for them, however, to study the periods from 1865 to 1873 and from 1920 to 1929. The years from 1965 to 1975 also make for a valuable lesson. One of the most outstanding examples is the Fugger group with its rise and fall between the late 15th and about the mid-17th century. Details and concepts vary but the basic pattern of cause and effect is the same.

I am *not* referring to wrong entrepreneurial decisions *in general*, which can never be entirely avoided even if people perform their tasks very diligently. Nor am I referring to things that nobody could have predicted, and which therefore have to be taken as a stroke of bad luck, or simply fate. I am speaking of maneuvers and behaviors which we *know* to be *wrong in most cases* and to be justifiable *only* if the *most favorable* future developments can safely be assumed. The future, however, does not always take a favorable course.

Mistake #1: Diversification for All the Wrong Reasons

Many sources illustrate the difficulties and stumbling blocks associated with a misguided *diversification strategy*. I am *not* saying that diversification never works. There have been a few cases where it did. But they are *few* and far between. The vast majority of diversification strategies has either failed or led to marginal achievements. There is a great deal of truth in the old saying *"If you don't know how to run your business, diversify."* The majority of corporate success stories are owed to *concentration*. In most cases of successful diversification efforts, this success was either due to *exceptionally favorable circumstances* (such as extended phases of undisturbed economic prosperity) or owed to a very *precise underlying logic*. To successfully diversify, a company must have one or two *existing* foundations to build on (rather than having to build them). Potential foundations can *only* be the *market* and/or *technology* – nothing else. There have been precious few cases where other factors (such as financial resources) provided a sound basis for successful diversification. But even the terms "market" and "technology" are still too general. Almost always, very *specific, narrowly defined* strengths and capabilities in these two fields have been the key to success. Examples include the special ability to successfully market bulk consumer goods, or – according to an even narrower definition – marketing expertise specifically for branded bulk consumer goods. One case in point is *Philip Morris*: the company was forced to diversify due to the problems of the tobacco industry and, by all accounts, managed quite successfully.

In most cases, however, managers give three very different purposes for the diversification strategies they pursue: *growth and expansion, the spreading of risk,* and *synergies*. Usually an overriding *vision* is stated, as some kind of umbrella spanning everything, and those publicizing it can be fairly sure of getting plenty of applause by the zeitgeist crowd. Yet these three reasons commonly given are the *main* sources of risk, and the "vision umbrella" is only covering them up.

1. Growth and Expansion – or: The Difference between Size and Strength

Growth and expansion as such must never be made overriding corporate goals. Growth for growth's sake or for size's sake is a wrong strategy.

This has nothing to do with being averse to growth. There is nothing to be said against large and expanding businesses. However, a company should never take a certain step simply because it *aspires to grow*. It might have to grow in order to achieve entirely *different* objectives, such as a sufficiently defendable *market position*. If *this* reason applies, growth is *necessary* – otherwise it is not, at least not exceeding the extent required to offset inflation. There are still too many managers who do not know the difference between *size* and *strength*. Growth of the kind that increases strength is good for a business – and strength is about market position. Growth that only increases size leads to "obesity" in the best of cases – and produces "cancer" in the worst.

Misguided growth targets are either due to *lack of knowledge* about corporate management, or to an *imperialist* attitude on the part of top management – sometimes even the desire (though unspoken and never admitted) to build oneself a monument. It is not the purpose of companies, however, to build monuments to ambitious managers, not even to entrepreneurs. Growth is not a goal in itself; it needs to be put in the service of *other*, clearly defined goals. Growth must not be an end in itself; it must be a means to an end which, in turn must be purposes *above* and *beyond* the personal ambitions of individuals.

Even the chance of achieving higher profits is not sufficient to justify a policy of forced growth. Often, this path leads straight to disaster. Profit – and I will elaborate on this in chapter 4 of part I – must never be an overriding corporate goal, either. It must be perceived as the key *measure* of how well a business fulfills its *true* purpose: *creating satisfied customers by delivering a service to the market.*

This notion is still largely unknown to major parts of the business sector; it also contradicts the shareholder value theory. I consider that theory *wrong* and *dangerous*, as fashionable as it may be these days. It will prove to be a short-lived fashion, and a cause of further corporate collapses (see also part I, chapter 4).

2. Spreading Risk – or: The Illusion of Successfully Battling on Many Fronts

A frequent reason for diversification is the desire to spread risk. Spreading risk, however, must *never* be a reason for *management* to diversify, though it can be a *good* reason for an *investor*. But these are two very different things which must be clearly distinguished. Managers certainly make investments but in general they are not investors – except for a few banking segments and parts of the insurance industry. The notion may also be acceptable for pure holding structures, though a great deal of skepticism is appropriate here with regard to their long-term viability and performance.

In the majority of cases, diversification results in an *accumulation* rather than a *spread* of risks. The bigger the number of diverse businesses, the more can go wrong. Every engineer knows from experience that there is a lot of truth in Murphy's Law – specifically the three phrases that say, *"Whatever can go wrong will go wrong," "Every solution creates a new problem,"* and *"Problems always occur at the worst possible time."*

Experience has shown that when diversification does not result in failure, the very least that will happen is that the resulting business conglomerates generate *mediocre* financial results over an extended period of time.

3. Synergy – or: Reaching for the Rainbow

Synergy is the *most dangerous* of all reasons to diversify. I am not saying there is no such thing as synergy, but it is a very rare thing in business. Wherever synergies are just a *rationale* or *justification* for diversifying, it is advisable to watch out and have a very close look at things.

When I ask managers who frequently use the term what it really means, they usually tell me, *"Synergy is when one and one equals three."*

Getting down to the core of the matter, it usually turns out that what managers refer to as synergies are actually well-known facts of business which neither pose new problems nor require new designations. Here are two typical examples I have not invented but distilled as a kind of "net present value" from many discussions on synergy: (1) Better use of a company's capacities by taking over a rival company and closing down its capacities. This has nothing to do with synergy. It is *"better use of capacity."* (2) Better use of the know-how existing in two corporate divisions, which was dormant because the two divisional heads could not stand each other and did everything in their power to wall off their respective operations. For months on end the company ran time-consuming corporate culture programs and synergy workshops, when all it took was for the two adversaries' superior to do his managerial duty and tell them in very clear terms what their obligations toward the company were and what they were paid to do.

4. Visions – or: The Metaphysics of Corporate Management

Fads and zeitgeist trends in management are often cloaked in the veil of "vision", a word which has enjoyed great popularity since the mid-1980s. It is considered an expression of modernity, symbolizing the top management qualities so loudly demanded: creativity, entrepreneurial foresight, risk appetite, pioneer spirit, and a charismatic personality.

There is no denying that managers need to look beyond the confines of operational business, that they need a clear idea about where the business is developing, a carefully thought-out business mission, and a precise and robust corporate strategy. These are among the *most essential* tasks of management. Visions, however, are *a different thing*. A German encyclopedia succinctly defines vision as *"deception in appearance or sense"*. And that is precisely what it is, even if some fashionable authors make desperate, partly amusing and occasionally even ridiculous attempts to give the word another meaning. It is much more than just linguistic sensitivity which is at stake here. Language influences our thinking, and thus our decisions. Good managers have always known that – and so have the pied pipers.

What the apostles of vision have not given us to date, despite the enormous amount of papers created, is a method, based on precise criteria, for distinguishing between visions that provide a sound basis for investment decisions, and visions that are little more than the day dreams of post-pubescent stargazers, or in other words: for distinguishing *good* from *bad* visions – if we do have to use the word at all. If it was up to me to decide, I would banish it from the vocabulary of any company.

We know today what a good strategy is, and we can clearly distinguish it from a bad one. We *know* what the requirements are that a neatly phrased business mission has to meet; we *know* how to distinguish a set of meaningful guiding principles from a set of hollow phrases. These advances in management theory, which have been made in the past three decades, have been generously overlooked by the proponents of vision. They do not waste their time on the depths of laborious research, as they have to devote themselves to "higher" purposes. They deal with the metaphysics of corporate management, and they proudly point to the fact that they know nothing about balance sheets and are unable to read a report from financial controlling. The difference between them and a reasonable and responsible management theory is the same as that between astrology and astronomy.

A *successful* diversification policy must, above all, be based on a *clear and precise logic*, not on pompous buzzwords which upon closer inspection turn out to be largely meaningless and simply mask a lack of management knowledge.

Then, *if* and when the logic of the business is right, a second element is needed: *professional and experienced managers, and a large number of them*. Even major corporations usually do not have enough of them. The synergetic-visionary diversification disasters that made the headlines *might* have worked if there had been a management "dream team", and they *might* have worked if instead of finding ourselves in turbulent times we were enjoying two decades of economic boom. However, to base investment decisions on these assumptions is pure daydreaming, which is why the chances of success were slim from the outset – something that *could* and *should* have been known by those involved. A supervisory body which does not do everything in its power to prevent such mistakes fails to perform its most important duty.

Mistake #2: Integrated Technology Corporation and the Fascination of High-Tech

In the problem cases of recent years, the notion of building "integrated technology groups" played a significant role. The business mission of a company could hardly be formulated in an even *more misleading* way. When writing up the fundamental *purpose and mission* of a business, the first and foremost requirement is a rigorous outward focus, aligning the entire organization towards the *market* and *customers*. This does not only include actual, *current* markets and customers but also potential ones – the markets and customers of *tomorrow*. Anyone who has studied the relevant literature and done his homework will be aware of this.

None of the above, however, is comprised in the term "integrated technology group". It expresses a purely *inward focus*. Actually, there could hardly be a better way of expressing inward focus. The term concentrates the business on precisely the things that the world is *least* interested in. The world does not need integrated technology groups. What it needs are cars (presumably for a long time to come, and preferably good ones), computers and software, airplanes, machine tools, ships, televisions, refrigerators, and so on. Exactly how all these things are designed and manufactured makes no difference whatsoever to the world. Likewise, the technology used – be it integrated or not – is of no interest. Apart from that, it is not very clear what "integrated technology corporation" really is, where it starts and ends, what it includes and what not.

Even if the concept is better understood for lower levels of the organization and for subsidiaries, because this is where it is applied to concrete products and services, the fact remains that this is a *wrong* orientation for an overall company.

It is nothing new that sometimes *several* technologies have to be combined to manufacture a product. Seen from this perspective, "integrated technology" has long been around in the automotive industry, as mechanics and electrics had to be brought together from the outset, and electronics and a few other areas were added later; in addition, some knowledge about steel and other materials has always been required. Something similar is true of almost every industry. So what is the point of using these linguistic monsters?

The misguided orientation expressed in the term "integrated technology group" is closely linked to another notion which is just as wrong and disastrous – at least when generalized and *applied* to more than just a few companies. It is the notion that every business must be "high-tech" (or "high-chem" or "high-whatever") and that the future and business success lie exclusively in high-tech. There are many politicians who talk of nothing else these days.

No doubt we will have *more* high-tech in the future, and there are companies which really *must* delve deeply into it. But it is completely wrong to generalize this, and harmful to the overall economy if the entire business sector is aligned towards high-tech. The enormous business opportunities in low-tech or no-tech areas would then be missed. Innovations are important, of course, but only a small proportion of them involve high-tech. High-tech grabs the headlines, attracts attention, and makes a lot of noise. Besides, it fascinates young engineers, and understandably so. But that is not essential.

To deliver value to the customer, the *right* technology is needed. The question of whether it should be high, low, or no-tech must be determined by the customer value consideration. Just as we used to have (and still have) the phenomenon of over-engineering, allowing the Japanese and other Asians to outflank us, we are now witnessing a misguided development leading toward general high-tech, and thus *over-tech*. As a general orientation for business this is highly questionable, a fact which even Silicon Valley has been forced to accept.

Mistake #3: Proliferating Complexity

It has become fashionable among intellectuals and managers to talk about the complexity of the world. Indeed, it is a fact that it is complex, and becoming more so by the day, and this fact has its implications. However, many use this as an excuse for pursuing strategies that are just as complex, for allowing product ranges to explode, for tackling three dozen things at once, for launching countless projects, for expanding central departments to unreasonable extents, for acquiring one business after the other, and generally for surrendering the business to the cancer of proliferating complexity. That is not the right way to deal with complexity.

Management's role is exactly the *opposite*: To define the business so that the company can stay *simple enough* to be *manageable*. Nothing is easier than driving a company beyond the bounds of manageability; it takes neither managers nor consultants to do so.

Good managers are people with the good sense to *restrict* the company to things it has really *mastered*, and to organize it in such a way that *ordinary* people can cope with the tasks involved. Good managers have the courage to oppose the modernist zeitgeist, and they make sure that they and their people are not enticed by the tunes of the pied pipers. Good managers select strategies which make the company as robust as possible against the inevitable vicissitudes of economic development, be they recessions, currency fluctuations, or political changes.

Mistake #4: Personality Cult

When the new financial officer was appointed, his first official act was to request a list of his colleagues' company cars. He found that board members averaged three company cars while he had only one. His employees had been seriously hoping that at last there would be someone with the courage to kill the "sacred cows" and put an end to such excessive privileges. They were bitterly disappointed. His second official action was to order two more cars for himself. What should we think of such people? I have not made up this story; it is sadly true.

Another true story is about a manager who, as newly appointed CEO, was intent on getting a desk so big that it would not fit through the corridors and doors of the building, and so an external wall had to be knocked down to get the impressive piece into his office.

What are we to make of people who act like the Sun King, who are willing to go to any length to add gloss to their image; who regard those around them as idiots, making it clear for all to see that they consider themselves infallible; who at every symposium pose as the schoolmasters of business, instead of taking care of affairs at home; and who surround themselves with half a dozen ghostwriters to pen their speeches and books? Any reasonable person would not think much of them. Hardly anyone will respect them and perceive them to be credible or even role models.

Unfortunately, however, there are supervisory bodies that appoint such people to the most senior positions, or at least are content to leave them there. Nobody should claim these behaviors to have been unforeseeable. Anyone who, having reached a senior position, pursues or encourages a personality cult in favor of his own privileges, his own glory and image, must certainly have left a number of early warning signals in his CV. Science calls them "critical incidents". Nobody appointed to such a position is a dark horse. All it takes is to look out for the signs, to pay attention to them, and to be willing to read them. A penchant for personality cults shows *early* and *clearly*, even if initially only in little things.

Fortunately, there are still enough true role models in the top management ranks. As I said before, the cases mentioned are no fictions; they actually happened. They are not isolated cases, either, but they are *not typical* of business as such.

If, however, they occur in companies of major significance for the overall economy or even a region, then even isolated cases cannot be tolerated. It is the responsibility of supervisory bodies to prevent excesses or correct them in good time. Performing these duties may be unpleasant and difficult at times, and there will be cases were some courage is called for. But that is precisely what these bodies were established for, and it is precisely situations like these that reveal whether they demonstrate leadership or content themselves with mediocrity and opportunism.

Some people think that the business sector is too important to leave it to the managers. *It is not.* But it is too important to leave it to *bad* managers.

Chapter 3

Is Management Ready for the Future?
or: The Great Transformation

Misinterpretation of the last two decades

Statements about the quality and effectiveness of corporate management require a benchmark against which to measure them. Despite all I have said in the previous chapter about undesirable developments and how they should not have come about if management and corporate supervision had been effective, there was indeed a reaction, though a somewhat belated one. An occasional objection is that a major share of the difficulties were not caused by the business sector itself but by politics. However, neither dramatization nor appeasement are good counsel, and even if the causes were political, it does not help much to point this out. All that counts is the outcome, not the causes.

If, in a spirit of generosity, one were to judge the past favorably over-all, and if one came to the conclusion that there was no need for major changes to overall management, the question still has to be asked whether the management currently practiced will also meet future requirements. My answer is *No*. I have two reasons for this:

First, the overall management of a company must be designed to meet the requirements of the most difficult and toughest situation. As mentioned earlier, executive bodies and in particular supervisory bodies do not really have to master major challenges in times of a normal economic climate. Their effectiveness and quality are put to the test when the going gets tough. Only exceptional situations – be they positive or negative – reveal whether management bodies are up to their tasks. Therefore, the challenges such situations involve for management – no matter whether it is a crisis or a unique opportunity – must serve as a blueprint for the design and function of senior-level management bodies.

The second reason why the effectiveness of top management bodies should be geared to the most exacting standards lies in the future developments expected.

"If the gods want to destroy someone they first send him forty good years," an old saying goes. Never before have so many people benefited from such lasting economic growth. And when a development has lasted for an extended period of time, it will inevitably be extrapolated into the future. Linear trend extrapolation is an almost compulsive reaction, and the longer a trend has lasted, the more the extrapolation seems justified. It does, however, nourish false hopes and represent one of the biggest dangers to any society. If there is one group that is able to recognize this danger, prevent it and respond the right way, it is the leadership elite – by preparing for the worst case. Not the ordinary but the extraordinary situation must be the benchmark; not the trend but its disruption; not continuity but discontinuity.

In the late 1980s and early 1990s, there was a general consensus that the upward trend would continue. It then increasingly gave way to disillusion and skepticism. But only very few companies were prepared for the recession that occurred in the 1990s, apparently to everyone's surprise, although the situation could be seen coming.

In early summer of 1990, I published a book about the crises looming for the global economy,[17] taking a position clearly opposed to the one held by most economists, top managers, and politicians. I had to stand my ground in numerous fierce discussions, in which the very situation that would occur later was called utterly improbable, even impossible, and the views I had expressed in my book were rejected, in part quite fiercely. This is why I so vividly recall those times and the widespread lack of managerial preparation.

According to the consensus among mainstream economists and large parts of the political and business leadership elite, the 1990s should have been the golden decade of the 20th century. There were good reasons for this view. It was largely based on two elements: first, on the forthcoming European Internal Market and the high expectations regarding the impact of integration on consumption and investments; second, on the collapse of the communist regimes and the new untapped markets that would emerge. Could there have been a better constellation for a spurt of growth?

---

17 Malik, Fredmund/Stelter, Daniel: *Krisengefahren in der Weltwirtschaft*, Zürich 1990.

My own considerations and analyses had led me to take an altogether contrary position. My view – as laid out in the aforementioned book – was that all the conditions were there for an extended severe recession with high unemployment and an economy with deflationary rather than inflationary tendencies (as had been the case for the previous 20 years). I took the view that, for the first time in 60 years, all the sufficient (though not yet the necessary) conditions were in place to allow a recurrence of what had happened in the 1930s. As a consequence of my analysis I warned against a linear extrapolation of the past four decades' trend, and recommended preparing for a long and harsh "economic winter". I believed that the economy was facing a period of forced, profound adjustments which would not only consist in superficial corrections to the welfare state and welfare society but might affect the very foundations of a democratic society – unless it was possible to mobilize the most prudent leadership skills in business and politics.

The actual developments of the 1990s then disproved all the scenarios built on extrapolations of previous trends. And we have not reached the end of this difficult period as yet, contrary to what many like to believe. I suggest assuming that we have completed just one-third, perhaps only one-fourth of a fundamental transformation of the economy and society. The biggest problems are still ahead of us, and their solution will require outstanding management skills.

The economic development in the 1990s may have differed in detail from region to region, but only in very few cases was it *fundamentally* different from the description in my book. *Japan* is where the course of the transformation can be seen most clearly. The country is undergoing a severe deflationary crisis. The situation *in Europe* is familiar to the reader and does not need to be described in detail. However, it is worth mentioning that hardly any of the hopes pinned on the economic development of Eastern Europe has been fulfilled. Former East Germany is far from enjoying the "blossoming landscapes" that former Chancellor Helmut Kohl had promised – despite the massive aid it has received – and even the comparatively best example, the *Czech Republic,* is facing difficult problems. In Western Europe, the *Netherlands* and *the United Kingdom* seem to be faring better now, but even they have not reached the end of their need for change.

At the same time as Europe or even earlier, the United States was caught by the recession as well; however, American companies and in particular unions responded more quickly and more radically than their European counterparts did. As a result, the US have managed to recover more quickly and more impressively; yet this recovery will prove to be temporary. Besides, the social cost of the American adaptation is not yet visible in its totality. After all, the adjustments required so far have caused the average income of US citizens to drop back, in real terms, to the level of 1956. The central problem of the US, however, is the financial bubble that has formed.

Some Southeast Asian countries may have taken another course of development, but their success is by far not as great as the media pretends it to be and as most managers believe. In addition, there is plenty to suggest that precisely the most successful Asian countries will suffer serious setbacks before long. Some South American countries have also made great progress, but they are a long shot from having solved all their problems. Africa, with few exceptions, must be considered a hopeless case for the time being.

The business sector and society as a whole are going through one of the most fundamental transformations ever to have occurred in history. In terms of both its extent and significance it is comparable to the developments which, quite surprisingly, have been found to occur every 200 to 250 years.[18] A transformation of this kind took place in the 13th century: it was marked by the Gothic era, the emergency of the modern city and the first universities[19] as centers of intellectual life, the new, urbane orders of the Dominicans and Franciscans, the emergence of the guilds as the dominant social structure, and the reemergence of large-scale cross-border trade.

Another, similarly profound transformation occurred between 1455 and 1517, starting with the invention of printing and culminating in the Reformation. This was during the Renaissance, the period when America was discovered, the emergence of sciences and the revival of medicine (in particular anatomy) took place, Arabic numerals were introduced to Europe, and the first standing army since the Roman legions – the Spanish infantry – was established.

---

18 See also Drucker, Peter F.: *Post-Capitalist Society*, London, 1993.

19 Such as Oxford as early as in the 12th century, followed by Padua in 1222, Naples in 1224, Paris in 1253, Salamanca in 1254, Lisbon in 1290, and Rome in 1303.

The most recent transformation of this kind began in the mid-18ᵗʰ century. Key events included the constitution of the United States, the development of the steam engine by James Watt, signaling the beginning of the age of industrialization, as well as the French Revolution and the Napoleonic Wars. This transformation did not only change the political structure of Europe; it also created the modern university and led to the emergence of liberalism and Marxism, or capitalism and communism, and it gave rise to a completely new structure of society in Europe.

The common denominator of these periods is that in each case society, and indeed the whole contemporary world, changed so radically within a period of about 50 years that later generations literally had no idea what the world of their parents or grandparents had been like. Fifty years may seem a lot in the life of a human being, but in historical terms it is a short period. But in relation to the life expectancy of someone living in the Middle Ages or the Renaissance, or even in the times of the French Revolution, fifty years was a long time. The transformations in those times thus spanned several generations. Nowadays, fifty years are not that much any more, even in the life of a single person.

The current transformation is therefore going to be much more profound than its predecessors: it will be perceived to be more dramatic because the demographic and psychological baseline is different. The pressure for adaptation, which in earlier time spread over several generations, today affects a single generation. This is the demographic aspect. Moreover, today's generation is the first in history which had reason to believe that things could go on as they were. No other generation before has seen the masses enjoy a comparable level of affluence, none has been so spoilt. This is the psychological aspect. People of earlier epochs did not expect much of life, society, and the state. They had no illusions. Most people were not particularly well off both before and after a transformation, so they had no particular expectations or demands. Things are very different today. The ongoing change hits one generation which has been extremely spoilt by circumstances. As a result, even minor setbacks in the general standard of living are perceived to be dramatic. Consequently, the demands made on leadership, on the navigators through this transformation, are much greater.

There all the indications that we are in the midst of a period of change which is similarly comprehensive, profound and rapid as those in the examples outlined. In 10 years, 20 at the most, little will be as it is now, and it is a moot point whether things will be better or worse. All times of radical change of the kind described have resulted in declining affluence, at least temporarily, as well as in a shift in power centers and in profound changes to political and social structures.

It will not be possible to describe the course and the consequences of this transformation in detail. We have never had as many futurologists and trend gurus as we have today, but the fact of the matter is that the future cannot be predicted. What certainly can be described are some developments that have set in, or are about to set in, and their consequences. That may seem like a forecast, but it is something else: it is thinking through the basic patterns of given realities and their logical consequences.

Almost Everything Will Change

Below I will sketch out some of the discernible elements of this transformation. One will always have to consider several alternative scenarios. I suggest, however, working at least with one scenario containing these elements and thinking about how the management would have to be and how it would have to function if this scenario came true.

My first hypothesis is:

The word of business and society at large are going through one of the most fundamental transformations that ever occurred in history. The nature of this change has not been fully understood by many decision-makers in politics and business. A major part of public debate focuses on the wrong points; it is conducted using the thinking categories of the past 100 years, and this involves the risk of being unprepared for the truly essential factors of this transformation and their consequences. There are many excellent answers today – but unfortunately they are answers to the wrong questions.

My second hypothesis is:

The pivotal function of society for this transformation will be management, both for exploiting the opportunities and for avoiding the pitfalls associated with it. Management itself, however, is one of the least understood societal functions, which is why the existing problem-solving potential will not be fully exploited – unless its understanding is substantially improved. Not only is management not understood; the generally

accepted ideas about it are dangerously wrong and collectively mislead-
ing.

As a result of the current transformation of society, we will see fundamental changes in almost all of *what* we do and how we do it, and equally
fundamental changes in *why* we do it. One approach to coping with the
problems typically associated with such transformations would be to
change just as radically the way we shape and control such processes, their
course and direction, as well as the associated institutions.

Change of the What and How

The driving forces behind this transformation can be grouped in four
or perhaps five major problem areas: *demography, technology, ecology,*
and – affecting all other areas – *debt.* A fifth problem area which could
be termed *complexity* results from the fact that the first four are interde-
pendent and interlaced.

Consuming

I said that almost all of *what* we do and *how* we do it will change, such
as what we *consume* and *produce* and how we go about it. Between 50
and 60 percent of the gross national product in developed countries comes
from consumption. In the fifty years or so of economic prosperity following the Second World War, we have reached an unprecedented level
of consumption and saturation. This is an achievement that would have
been hard to envisage for earlier generations. Of course, there is still a
much larger level of unsatisfied needs on a global basis; but an economy
cannot satisfy *needs*, it can only satisfy *demand*. And demand includes
only those needs which someone can pay to be satisfied. There is no natural law according to which all needs will be satisfied. That this could or
ought to be so is an illusion which was allowed to develop in the countries
benefiting from said period of prosperity. From there, the media and some
economic theorists carried it to those countries that have not been able to
participate in the affluence yet, and which now, driven by understandable
and in part aggressive envy, try to catch up with the development.

Still, it is an illusion. So far, historically speaking, most people died with the same needs they had when they were born. Demand – the only thing the business sector can cover – does not require needs but *purchasing power*. In view of the *global level of debt*, it is rather difficult to imagine the existence of any purchasing power, let alone any purchasing power *beyond* the current level. Purchasing power is either available money, resulting from economic activity, or credit granted against property. Both have been used up by the credit economy of the last thirty years, even in the world's richest countries. For this *first* of two reasons, consumption will be an unreliable pillar for economic development.

And there is a *second* reason. In the developed countries, and in particular in those parts of the population which still have buying power, the *nature* of consumption has changed. Apart from food, drugs and the like, it is no longer primarily used to cover urgent and basic *needs* – as it was, for instance, after the Second World War – but to fulfill *desires*. Most people, if they were to buy nothing but their daily groceries, would not be short of much because they already have virtually everything they need. This is true in particular of consumer durables, such as cars, washing machines, refrigerators, televisions, and so on. While purchases of new items cannot be postponed forever, they can be put off for a considerable length of time without any real sense of deprivation. One would not have the latest, technically most sophisticated model of a given piece of equipment, but that is something one can get over.

Of course, there will be a certain degree of *replacement demand*, and above all, *substitute goods*. As a consequence of technological and partly ecological development, however, they will be different from their predecessors, be they genetically modified food or electronic robots.

Similar is true of the *capital goods sector*. The infrastructures of the developed countries are in place: industrial plants, transportation systems, schools and universities, swimming pools, office buildings, and so forth. If anything, there is a lack of affordable and subsidized housing. This infrastructure is of a high standard; it is efficient. It is not even close to being fully depreciated in the balance sheets. Of course, it is always possible to imagine something better, and some repair and replacements are needed, but only in very few cases is there a pressing need for capacity expansion.

Again, what will be needed is *substitution* rather than expansion. And while substitution always brings something new, it also jeopardizes some of what is already there. When solar panels are used on a roof, fewer roof tiles will be needed; when a fiberglass line is installed, copper cable is no longer needed – with fiber-optic cable providing approximately 300 times the capacity for a fraction of the cost of copper.

But even the undisputed need for repair and substitution is subject to very narrow *financial* constraints, due to the current level of *debt*. It is almost always for the same reason that, for instance, public funds are not granted even for clearly needed renovations or replacements: financing. And there are almost always two reasons why ecological investments are not undertaken: either because they affect the competitive situation of businesses, industries, and countries at least temporarily, due to the costs involved, or because they cannot be financed in the first place.

Producing

For a series of reasons, the way in which we manufacture has started to change permanently. This change is driven by existing *overcapacities*, as well as by *productivity differences* between competing companies and countries. The underlying *premises* are these: Everything that can be automated will be automated over the next ten to twenty years, and everything that can be digitized will be digitized. Everything that can be omitted will be omitted; everything that can be outsourced will be outsourced.

Despite occasional reports about the level of automation having been scaled back here and there, or about considerable problems with outsourcing, these are the premises from which we need to proceed. We are standing at the threshold of these developments, not – as some would have us believe – at their end. In the context of such profound changes there will always be mistakes and exaggerations which will have to be corrected. But it would be very dangerous to conclude that these are only temporary trends or that major changes have come to an end. Just like business *process* reengineering, business *restructuring* also follows a sound logic and achieves remarkable results. They may not be the only, but they are at least one answer to the fundamental shifts in economic and social structures.

Transporting and Distributing

In the course of this development, *modes of transport* and forms of distribution will change just as radically. We are right in the midst of this development. In the past ten years, hardly anything has changed so much, in almost every country, as sales channels and the way goods are distributed and traded. But here, too, the change is far from completed. For instance, the insight has taken hold that it makes little sense either economically or ecologically to transport goods from one end of Europe to the other, and then to return the transport vehicles and containers empty. As a consequence, logistics worldwide is being reorganized. Whole levels or stages of goods distribution systems are being eliminated, transshipment points and flows of goods are being shifted. New services and business opportunities arise, rendering previous ones obsolete and their replacement unnecessary.

Utilizing Knowledge

There is yet another, entirely new development: The economy of the past 100 years worked, as Peter Drucker so aptly put it, by "making and moving things and people". Apparently, this type of economic system has now come to an end. "Making and moving things" is hardly an issue anywhere in the world. Even very underdeveloped countries are able to have surprisingly quick successes, as numerous examples have proved, in terms of not only catching up but even gaining a lead. *"Using knowledge"* is the new challenge, and we will come back to this later. "Moving people" has also reached its limits, at least for the working world, what with all the traffic jams, congested inner cities, air pollution, and the utter disproportion between the time spent commuting and actually working. All the more so as we have the technology permitting us to bring work to employees rather than making these people travel to work. This will result in radical changes to the workplace, the forms of work and the working hours, perhaps even to the attitude towards work – some of them negative, others very positive.

Mind you, I am *not* envisaging people sitting in front of their computers at home and doing "telework". Human beings are social creatures, and will probably continue to be for some time. Rather, I believe that the administration centers and the brainworkers' "citadels" will move from downtown to the suburbs, and that work will be done where people are based. There are already several examples for this, such as an American insurance company which has its policy administration located in Ireland, which, thanks to satellite connections, is easily possible without anyone needing to travel from Ireland to New York.

Raw Materials

Raw materials will no longer play an essential role in the new economy. They will continue to be needed, but they will cease to have the significance they had in the past centuries, when the possession or control of raw materials was the key to power, influence, and global importance. The era of raw materials essentially culminated in the establishment of the OPEC cartel.

First, we do seem to have greater reserves of raw materials, even of key ones such as oil, than previously assumed. *Second*, recycling and substitution are starting to have an effect. For the most ecologically committed, it may still be far from being enough, but even in the countries where the greatest waste of energy occurs, energy consumption per unit of national product is declining, and as much as 80 to 90 percent of the raw materials used in building modern automobiles are reusable. *Third*, the new economy will need smaller quantities of raw materials: The automobile, being the perhaps most typical product of the 20th century, has a raw-material content of 30 to 40 percent, and we are talking about very expensive raw materials. The product most typical of the 21st century – the microchip – and everything around it accounts for only two to three percent in raw material content. And these are cheap raw materials – ultimately, nothing but sand. What will be in short supply is a raw material of an entirely different kind: it is *knowledge* – such as the knowledge needed to turn a substance like sand into a microchip. It is becoming increasingly clear that the crucial and, in the end, only wealth-creating resource is knowledge.

Brainwork

In connection with knowledge, a fundamental demographic consequence cannot be overestimated: it is the replacement of the *manual* worker by the *brainworker*. Given the premise of increasing automation which I mentioned above, there are two prevalent notions I consider highly questionable: One is the notion of a *high-tech economy*, the other that of a *service society*. We will certainly have some more of both than before, but we will not have substantially more.

High-tech dominates the headlines; it attracts a great deal of attention and interest and it also is a source of many fears. By far the largest part of the manufacturing sector, however, is still low-tech and no-tech. What we will certainly need more of is *high engineering*, and what will grow more than anything is the *knowledge content* of all activities.

This is evident from the fact that an increasing share of tasks for which until recently the ability to read and write was more of a hindrance than a help now require a considerable degree of school education in addition to the vocational training needed. Years ago, a bricklayer could do his job based on a few hand-drawn sketches which hardly deserved to be called blueprints. The bricklayer of tomorrow will probably start his workday by booting his portable CAD system and going online via satellite, to see what the latest stage of planning is after someone else has modified and updated the blueprints in real time over night – either in another part of the world where it was daytime during the bricklayer's nighttime, or at a location where work is done in three shifts around the clock, as software engineers in India are doing already, to ensure the best possible use of this costly resource.

The substitution of the manual worker does not primarily mean a shift from value-added manufacturing toward services, but from the *industrial worker* to the *brainworker*.

The term "services" in itself is questionable. Existing economic classifications, statistical categories, the data material based on them, and thus the conclusions drawn from them are meaningless and even dangerous because they are misleading. "Services" is a meaningless category. It includes both the industries with the *lowest* wages (such as restaurant chains and supermarkets) and those with the *highest* income (such as banks, insurances, or software). This formerly plausible moniker (it was a catch-all for everything not fitting into any other category, accounting for approximately five percent of the gross national product) now covers activities that require *no* professional qualification whatsoever (simple cleaning services) as well as those requiring the *highest* level of education (research laboratories). In it we find both businesses with *negligible* assets and those with very *sizeable* ones. There is an increasing number of businesses which do not fall in either the industry or the service category. For instance, where does General Electric belong, when 40 percent of its turnover come from services and, via its customer finance and leasing companies, the company has long been one of America's biggest banks – even if it does not even appear in the often-published lists of banks? A similar question applies to General Motors and Ford.

Unemployment

The shift from manual labor to brainwork and a number of the other developments outlined here mean that there will be even more *unemployment* than before, and it will last for an extended period of time, and/ or that a substantial number of people will have to *reorient themselves* completely in occupational terms. This is, however, by no means a consequence of the *failure* of the capitalist economy as many believe; quite to the contrary, it is a consequence of its enormous *success*.

Over the past 100 years it has managed to make workers so productive that they are no longer needed. This success is rooted in the fact that there were enough people who ignored the fallacious doctrines of Marx and his followers, instead setting out to constantly improve the productivity of manual work. As a consequence, the workers were not impoverished, as Marx had prophesied, but became the new middle class who lived reasonably well and were able to send their children to school and to university. Now, however, the industrial worker shares the historic fate of the agricultural workers and domestic staff of former times, who in the developed countries transitioned from a dominant majority to a negligible factor. Along with the workers, the organizations they established and which dominated society for 100 years will also vanish or have to change radically: labor parties and trade unions.

For those directly affected, this development is tragic, and the welfare state must take some measures to soften the blow as far as possible. The result will be a major burden for the welfare system. And while this development is unstoppable, it is just as certain that every last vested interest will be defended with grim determination. Still, these discontinuities are a consequence of success rather than failure, and a consequence of a fundamental shift from an economy reliant on *raw materials* and *manual labor* to one based on *knowledge* and *brainwork*. However, to draw from this the conclusion – as many people do – that we will no longer have manufacturing in the future but only services would be wrong in my opinion.

Manufacturing and value creation from manufacturing will continue to be necessary, and will continue to exist even in the developed countries. The case is simply that far fewer workers will need to be involved.

Labor Cost

For all these reasons, the wage *negotiations and conflicts* we have today, and which are focused on workers' wages, will cease to have any significance because wages will account for a marginal share, perhaps 5 to 10 percent, of total cost. These are the proportions that are already a reality in the world's best-organized factories. The impact on trade unions, political parties, and politics in general will be considerable.

Again, it would be wrong to conclude that aggregate wages will decline as well. Virtually nowhere have *aggregate* wages decreased *due to* computers and automation. What has decreased in some cases is not the absolute wage total but the wage total as a percentage of value added, or in relation to the volume of goods handled. In other words, computerization allows companies to deliver higher performance on the same basis, which, of course, is an improvement. What has increased, above all, is the level of *people* needed. What in the times *before* computerization and automation used to be done by large numbers of people in relatively *cheap* manual labor, is *afterwards* done by much fewer, but also much more *costly* brainworkers. Traditional steel production required a large number of relatively cheap steelworkers. A modern steel plant requires relatively few staff, a marginal share of whom are traditional steelworkers. The rest of the "few" are highly qualified, very costly brainworkers – specialists such as computer operators, metallurgists and process engineers, whose education has often cost more than the capital investment in one job.

Hence the new economy will no longer correspond to the *economic* theories we have today, which are actually theories for the economy of the past 100 years. One of the most fundamental of all economic theories is that an economy, an industry, a business can be either capital-intensive or labor-intensive – but never both. This was certainly *true* for the past 100 years; the theories were right. Now they are getting close to the point where they will be *wrong*. For the modern economy will be *both*.

At the forefront of this development is a type of organization which is giving us substantial cause for social concerns: the hospital is the first organization existing in large numbers, which is both capital- and labor-intensive. Only a small part of the costs of the healthcare system are unacceptably high, due to wasteful use of drugs or unnecessarily long hospital stays. The main reason healthcare costs are so high – and will not go down – is that hospitals need *both*: very costly equipment *and* very costly, highly specialized personnel. An X-ray machine, which was relatively cheap in itself, could be operated by cheap workers. An expensive CT scanner, however, requires a whole team of well-paid specialists: electronic technicians, nuclear physicists, and highly qualified medical staff.

Now we could call this phenomenon an "industrial revolution", as has been done in the past. With regard to the impact they had, however, industrial revolutions have primarily been *social* revolutions and transformations. While key effects of this "revolution" will include technological and industrial consequences, the most significant ones will be of a social nature. Technical and technological changes cannot really be understood if they are regarded solely or primarily from a technical and technological perspective.

Change of the Why

At the beginning of this section I said that the ongoing transformation process was changing almost everything we do, and how we do it. It will, however, also change the reason *why* we do it. It seems as though we ought to discard the economic theories according to which an economy can be either capital-intensive or labor-intensive, and which can therefore give us no guidance whatsoever when the "theoretically impossible" does come true. And not only that: several factors suggest that we will need a completely *new* economic theory and a *new* economic understanding. What are they?

I have already mentioned that one of the driving forces behind the profound changes is the level of debt found worldwide and across all sectors of society. Not only is this one of the driving forces of change, it is also an all-limiting factor. We have the highest level of debt in history, both in absolute and relative terms. No country in the world, except for Switzerland and a few small countries such as Luxembourg, is able to service even the interest on public debt from its tax income. It has to be covered by *new borrowing*, which means that *compound interest* is taking its devastating effect everywhere. All sectors of society are indebted: public budgets, private households, and the business sector. In none of the countries do the figures published depict reality; everywhere the truth is glossed over, concealed, or played down. Improving the debt situation by "soft" means will hardly be possible in the foreseeable future. Raising taxes is impossible in some countries; it is difficult and politically inopportune in all of them. The art of social redistribution has reached its limits. From whom could we take away even more – enough indeed to give it to others and achieve a perceptible effect?

When debt is high, so an often-heard argument goes, there must also be a high level of receivables. Where there are debtors there must also be creditors. But what if the debtors can no longer redeem or even service their debt? Then these receivables are worthless, or at least their value needs to be adjusted. Existing real wealth – that is to say, capital assets – is not "worth" very much in situations like these because, contrary to popular opinion, value has a very conditional existence in an economy. As a matter of fact, and regardless of all the theories and valuation methods, there is no such thing as value – only *price*. The value of an economic good is what the *next* buyer is willing to pay for it. An object only has "value" as long as this value does not have to be realized. This concept is most clearly illustrated by the steep drop of property prices in many countries: in Switzerland alone, over 40 billion Swiss Francs had to be written off as a result in the 1990s. When, in 1990, I gave my first speech about the dangers of falling property prices, it was met with incomprehension.

Once an economy is forced to create liquidity, there are narrow limits to the realization of even very "valuable values". This is true even for the liquidity created by printing banknotes. If we had this situation after several years of economic depression, there would be nothing more to be said about it. But it follows one of the longest periods of prosperity that history has ever seen. In fact, all sectors of society should be bursting with financial health, and if they were, we could face the future quite calmly. However, the opposite is the case.

The financial situation is alarming. In almost every country, above all in the United States, the stock market boom has led to a situation which could result in the *collapse of the financial markets* any minute. In Japan, the financial bubble burst in late 1989 and, as mentioned before, the country has since been in a deflationary crisis, with no end in sight. The reason there has not been a social catastrophe there – not yet, anyway – is that *first*, the general environment continued to be favorable and other markets remained intact and, *second*, that the Japanese mentality does not tend toward rebellion.

If the stock market in the US were to collapse, however, it would hardly be possible to cushion it. In all likelihood, all other stock exchanges worldwide would be affected – including not only the stock markets but also bond markets along with currency and commodity markets.

What makes the situation in the US particularly troubling is that the savings of two generations are at stake: as the general euphoria was building up, the Wall Street industry channeled these monies into the securities markets, via pension funds and investments funds, luring the owners with totally untenable promises and unrealistic expectations. By now, the general public has been persuaded to believe that the stock market will rise forever, at worst interrupted by minor glitches which, however, are viewed as "favorable" opportunities to invest even more.

How and why could things take this course? Part of the reasons may lie in the behavior of certain politicians and in a certain policy. Perhaps our *economic theories* are wrong. They do not explain anything; it only appears as if they did. As complicated though they are, they still have very little substance. They do not explain why people undertake a given economic activity, or how they do so. They do not explain why there is such a thing as money and what it is; why there is interest and why interest rates can vary; why an economy grows and why it does so at a certain rate; or why some countries' economies do not grow despite all the efforts, aids, and programs. Even the explanations of what a market is, what its purpose is, and where capital comes from are unsatisfactory. They provide prompt answers to all questions, and most sound plausible enough to be readily accepted. Upon closer examination, however, one will find a minefield of contradictions, inadequacies, and in some cases sheer nonsense.[20]

The transformation of the economy and society and the related driving force of international debt, in particular of the "richest" countries in the world, will probably force us to come to a completely new understanding of economics and business, and for why we do things the way we do.

So much for the illustration of my first hypothesis, the fundamental

---

20 See also the papers by G. Heinsohn, O. Steiger, and P. C. Martin listed in the references section.

transformation of the economy and society, and of the change of what we do, how we do it and why we do it.

Management: The Most Important Societal Function

How does this discussion relate to my second thesis, that management is the most important, albeit most poorly understood, societal function?

The fabric of society will probably have to undergo profound changes because of these developments, and in this context the following categories of thinking are perhaps the most dangerous of all. This is why politics and management will have to change.

The development of the *welfare state*, which began with the introduction of the first social security system by Bismarck in the 1880s, has reached an enormous and previously unimaginable level – but now it seems to have run its course. The welfare state is at an end; not because it has served its purpose, but because it can no longer be financed and because its forms of organization have become obsolete.

The welfare state is at an end, but the welfare *tasks* have remained, or new ones have emerged. We have an increasing number of elderly people, and how they will be provided for is not at all clear, given the state of pension funds and the speed at which we are heading towards an aged population, in which *one* working person will have to support *two* retired people rather than vice versa. Old people live much longer today, so society has to pay more and longer for them because they need more medical care over a longer period of time than they used to. We have sick and handicapped people, alcoholics and drug addicts, homeless people and those living below the poverty line. We have unemployed people, and in many countries a substantial percentage – up to 30 percent – of unemployed young people. The older unemployed person is a tragedy. Youth unemployment is a source of social unrest, a potential for political radicalization, for violence and crime.

All of this is the upshot of a century of welfare state development, and presumably of an even greater amount of intelligence, commitment, pity, compassion, and any other ideals and noble motives there might be. Do we currently find ourselves in this state despite or because of them? The answer to this question depends on one's philosophical and ideological position, but the facts remain. We cannot go on like this, irrespective of ideological positions. There may be some consensus about goals but not about ways and means. No matter what it is, we have an apparatus, an authority or an office for anything, but whether they fulfill their purpose and work efficiently is highly questionable. And while their costs are included in the national product they are hardly productive. Our present forms of organization, processes, and management structures, as useful as they may have been years ago, have become obsolete. They certainly cannot provide models for emerging economies and developing countries.

The *politics* which has "managed", shaped and controlled all these things has become unpredictable, ineffective and untrustworthy in nearly all dimensions, no matter whether we look at external or internal policies, security or social policies, economic or financial policies, ecological, family, educational or science policies. None of these areas can continue to be managed as before.

Successes have been greater than could ever be expected. However, they overtook themselves and created new problems. What should the family policy of the future look like, now that it has successfully solved the problem of lifelong cohabitation imposed by the Church and enforced by economic circumstances; now that marriages can be divorced and over a third of them actually are; now that an increasing number of people choose to live independently in single-person households and with changing partners; now that women, after a century of struggle, no longer depend on being supported by men but are free to shape their lives and careers as they please, so their perception of what they want to do in life and what they want to achieve differs greatly from what they wanted and thought in the past millennia?

What will external and internal policies have to look like, now that they have been so successful in integrating living spaces and economic areas, so that people enjoy the advantages but refuse to accept the disadvantages – such as major migrations and being "inundated" by foreigners, even more and even fiercer competition, job insecurity, currencies threatening to become unstable, anonymous heteronomy, loss of autonomy, incomprehensibility of decisions, and cross-border crime? Even if the interpretation of certain developments is based on *perception*, influenced by fears and anxieties that may be hollow and unenlightened in themselves, this interpretation is still *reality* and it influences people's behavior.

When, on top of everything, people are told by the media every day that all over the world wars are waged in categories and based on motives stemming from the 19th or early 20th centuries, as are the responses to them in international politics; when they see that interventions of international organizations, whatever the intentions behind them, almost always achieve the opposite of what has been intended or at least declared; when they see that the "blossoming landscapes" they were promised can only be kept alive with much "irrigation", it is hardly surprising that politics nowadays has little power of conviction. The appeals made, in particular those for support and solidarity, also come from an era and a societal situation that no longer exists precisely due to these policies. To whom should you show solidarity when you no longer know anyone, and whom should you help when you are no longer able to see the effect of that help?

Isn't solidarity a property of small spaces, comprehensibility and overview, of at least potential face-to-face contact, of communication that can be experienced with all senses? Does it not manifest itself in regionalism, nationalism, ethnocentrism, in the formation of neighborhoods, groups and "gangs", in the family, in the clan, in kinship and in the tribe? For millennia, these were the parameters for the evolution of human emotionality, the rules of play for living together, and the ties within a community. The large organizations of earlier eras, such as the Catholic Church – though comprising hundreds of millions of people – understood this fact quite clearly. They were big, but they had a small-scale cell structure. Even battalions and regiments of the major armies were largely organized along local lines.

In my opinion, an inevitable and quite predictable consequence of integration policy and economic globalization will be a countermovement whose nature, characteristics and manifestations cannot yet be foreseen. I consider it highly probable that we will soon enter a phase of general *disintegration*, or perhaps to be even more precise, of *exclusion*. This may seem hard to believe at the moment because we are still so busy completing the final steps of integration or inclusion; for example, in Europe and the Middle East. But the collapses of the Soviet Union and Yugoslavia were the first examples. The next to follow may well be China; the country is far from having achieved the homogeneity and cohesion that its name implies. Too many things that do not belong together have been brought together, and the advantages promised to the people have not materialized.

The same could happen in Europe. The integration of the European markets is not irreversible. Even if the common currency can be sustained – which can be enforced *politically* – this does not necessarily mean that it will become an *economic* reality. It may just as well be sidelined by the other national currencies, which could continue to dominate for a long time. A phase of disintegration or exclusion does not necessarily have to imply a return to the old nation state, let alone a functioning nation state. Ethnic and regional aspects will also play a role, as will interests – but not the type of interest organizations that led to the emergence of today's major political parties.

Economic class interests and consensus about ideological-religious values will hardly provide a basis in the future, except perhaps in the Islamic world. Something else is easily possible, however: in collaboration with the mass media, the extortion of any conceivable majority by any conceivable minority, by action groups of any variety, by small and even tiny groups forming around ecological, social, or other interests, some permanently, others only temporarily and situation-based, some acting democratically, others using all the means of modern-day terror against which every developed society is almost defenseless.

Economies and societies in which developments of this kinds are going on are under *considerable stress*. They can break apart in many places or even collapse, partially or completely. They can drown in erupting terror and end in economic disaster and anarchy. This is one possible scenario. The other has them wasting away lethargically, watching in a state of paralysis as the centers of activity and influence shift in both geographical and political terms, and that they fall into pain and despair. Historically, both situations have occurred over and over again. There is ample documentation on the rise and fall of nations, powers, and empires.

Nevertheless, there is no need to regard it as an *iron law*. For there is also a *third* possibility, which is to proactively face these challenges – the *revitalization* of economy and society, as well as their organizations, from within. Admittedly, powerful efforts of this kind have often been arisen from disaster: examples include the United States' development after the Civil War, Roosevelt's New Deal, and the rebuilding of Germany and Japan after the Second World War. But there were also phenomena like the Renaissance in Europe and the Meiji Restoration in Japan.

No matter what the origin of a reform or revitalization movement, its key has always been a *new form of leadership*. Let me stress this again:

the key was leadership – not a leader. Of course, new leaders have also emerged in such situations, but in most cases it was only to create another, often even greater disaster.

So what I am talking about are not leaders, and most certainly not a single leader, but *leadership*. The history of leaders has been written in sufficient detail for us to learn from it. The history of leadership has yet to be written.

As contradictory as this may sound: the conditions for a profound revitalization of leadership are both the best and the worst we ever had. They are the best in that we have a pluralistic society, which is usually taken to mean a diversity of values and opinions, purposes and goals. This is an important fact. What I consider *just as* important but less prominent is that, instead of having *one* center of power, one or very few centers of influence, steering, design and control, we have an extraordinarily *large number.*

We live in a society of *organizations* – more, larger, and more varied than ever before in history. Whatever man does, he no longer does it as an individual but as a member, an employee, and/or a user of organizations. All of them are centers of influence and power, of design and control – some to a greater, some to a lesser extent. Never before in the history of mankind have so many people, both in absolute and relative terms, actually performed management tasks. This is a good basis for vital leadership; it is a strength.

The weakness that simultaneously exists is, in my view, that only few people have *systematically* been prepared for performing these tasks, that in this area there is no training nor education, least of all any wisdom imparted, and that we lack both standards for good and sanctions for bad management.

Here we have a truly peculiar, even paradoxical situation: Never before have there been so many books and magazines on management, never have there been more seminars and larger training budgets. We have famous business schools and more MBA programs than ever before. So much for the quantitative side. But what about content? According to the names and labels, what is taught and learnt appear to be leadership and management; a closer look at the content, however, reveals otherwise. Never before have we had less of a consensus regarding the right answers are, let alone the right questions.

The main thing taught at business schools – in line with their original purpose – is business administration. Courses are called Production und Corporate Finance, Human Resources and Marketing, International Relations, Corporate Strategy, and Corporate Structure. You can put the word "management" in front or after each of them, if you want, but that does not change the fact that what is taught is production, not production management, and marketing, not marketing management.

Mind you, I consider all these subjects important. There can never be too much knowledge about them, and there can never be too many people with a sound education in these areas. I do not share the view that young people should not have a higher education; much to the contrary. It must, however, be made very clear to them that "technical" knowledge in these subjects is not enough and that in addition they need to learn how to transform knowledge into benefit and, above all, how to do this in an organization.

The changes outlined involve enormous challenges for managers in all organizations. Clarity of thought, precision of action, role-model behavior and credibility of management will be tested to their limits.

Even the changes in the markets, the technological developments, the need for innovation in products, manufacturing, distribution, and information systems, all these things and many more will entail tasks of substantial scope and complexity. The key difficulty, however, will lie in the *social* consequences of all these changes. Not only will we change what and how we produce, distribute, and consume; we will also have to change what and how we work, learn and teach, know and master, talk and listen. We will have to change the way we act and treat others, and in particular we will have to change the way we manage.

All of this is about management, a term I use when referring to the totality of all shaping, controlling, directing, and developing functions of a society. While I basically do not distinguish between management and leadership, I can accept a certain differentiation which, however, was hugely exaggerated in the 1980s and 1990s.

The context of management is the organized society – a society in which anything done by human beings is done in an organization, be it consuming or producing, teaching or learning, giving birth to children or burying the dead. It will also be a society in which, as pointed out before, raw materials and manual labor will no longer be the essential resources; instead, knowledge will be the key component for achieving performance and creating wealth.

I therefore suggest understanding management to be the *transformation of knowledge into performance and value*. I believe that this perspective permits the best and most productive understanding of this function. This view determines better than any other the tasks, tools and principles that managers have to perform, master, and comply with in order to be effective and productive in the organized knowledge society; it also permits the relatively most useful definition of the standards to be set for managers, their responsibility and liability.

Management must meet constitutionally based, clearly defined standards and criteria. Establishing them is not an easy task, no easier than producing modern national constitutions or putting in place the institutions required for their enforcement and compliance. It will also not be more difficult than that.

Over thousands of years, what managers did and how they did it could be regarded as secondary, since people were only marginally affected by it. And when they were affected it had to be accepted as their inevitable lot. What did the fellahin in the Lower Nile Valley care what the pharaoh was doing in Thebes, hundreds of miles away – and if it mattered to them, what choice did they have? Management did not count for much; what counted was survival. Today, however, management does count, on all levels and in all organizations. Almost everything depends on the quality and competence of management: standard of living, state of health, upbringing and education, and the question as to whether in the end a life can be regarded as worthwhile.

The behavior of noblemen could be considered a "matter for the nobility", as it was linked to privileges of birth; the behavior of clerics was a "Church matter", for it was religious and thus not up for discussion; the behavior of an entrepreneur could be regarded as his own matter, for he risked his property.

By contrast, the behavior of managers in the organized society is public, for they are *employed* by the organizations they work for; they are paid with *other people's* money and they work with *other people's* money. Their behavior is visible, for in a world of mass media nothing can be kept secret or covered up any more. Everything is discussed, criticized and assessed, as more and more people are able to make comparisons and form opinions on these things. Above all, more and more people have alternatives. In the past, people had to *endure* management; today they can *accept* or *reject* it. People can turn their backs on politicians and, at least for a while, leave organizations; brainworkers can even take their resources with them. I am not attempting to trivialize the dependences that still exist, but they are not as great as they used to be.

Managers have to *live by* standards which are important for the stability of society, and they have to make these standards visible. *Trust* and *credibility* are fragile goods. They cannot tolerate too many mistakes, some mistakes they cannot withstand at all. To cope with the current transformation of society, management's trustworthiness and credibility are of utmost importance. It is therefore equally important to develop mechanisms and institutions for the education and training of managers, for their selection and placement, for assessing their performance – before it manifests itself in poor business results or a visibly failed business purpose – for sanctioning their potential misbehavior, and finally for removing them from the positions they are holding.

To some people it may seem absurd to try to define the standards of competent management in a sort of constitution, yet this is precisely what was done historically in turning *arts* into *professions*. This did not lessen the importance of the arts. Whatever is unique and special about them will remain so, and will be restricted to the few who have access to it. It will presumably also be the arts which, time and again, create new and better standards.

When we look at what *changes* the world and the lives of human beings, however, it is not the arts but the professions, not the top performance of geniuses but the fact that art has turned into a learnable and teachable craft. This is what has brought progress in medicine and, above all, made it possible for millions of people to have access to remarkably good medical care. Those following in the steps of Leonardo da Vinci are not geniuses but hundreds of thousands of skilled engineers; those following in the steps of Imhotep, Phidias, Bramante, and Le Corbusier are the countless architects who do not create works of art but provide real and worthy services to other humans; and those following in the steps of the Wright brothers are the thousands of airline pilots who fly tens of thousands of passengers to their destinations every day, safely and reliably.

The achievements of pioneers and geniuses are still marveled at after thousands of years; those of professional craftspeople are less spectacular, yet they are what change our lives.

What has been achieved in hundreds of disciplines should not be considered impossible for management. Winston Churchill once said at an informal meeting in 1946 with around thirty of the most outstanding members of the US military, that while he had been aware that the United States with its immense economic power would be able to provide the necessary war materials, he had truly been surprised that the US had been able to deploy so many excellent officers in such a short time.

There is a simple answer to the question as to where the thousands of commanders leading the US armed forces – with an overall headcount of roughly 10 million – came from: They came from military academies where they were trained and prepared, as well as from training camps which had been established as part of the mobilization initiated after Pearl Harbor.

What was achieved in the field of military leadership can, of course, be achieved in the field of civil leadership as well: turning an art mastered by *few* into a craft or profession for *many*. The content and methods will be very different, and many principles may be similar, but the need for leadership exists in both fields. To successfully cope with the ongoing transformation in a peaceful, humane way, every society needs a large number of competent, effective, and responsible leaders/managers. Not only engineers are needed but engineers who can manage; not only scientists but scientists who can manage themselves and others, not only business economists but economists who can translate their own and other people's knowledge into value through management. This applies not only to business but to all organizations, not only to senior levels but to everyone with leadership tasks.

Investments in management and management skills are impossible to calculate at present, but they will determine the performance and competitiveness of organizations, industries, countries, and economic blocs to a greater extent than ever before. They will be crucial for ensuring wealth, eliminating poverty and misery, and correcting ecological damages; and they will determine whether our young generation has a future and what it will look like.

Chapter 4

Corporate Governance

The Significance of an Effective Corporate Supervision

The need to avoid company collapses and turnarounds, as well as the destruction of capital associated with them, is a good enough reason for strong and effective corporate supervision. But there is more. A strong supervisory body is not only needed to *avoid* something but also to *achieve* something: the best possible use of capital and all other resources.

Not only for reasons of competitiveness – of the business itself – but also for reasons relating to the economy as a whole, the supervisory body has to ensure that productive work is carried out and results are achieved. The yardstick for this must be the world's best productivity rates and results.

To this date, nobody knows just *how* productive "productive" really is. Economic theory has not provided any absolute standards for the use of resources. Maybe there is no such thing. So far, it is not even possible to say *what* economic resources are, for that, too, is subject to constant change. This is why the social "cell" of economic activity requires a body of people who permanently monitor and ensure a continuous search for the best possible use of all current and potential resources – not only in abstract terms but referring to the concrete, individual case. The only body that can perform this task is the supervisory body.

The executive body's job is to *do* the work; *making sure* it is done is the supervisory body's job. This implies much *more* than control, even something entirely *different*. It requires taking influence on objectives, as well as on the standards for the assessment of performance and results. Although there may be people who can perform three functions simultaneously – *setting* goals for themselves, *delivering* the performance (or making sure it is delivered) *and assessing* the quality of objectives and results, they are an exception. Not the rule. In other words, it should not be left to the discretion of the individual whether he or she will do something or not; instead, performance of these functions should be safeguarded *constitutionally*. That requires *two* constitutional bodies at the very least.

And another factor must be taken into consideration: The supervisory body can almost be regarded as the twin of the *market*.

As pointed out in the last chapter, we live in an *organized* society – a society consisting of organizations and institutions. Every organization requires management (or whatever term may be used for it) as a shaping, moving, and steering entity. It is the *management* of social organizations that determines *their* efficiency and performance, and thus the efficiency and performance of *society as a whole*.

Management is the profession with the strongest *effects on society*, be they positive or negative. Through management, the resources of a society, in particular capital and human resources, are put to productive or unproductive use; it is management which creates or destroys value, pursues or blocks innovation, creates or obstructs the future.

This is why the highest demands must be made on the training and execution of the profession, and why there must be an effective control of how the profession is executed even at senior and top management levels – and why all of this has to be done before the market takes its effect, *because once that happens it is too late*. The risk of management failure is too great to leave it to the market *alone*, although it may once have been a perfectly adequate means of control and correction in times when a company's collapse would hardly have any significant consequences. Moreover, the market alone cannot *bring about* economic performance, let alone social performance.

This statement is far from being a concession to anti-market views. Some people are dissatisfied with the market and market-economy solutions because they do not agree with the results of market-economic processes, such as the distribution of income or the performance pressure. That is *not* my argument. I have other reasons for being dissatisfied with the market: it is too *slow*; it is not *proactive* but *reactive*, and its effect is essentially only a *punitive* one.

The market does not tell us where and how resources *should be* used, only where and how they *should have been* used. When this signal comes from the market, however, it is *too late* for the individual company, in particular for *large* corporations. Even the fastest-moving company has its "dead time", as the time lag between stimulus and response is called. The market as such does not bring about *anything positive*, and it does not *prevent* mistakes from being made. It only *punishes* them – but only after they have happened, which is too late. That must be clearly understood, *in particular* by the proponents of market-economic solutions.

Another factor to be considered is that – as important as small and medium-sized companies may be in other respects – it is the *large corporations*, more than anything, which have to be the center of *societal adjustment and renewal*. It is an illusion to think that politics could fulfill that function, and an even greater fallacy to believe, as many people do, that the truly important innovations can be achieved primarily by small or medium-sized businesses. The latter lack both management capacity and capital. Management will turn out to be the key factor of competitiveness, both for businesses and society at large. In part this is already the case.

This does not only refer to *technological* innovation. Companies will have to face *the biggest challenge* somewhere else: in the area of *social innovation*. This development is not to be welcomed, but there are numerous signs indicating that it cannot be stopped, even though it may not yet be visible with all its consequences.

The welfare state has had its day – as mentioned before – but it has not solved any of the pressing issues. Both the healthcare and the education systems are in a lamentable state, and it is highly questionable whether these systems can be reformed within an appropriate period of time. Only the business sector has managed to prove, time and again, that it is able to make the necessary changes – if sometimes belatedly. Its structures and forms of organization, its systems and processes, its efficiency and performance may not be consistently excellent, but at least they are not as bad as those of other institutions of society. It is all the more important, then, to pay attention to the *quality of its leadership*, apply the highest possible standards, and take countermeasures against even the minutest signs of erosion.

The reason that large-scale enterprises in all industries are particularly important is not only their financial capacity, and thus their power, but above all their *visibility to the public. They are relevant as the standard-setting institutions; they either determine the points of orientation or ruin them.* Thus, they also play a decisive role for *leadership* or *mismanagement.* The performance, responsibility, liability, and role model function of the persons acting on behalf of large corporations, their credibility and the trust people have (and can have) in them, are put to an extreme test in times of profound change – when it comes to taking the difficult, unpopular, radical, tough and painful decisions that are necessary to transition from the present to the future. For obvious reasons, political institutions cannot make these decisions, even if they wanted to.

People have always had the *capability* for adjusting to new circumstances and, if necessary, for making sacrifices; they have always been able to work hard. Sometimes they were driven by violence and terror. Beyond their mere capability, however, people have always had the *will* and *motivation* only when and as long as they *trusted their leaders*, finding them *credible* and facing up to their *responsibility*. Only then could work result in *performance*, creating *wealth* and *value*, and only then did people find meaning in their work.

For all these reasons, corporate supervision is not only a question of legal forms but, above all, one of *factual* impact and effectiveness. The question of non-violent but effective control of people by other people has remained unsolved to this date. Years ago it was not that important because we used to have another societal structure, because life was different. Moreover, mistakes and failures had only local and rather limited impact. *For the first time in history, it is truly important to solve this issue.*

If my analysis in part I, chapter 3 of this book is correct only in part, the significance of the management of businesses cannot be overestimated. As a matter of fact, it will be the management not only of businesses but of all societal institutions – of trade unions, educational and healthcare institutions, administration, and above all, the non-profit sector – which is increasingly gaining importance. I am excluding politics here, not because it is fundamentally insignificant but because it will have less and less importance within national borders, and because it will take a long time until we will have truly effective transnational politics.

National politics is more likely to keep putting the brakes on the transnational play of forces for another while, at least, if the British stance vis-à-vis the European Union is anything to go by. As no single government will be in a position to bring about the solutions that would benefit its own country (and that would secure its reelection), it will at least attempt to prevent, as best it can, any developments that could adversely affect its country and its reelection. Thus, politics will practically paralyze itself, as has been the case in virtually all recent instances where real solutions would have required joint and internationally coordinated action – including everything from Bosnia to the Middle East, and from ecological issues to food controls. For all these reasons, the effective management of business enterprises will carry much greater significance than ever before.

A company is an economic institution, and as such it has a clearly defined purpose to fulfill. But a company is much more: it is a *political* and *moral* institution, and must therefore abide by certain basic conditions and rules of play. The former statement generally meets with agreement. The second is highly controversial. The controversy is pointless, however, as it is not for anyone to decide whether companies are also political and moral institutions – it is a *fact* that they are, in particular large-scale companies. Efforts to factor out this second aspect, as has become fashionable again in the context of a misunderstood (pseudo-)liberalism, are naïve at best but actually dangerous.

This point becomes evident when one considers the conditions in which a business can be operated in the first place. In a decayed society it may be possible to make *deals* but not to operate a *business*. Any degenerated, ruined society offers plenty of evidence, from the failed Communist states to the corrupt regimes in Latin America, Africa, or Asia.

How this problem can be solved is a central issue of modern society. If business leaders do not make visible, proactive and constructive efforts to find a solution, it will be found by others outside the business sector, and judging from past experience it will usually be to the disadvantage of business. Even dodging the problem by going abroad – as is currently done under the globalization label – does not really help.

This problem is the central theme of corporate governance. The essential issues are linked to the *nature and function of profit*, as well as to the question as to *in whose interest* and thus *by what standards* a company should be managed. There are plenty of misunderstandings and errors with regard to both questions. In the following sections I will briefly deal with the most prominent of the false doctrines, and sketch out what I consider to be the right position. These are, of course, questions that need to be *discussed* in the context of overall management of a business. In related discussions, supervisory bodies need to play a decisive role and have the *final say*. Whatever the final decision may be in the individual case, I recommend that the following considerations at least be taken into account.

Profit Maximization Destroys a Business

Profit is still one of the most misunderstood elements in an economy. It is misunderstood by the general public mainly because most managers and business people misunderstand it and thus communicate it incorrectly to the outside world.

But profit is also misunderstood by large parts of the scientific community. In most (market) economic theories, we find the concept of the *profit motive* as a driver of economic action, and of *profit maximization* as its topmost objective. This kind of thinking was brought to the fore again by the recession, though in part under different labels.

In principle, you cannot stop anybody from viewing a business enterprise from the profit perspective and using it as a means for profit maximization. The relevant "theories" seem so plausible that they are barely questioned, and if they are, it is mostly for political-ideological reasons.

Yet there has long been serious criticism even from proponents of the free market economy. *Particularly* when one favors a free enterprise system one *cannot* accept profit as the overriding goal of an enterprise. Time and again it has been demonstrated and conclusively proven that both the profit motive and the economics of profit maximization are concepts *devoid of substance.* Even more importantly, they are also *misleading* and *dangerous* in several respects. Profit as the *topmost objective* undermines the earning power of a company and causes it to risk ruin.

It goes without saying that businesses have to make a profit. Financial discipline must satisfy the highest standards. That, however, has little to do with making profit maximization the overriding goal or purpose of a business. *First,* the ways and means of determining profit are highly questionable; deep down they are quite arbitrary and derive what legitimacy they have from convention. *Second,* some essential elements of a company's *value* cannot even be depicted with accounting tools, not even by the most advanced and sophisticated ones, and so it is impossible to evaluate or manage a business based on balance sheets, profit and loss accounts, or accounting in general. Management based on financial indicators is *operative* management. Once a company's problems start showing in the accounting figures, it is usually too late to correct them.[21] This is

---

21 These considerations, as well as those that follow, also apply if the term "cash flow" is substituted for profit.

why businesses also need strategic management, which focuses on entirely different parameters but is also disciplined by financial measures. This is why in part I, chapter 5 of this book I suggest other *evaluation parameters* and why the supervisory body should only have limited exposure to accounting figures. There are more important things.

I suggest regarding profit as an *outcome* of business activity, not its *cause* or driving force. Profit is the *yardstick* for the correctness and effectiveness of what a company does, not the *reason* for what is done. Profit and profit maximization cannot tell anyone what he or she *should do*. The real causes of good results are *innovation, marketing* and *productivity*, and they are the points of orientation long before profit can be discussed at all or determined.

The purpose of a business must come *from without*, from the market and from society. The legitimization of the company lies in making an economic contribution to the market and to society.

Its purpose is *to create customers by delivering value to the market and to transform resources into economic value.*

The customer does not buy and pay so the business can make a profit, but because he receives value in return. Profit, however, is the yardstick for whether the business serves that purpose correctly and well.

But is there no truth in what is often said about the *profit motive* being the main force driving people to become entrepreneurs? There may be people for whom it works that way. However, as we have yet to find ways of convincingly proving motive, it is probably better to leave this question open. Current economic theories simply assume the profit motive as a premise, yet they cannot provide any evidence of its existence. With profit motive as a premise, theorizing and in particular calculating is easier.

In any case, a closer look at the biographies of business pioneers and tycoons as well as conversations with many of today's entrepreneurs will reveal that they were far from being driven by profit motive when they founded their companies. There are numerous factors indicating that entrepreneurs, at least as often as they claim to want to make a profit, actually strive for something else: for delivering performance, marketing a product, implementing an idea. Many have given up everything for years, gone through bankruptcies, started anew, tried new ways over and over again, before they finally had entrepreneurial success which could also be measured in profits.

Now it would be easy to assume that they, too, are driven by nothing else but the urge to make a profit – though not in the short but in the long term. This, precisely, is one of the deficiencies of profit-focused theories: they have to keep shifting *back and forth* between the short and the long term, between the concrete and the abstract, thus draining themselves of all content. They immunize themselves against the test of reality. There are people who have given up happy, secure livelihoods to become entrepreneurs with the most risky prospects. If they had done economic calculations, perhaps determining the net present value of their calculable, secure income and comparing it to the entirely incalculable net present value of their entrepreneurial activities (which, if it was calculable, would be disastrously negative) they would have never taken that step according to the standards of profit maximization.

Nobody knows what the motive is. Some may want to maximize their profits, others may want to create a life's work, yet others may aspire to power or fame. We do not know – and most of these people probably do not even know themselves. It therefore makes no sense to engage with motives. Instead, it is essential to look at *what* people do, not *why* they do it. In doing so, one will notice that many of the entrepreneurs and managers so proficient in the rhetoric of profit maximization are actually far from behaving in a profit-maximizing fashion. And those who do soon get into major difficulties or go bankrupt.

Of course, anyone establishing a business must submit himself to the *discipline of economic laws*. He must do what he does in a profitable manner, but that does not mean that he has to do it *because* of profit. Profit is a *necessary* condition of entrepreneurial existence, but it is far from being a *sufficient* reason for *what* the company does. Consequently, it is impossible to explain based on profit what the company has done in the past and why, just as it is impossible to deduce from profit what a company will due in the future and why.

Profit is the *result* of *and yardstick* for the quality of corporate action. It is the acid test for the mostly unspoken premises and theories underlying corporate action, but not the reason for them.

One of the key questions in this context is: what kind of profit are we talking about? Basically, from the point of view of running a company it is better to speak of *costs* instead of profit. Once we apply this perspective we realize that even the most advanced accounting system captures only a part of the relevant costs, so what is reported as profit – the difference between revenues and expenses – is either false or misleading.

There are two kinds of costs: those of *today's* business and those required *to stay in business*. The latter are not *costs of tomorrow* but *today's* costs: costs that have already been incurred but have yet to be paid. They are what could be called *"deferred"* or *"accrued costs"*.

The question that needs to be asked is not: *What is the maximum profit?* Remarkably, business administration theory has not provided an answer to this question to this date. The crucial question must address the very opposite. It must be: *What is the minimum profit a company needs in order to still be in business tomorrow?*

This question has nothing to do with hostility to profit; quite to the contrary. Anyone thinking this question through will inevitably find that the minimum, defined along these lines, is considerably *above* what most people would be willing to accept as profit maximum.

The minimum requirement in terms of financial discipline is coverage of the cost of *total capital*. Thus, the main challenge to a company is not to maximize profits but to make *enough profit* to cover the *cost of capital* as well as the risks of future business dealings. Profit is the only source from which economic risk can be financed – including both those of the business itself and those of society at large.

Whatever the theory may be, the practice of managing a company according to the profit maximization principle inevitably leads to *short-term orientation and activities being focused exclusively on financial aspects. But are not American companies and their successes a perfect example for it being right to manage by the profit maximization principle?* America may be the stronghold of profit maximization; but savvy US managers know very well that it was this focus on short-term profits which led to the loss, to Japan and Germany in fact, of highly lucrative markets – such as consumer electronics, television, video, and fax machines, machine tools, and automobiles.

After the Second World War, these two economies practically had no chance of ever playing a role in the world economy again (which the Japanese so far had not done anyway). In both countries, leading companies were not and are not primarily oriented to profit, let alone short-term profit, but to entirely different goals: *long-term market penetration* (with the Japanese explicitly aiming to maximize their market position) and *customer value* as well as *quality*. Profits were an *outcome* of these strategies. In both countries, companies were always committed to serving social purposes – not always gladly, but still consistently. German and Japanese managers were acutely aware throughout the past 150 years that social tensions, class conflict, strikes and an impoverished population were not a good environment for entrepreneurial activities. In Japan, this view is still valid today. (The behaviors leading to the current crisis originated in the finance sector, not the industrial one.) In Germany and Switzerland, this attitude started eroding as late as in the mid-1990s, under the influence of shareholder value thinking.

After all the disasters that these countries (except for Switzerland) had to overcome – as opposed to the United States, which benefited from them – America's much-lauded economic success is put into perspective at the very least. It has largely been attributable to *political and military* circumstances since the Civil War, which were at least as causal as US management practices. Compared to them, the German and Japanese economic success should be rated *higher* in my opinion. The fact that these two economies are currently in serious difficulties does not change a thing about it, nor does it provide a reason to uncritically adopt US practices.

It should be noted at this point – not to add another argument but for illustrative purposes – that some of the most profitable companies are not focused on making profit. Examples include Migros in Switzerland, the Raiffeisen organizations in Germany and Austria, and in general – to a rather considerable degree – the cooperatives. Even the VISA credit card organization was originally established as a non-profit organization. Today, it is the largest and most profitable business in its field. Perhaps the reason is precisely that these organizations have fully dedicated themselves to delivering value to the customer – and their profits were a *consequence* of this attitude.

As I said before, every supervisory body will have to form its own opinion on these questions, in collaboration with the respective executive body, and every company is free to opt for profit maximization. However, it should at least be done in the full knowledge of the arguments against it.

Anyone deciding in its favor should be fully aware that it means making things *easy* for executive management. It is not that difficult to drastically raise profits for a few years, and the stock exchange will certainly reward it. The question is how it is done and what the consequences are.

As a general rule, one will find that the *conditions* for profit – the company's earnings potential – will suffer irreversible damage. There will be a strong temptation, for instance, to cancel planned investments in market position and to put the brakes on research and development, as well as on human resources development. Management is practically given carte blanche to let the long-term health of the business erode to make short-term profits. It is to be expected that, once the – initially invisible – erosion of earnings potential starts manifesting itself in the accounting figures, it will be too late to take corrective action. Profit as the *ultimate* and *only* goal and, a fortiori, profit maximization destroy the performance ability of a company.

Three Models of Corporate Governance – and a Fourth

In order to tell sense from nonsense in today's corporate governance, it is useful to have a look at how it originated. Corporate governance, as it is understood today, emerged from the earlier practices of overall management, in part as a consequence of its shortcomings and ultimate failure, in part from profound changes in international and global business and in the finance system, and for the largest part from errors.

The precursors of today's *shareholder* model are the *owner* model and the *stakeholder* model. Both have become obsolete or have failed, giving rise to the shareholder model in the late 1980s, triggered by the book by Alfred Rappaport.

The shareholder model spread quickly, which, in turn, caused people to believe that it was the right thing and everyone had to adopt it – a typical phenomenon of mass psychology that fit the zeitgeist of the 1990s. *Birds of a feather flock together,* as the old saying goes.[22]

The shareholder model found its breeding ground in the neoliberal thinking of the time. In addition, some more weighty reasons led to its dissemination and largely unquestioning acceptance. This involved the greatest risks of misleading corporate management.

The shareholder model seemed to make the management of a company *easier* in several respects. First, instead of having to balance several over-riding goals, which is always difficult, under the shareholder doctrine management had only to focus on *one* variable. Second, it is a variable that can be quantified, even in monetary terms. Third, it can be verified in the stock markets day by day, so there is basically no need for a finan-

---

22 Pelzmann, Linda: *M.o.M.*® 05/11.

cial controller. Fourth, the shareholder approach was taught in MBA programs worldwide, implying that one was in consensus with "the best" and had no reason whatsoever to question the good sense of the shareholder approach.

But the shareholder model only *seems* to make corporate management easier. In fact, companies are not one-dimensional, purely economic entities but *complex, multi-dimensional systems*. Sooner or later, their multi-dimensional nature will assert itself.

When the first scandals and company collapses revealed the limits of the shareholder model and that reforms were urgently necessary, the response – labeled as progress – was actually a giant step back, to the very model whose failure had caused the equally failed shareholder approach to arise: the stakeholder approach.

No one realized what the true alternative was: giving up the fixation on *interest groups* outside the company, and redirecting the focus of attention to the *company* itself. The logic of this 180-degree turnaround is simple and clear: *What is good for the company cannot be bad for its stakeholders. By contrast, what is good for stakeholders may spell disaster for the company.*

Historically, there have been *three basic models* which also represent the basic forms of a market economy system or of capitalism: owner capitalism, stakeholder capitalism, and shareholder capitalism, which is sometimes referred to as speculator capitalism.[23]

The Owner Model and Corporate Capitalism

In owner capitalism, only one owner or a small number of them control a business. This model is dominated by the figure of the classic *big capitalist*, the tycoon.

The tycoon model hallmarked the era from around 1850 to 1950. Every country had its industrial pioneers: in Germany they were characters like the Krupps, the Thyssens, and Siemens, in the US, the Carnegies, Morgans, Duponts, Rockefellers, and Fords, in Switzerland the Browns, Boveris, Sulzers, Eschers, and Wyss. Present-day examples of famous per-

---

23 With regard to the following, see also Drucker, Peter F.: *Managing for the Future*, London, 1992.

sonalities of this kind include Warren Buffet or Bill Gates. These people built up and managed their companies themselves; they were liable with their own money. In some cases they established entire industries and acted with the undisputed authority of *expert know-how*, combined with unlimited *ownership* and extensive *liability*.

In *Europe*, the classic owner capitalists were historically superseded by the *banks*, in Germany under the leadership of Deutsche Bank. In some countries, before deregulation started, it was largely – directly or indirectly the state or the government, for instance in Italy, France, and Austria. In Japan, the *keiretsu* are the successors to tycoons, and in the US, before pension funds acquired more weight, it was the public.

Ownership and control were thus in the hands of *institutions*, represented by delegates to the corporate executive and supervisory bodies. Thus arose what could be called *corporate capitalism* – or, to be more precise: *corporate capitalism I*, the first version of this model. For a range of reasons, *a long-term way of thinking* prevailed, orientated towards investment, market standing and in part – in close coordination with governments and trade unions – towards the objectives of economic policy and possibly even social policy.

The German "Hausbank" system, invented some 130 years ago by Georg von Siemens, the first chairman of the board of management at Deutsche Bank, was primarily concerned not with dividends and market profits from its portfolio, but focused on commercial business with its key accounts. The Japanese *keiretsu* were primarily interested in economic *power*, as well as in direct business with the "family" members, and not in revenue from shareholdings; and in politically dominated countries, it was and still is the *political interests* that determine the management of business enterprises. Hence, the determining factors in this model are business and political interests, rather than shareholders' interests.

While the controversial personal relations associated with this model have a number of serious drawbacks, an undeniable advantage is an essentially *uniform basic consensus* in large corporations as to the criteria by which a company is to be managed, what performance and results must entail, and by what they are to be judged. Objectives are long-term, fruitful business relations and a sustainable coexistence of political groups

Apart from cases where not only legitimate state and government objectives but also party-political interests were given priority over economic logic – as happened in Austria and Italy, among others – this model can be regarded as successful. Germany and Japan could hardly have achieved their global economic status in any other way, and France, too, cannot be understood without any knowledge of the cooperation between business and politics. The biggest drawback or biggest danger of this model lies in the fact that power is accumulated in the hands of a small number of people, so that the whole economy depends on their ability, quality and competence – which is fine if they are the right people, and dreadful if they are not.

In the United States, developments took quite a different course. Due to the significance that the financial markets – in particular the stock market – have always been accorded there, and due to the very different structure of the banking system, business ownership was very widely spread. With few exceptions, no single shareholder was strong enough to have real control over a corporation. Shareholder interests could not be organized. Control therefore lay in the hands not of the owners but of *management*. Due to the US board system, with its mix of supervisory and executive powers, the top management was not actually responsible to *anyone* – it was left to *define its own* responsibilities.

In the aftermath of the Second World War, this situation resulted in the emergence of two corporate governance theories: the *stakeholder* theory and, much later – starting in the late 1980s and entering public awareness as late as in the mid-1990s – the *shareholder* theory. Neither of the two has stood the test of time. The first has visibly failed; the second is currently in the process of doing so, even if many people are not able or willing to realize this – yet.

The Stakeholder Model

The first theory became popular under the name *"stakeholder approach"*. Its basic proposition is this: if management is not responsible to any specific individual group, the company must be run "in the best balanced interest" of *all* groups with "stakes" in the business – that is, all shareholders, employees, customers, suppliers, banks, and possibly local political institutions. As plausible as this universal "harmony model" may look at first glance, its consequences are disastrous. The company is exposed to the changing interests of a broad variety of groups, and is permanently at risk of having to satisfy special interests instead of fulfilling its economic purpose. In the US and in England it was the unions, in Italy and Austria the political parties which for many years took advantage of large parts of the business sector for their own ends.

The first person to formulate the stakeholder approach was Ralph Cordiner, CEO of General Electric in the early 1990s. It was an acceptable starting point, but the question it raises is what the "best balanced interest" is supposed to be, what *specific* performance and results the company is to achieve and how management's responsibility is actually to be introduced, to be honored, and to be enforced if need be.

A practical answer to this has never been found. This set the scene for what was to follow: in many cases, managers – in their common interest with the board – who, in the final analysis, were in fact responsible to no one, let the reins slip and became complacent, or behaved like what is referred to as "kindly tyrants" or "benevolent despots" in political science. In the absence of binding standards, they defined on a case-by-case basis – and to no small degree influenced by self-interest – what was in whose interest. This did not happen everywhere: there were also companies which were excellently managed at that time and which functioned extremely well. But wherever management was fine it was due to *people*, to the individuals involved, and not thanks to the intrinsic merits of the *model* as such.

It was this *constitutional* weakness in the American system, combined with the opportunities offered by the stock market, which led to the wave of takeovers gaining momentum in the 1990s, helped by the bull market, and on to the known excesses. This development was systematically inevitable although initially, the necessary funding was not available. American banks did not have the funds to finance hostile takeovers, due to the US system of specialized commercial banks; some were also reluctant as a matter of principle, or because they feared an excessive risk concentration. What prepared the ground for the wave of takeovers was the *investment* and *pension fund system*, which in turn led to an unprecedented *capital accumulation* in the hands of just a few institutions. The pension funds alone controlled some 2.5 trillion dollars in the early 1990s; today it is a multiple thereof. In the US they have largely replaced the banks as centers of capital accumulation

This accumulated capital is constantly on the lookout for investment and return opportunities. The majority of these funds have flowed into stock and bond markets. Thus, the American "working class" via their pension funds became the owners of the US economy. What has occurred is a phenomenon to which Peter Drucker, in his largely unnoticed 1976 book "The Unseen Revolution", has referred as "pension fund socialism" – or US-style people's capitalism. Pension funds hold more than 50 percent interest in large corporations, whether by shares or bonds.

The *owners* of large-scale US corporations are thus millions of American people. The *power of disposal* over these funds, however, is directly or indirectly in the hands of *pension fund managers*: directly to the extent that they hold securities, and indirectly to the extent that they have invested in investment funds. This inevitably has two consequences:

The *first* – negative – consequence is that this paved the way for the wave of *hostile takeovers*. Without the direct or indirect help from the pension funds, the early Wall Street raiders would not have been able to carry out their aggressive plans. Although more than a few fund managers were highly skeptical about these deals, they were forced to play to them, *de facto* and in some cases even by law, as otherwise they would have had to face legal action for breach of faith and claims for damages on the investors' part, and furthermore they would not have achieved their performance objectives

Competent pension fund managers were justifiably skeptical, for it turned out that hardly any of the companies which had gone through hostile takeovers ended up in a better position afterwards. Basically, only the management buy-outs produced good results. Hostile takeovers did not.

With few exceptions, the outcomes of these takeovers were over-indebted wrecks or totally disrupted firms. Even worse, they created bitterness, cynicism and lethargy in the companies' employees, for they saw themselves being treated as nothing more than merchandise, and dismissed en masse. Their managers, having previously operated with lofty words and great ideals – such as loyalty, motivation, and so on – simply "sacrificed" their staff while they themselves often profited handsomely from these deals. Whatever the intentions may have been, the employees could not help but feel that this was a betrayal of everything preached to them in the past. This lesson was in no way confined to the companies directly affected: it sent a strong and far-reaching signal, as every employee in every firm had to assume that the same things might happen to him. There could hardly have been a faster and more effective way of destroying the social cohesion of a society.

The raiders and their supporters justified these goings-on by saying that they were to the benefit of shareholders. Even if this had been the case, it would have still raised the question as to whether the social costs of these profits were not too high. In fact, however, it was not true, at least not generally. Broadly speaking, what happened was that the absurdly inflated takeover prices were only partly paid in cash, or not at all, but in the form of debt bonds of all kinds, mostly junk bonds. Most of these papers quickly lost value after the takeover coups. On balance, the only ones who gained from these hostile takeovers were the raiders themselves, their lawyers, a few managers and the investment bankers – sometimes to a shameless extent.

The *second* – essentially positive – consequence of the takeover wave was that the way in which American corporations are managed changed *radically* within just a few years. Suddenly performance was demanded, whether to ward off takeovers, be successful after a takeover, or in general give a good visual appearance. Almost immediately, however, the negative side effects of this basically desirable change started to show: top managers found they were forced to manage their companies focusing on variables that had nothing to do with sound entrepreneurship and everything to do with the short-term expectations of financial analysts, which were increasingly driven by time pressure and greed. Everyone had to take care not to become the raiders' next prey, and thus did everything to keep their corporation's stock price high.

The failed stakeholder model was thus replaced by the shareholder model. After all, the raiders could only realize their plans if they could make people believe that they were serving the interests of *shareholders* better than the management in charge. That that did not come true overall is one of the ironies of the market. Nonetheless, the hostile takeovers did fulfill one purpose: they gave a real fright to managers who were comfortably dozing along, safe and secure all around and responsible to no one, as well as to the supervisory bodies which had been tolerating the poor performance of these managers for many years. And they added momentum to the discussion on the basic questions of corporate governance.

The Shareholder Model

Shareholder value became the new creed and edged out all other considerations. In the context of shareholder value, everything is dedicated exclusively to return on capital employed, and usually also return on equity. This model cannot work in the long term as it violates fundamental principles of corporate management. Its most important problem, however, was that from the outset it could only gain a foothold in periods of bull market. Even in the US the model does not really fit. There are already political movements aimed at radically curbing shareholders' rights. Least of all does this model sit well in Europe's social landscape, where it is nevertheless being copied diligently and, as always, somewhat rashly.

What seems to have been overlooked here is that, *first,* the strength of the US economy – if it exists at all – is not owed to its profit and shareholder orientation but to other factors, including political ones, and to the fact that there are still plenty of top managers in the United States who may have adapted their *rhetoric* to Wall Street thinking but do not act that way. This is true in particular, and quite demonstrably, of the man whom the majority of the media have been misusing as expert witness for the shareholder model: Jack Welch, the renowned former General Electric CEO. A *second* factor which is overlooked is the reason why the shareholder orientation even came to be in the USA and that the situation there is quite different. *Third*, people are not aware that Europe and Japan are much more developed in major aspects of corporate governance than the United States is.

Putting aside all the rhetoric and declared intentions, what is the *inevitable practical* effect of shareholder value capitalism? Fund managers are rated by their performance, that is, by the financial growth of the capital they manage. Due to the competition between the 10,000 funds for investment liquidity, and in an environment influenced by the totally euphoric Wall Street industry, that means nothing but *short-term* performance. It simply *cannot* be otherwise: fund performance is published daily; dozens of rating agencies and investment services compare on a monthly or at least quarterly basis how funds are performing and publish ranking lists. Anyone who does not consistently deliver a top-level performance will invariably fall behind – with potentially disastrous consequences for the fund, in particular if money starts to drift out.

Fund managers therefore *cannot* act as *owners* of the "property" entrusted to them; they *have to* act as *short-term* speculators. They do not invest in *companies* but in *shares*, which they resell just as quickly as they buy them once dividends or prices do not meet the performance targets they require of them – for example, because the company itself has adopted a long-term investment or innovation strategy which temporarily squeezes profits. As a matter of fact, they are not interested in the company as such: they *cannot* be due to the logic of the financial system. There is no room for loyalty of any kind towards a company.

Today's high priests of shareholder value – fund managers and financial analysts – will even *actively* and *excessively* destroy shareholder value every time we have a bear market. When this happens, which means that fund managers can only achieve returns by selling short, they will keep driving stock prices lower and lower – unless they are hindered by exchange regulations. Financial analysts will advise them on their sell strategies.

Nor can corporate managers sidestep the dictates of shareholder-value-driven performance measurement. In public opinion, or, to be more precise, in the opinion of financial analysts, they face nothing but problems if their shares underperform. Therefore they avidly monitor stock trade records in the financial markets – they consult the *Reuters screen* instead of looking at what they should be monitoring: the outside *market*. They start aligning the management of their companies with the interests and behavior of the *stock market,* instead of that of the *customer.* They let themselves be guided by the interests of *speculation* rather than those of the *company.* This was clearly demonstrated by the dramatic crashes in stock prices, in particular with the previously spectacularly inflated initial public offerings.

Even those top managers who are smart and experienced enough to recognize the hazards of short-term action driven solely by financial figures, find that they are forced to conform to the expectations of the financial world by at least paying lip service to it. Their rhetoric may be music to financial analysts' ears, but it is harmful to employees, customers and suppliers, and unfortunately they cannot send out two contradictory messages at the same time without losing credibility.

The shareholder value theory may well prove to be *even more short-lived* than the stakeholder theory and possibly also *more damaging.* It could only have real impact in the context of one of history's largest bull markets, and it will surely disappear when it ends and the next bear market emerges, leaving behind economic devastation. This will also force pension funds to remember that there is a difference between ownership in *shares* and ownership in a *corporation*, although both are certified by the same document. While they will not be able to act as managers of the corporations they dominate, they will have to behave as entrepreneur shareholders – because they will no longer be able to sell their shares the way they did before. Once we are in a bear market, the market will not let them do so without suffering huge losses. They will then have to learn, like all "big capitalists" before them, that *"if you can't sell you have to care."*

As one of the consequences of the shareholder value theory, the difference between an *investor*-owner and an *entrepreneur*-owner or entrepreneurial manager has become completely clouded and confused. But this difference is crucial. Let me briefly summarize the key points here: The investor operates *temporarily*; entrepreneurial activity is designed for an unlimited duration. The investor *gives up when difficulties arise* – he sells – and if he is shrewd, he gives up before it ever comes to that. He makes his investments precisely so that he can get rid of them very quickly; the entrepreneur (-manager), by contrast, fights when difficulties arise – he cares. The investor maximizes *one* resource: money; the entrepreneurial task covers a combination of *several* resources. The investor is only interested in *financial return*, while the entrepreneur is interested in the *performance* of the business. To the investor, the stock exchange is *indispensable*; the entrepreneur, however, does *not need* a stock exchange. Companies exist without stock exchanges and even if stock exchanges were to collapse or temporarily be shut down, companies would still exist. The investor of the shareholder value type is only found in *bull markets*; the entrepreneur is an *all-weather type*.

The differences set out here do *not* imply that there is reason to be opposed to financial investors or speculation. Both fulfill important functions in a market economy. Only these functions are quite different from those of the corporation and the corporate manager. They are not interchangeable nor should they be confused with one another.

A summary of the most important differences is provided in the table below.

Investor	Entrepreneur
sells	cares
operates with a temporary focus	operates for an unlimited duration
gives up when difficulties arise, and sells	struggles because he is not able to sell
needs only one resource: money	combines several resources: money, people, machinery, materials, etc.
maximizes profit	maximizes market position
shareholder value	customer value
keeps the Reuters screen in sight	monitors the market
needs the stock exchange	does not need a stock market
only in bull markets	economic all-weather type
actively destroys value in bear markets	creates value even in bear markets

The Corporate Model, or Corporate Capitalism II

There is only *one* right way of managing a company – namely, *in the interest of the company*, not in the interest of a group or even all the groups together. The maxim must not be the "best balanced interests of interest groups" but the "best interests of the enterprise", because of the specific purpose it has to fulfill within the economy. Which brings us to model No. II of corporate capitalism.

True entrepreneurs throughout the world, the managers of companies that are truly strong and healthy today, the "empire builders", do not regard balance as a *supreme* principle. They do *maximize* something, but it is not profit: *they maximize the wealth-creating capacity of the company by delivering market performance for their customers to the best of their possibilities.* They *also* pay attention to profits, of course, as something to be reinvested and used to cover risk, rather than something that has been earned and can basically be spent. Their bottom line is not the *figures* the accountants come up with, but the *survival* of the company, and their primary objective is the *health* and *viability* (though the term sustainability is sometimes used) of their company. For precisely this reason, they are not interested in *growth* per se, but in *strengthening their market position*, and in growth only as its consequence. Not size but strength is their criterion. They distinguish very carefully between different *kinds* of growth – between growth leading to strength, growth which is simply an extra layer of "fat", and growth that is cancerous.

In short:

They maximize their market position, not their growth; they maximize customer value, not the return on equity; they maximize their innovativeness, not their profit. They are keenly aware of the difference between an investor and an entrepreneur. They focus on customer value, and on shareholder value only as a consequence. The starting point for their plans is not finance but their business mission.

As a consequence, they do achieve profits – which are usually higher than those of others – and so their shareholders, too, achieve capital returns; but it is a result of entrepreneurial success, not of letting the company "bleed to death" financially.

Only by an orientation towards the viability and health of the company is it possible to weigh up all interests against each other and against the company's interests, regardless of how vociferously they are expressed. This is the *only* way of integrating short-term and long-term thinking, and it is the *only* way to organize top management bodies properly, to determine what their responsibilities are and how they are to be distributed, and properly shape their collaboration, their relationships with each other and with the company. It is also the *only* way of having any chance at all of resolving the most *serious* conflicts: those rooted in fundamental value conceptions about the purpose and function of a company, or of corporate governance.

To some extent, this signifies a return to *corporate capitalism* – but only in a certain respect. Peter Drucker was very much to the point when he said that early corporate capitalism asked the right question but gave the wrong answer. It is possible, however, to give the *right* answer to this question. It lies in the six key variables – or Central Performance Controls (CPCs) as I call them[24] – which will be dealt with in the next chapter.

In the final analysis, it may be the most important task of corporate governance to produce an answer to this crucial question and to firmly instill it as the primary objective in the company. The answers found in *small* corporations may be relatively unimportant, but *large corporations* have a particular responsibility here. Extreme financial discipline and undisputed corporate performance are the *supreme rules* – there can be no doubt about this. The *old* form of corporate capitalism fell at this hurdle. And yet financial performance alone is not enough. Fixation on it results in a gradual neglect of other factors which are important from an entrepreneurial perspective. It also results in growth and size being misunderstood, with – in some cases – disastrous consequences, as demonstrated by any merger which finds itself in trouble. Anyone interested in a free enterprise system must consider more than purely financial performance.

Last but not least, consideration must be given to the business environment. No society can permanently function in an anti-business environment. It will be impossible to convince people, no matter in what society and what their level of wealth, that they have to perform better, be more productive, possibly even be made redundant in vast numbers – *just to make shareholders rich*. People are willing to perform – and possibly also make sacrifices along the way – if it is in the service of the company, but not simply to make "rich people even richer". This is how shareholder value, whatever the intentions behind by it, will be understood by anyone delivering performance – and there is no way of depicting it otherwise. This is how things will always appear – and in my view, it is the truth. It is dramatically proven by the almost total collapse of the stock options systems on the New Markets, where some believed they had found a miraculous formula for rewarding employees and increasing wealth.

Nor can people be made to accept that they must perform so that managers can get rich. The only things that words and actions to this effect will achieve are new class conflicts, belligerent trade unions, and a completely demotivated workforce. In past instances of parasitic, self-enriching board behavior, this is what happened. Luckily such cases are excep-

---

24 Malik, Fredmund: *Corporate Policy and Governance. How Organizations Self-Organize,* Frankfurt/New York, 2011 (Volume 2 of the series "Management: Mastering Complexity").

tions. But due to the power of the media they have a disastrous effect on the reputation of management. After all, it is – quite understandably – not the honest managers and sensible behaviors which are most interesting to the media.

What is at stake here is *far more* than economic performance, however important it may be. It is highly doubtful whether society can function in the long run if everything is subordinate to just *one* objective, even if it is a goal as important as economic performance. Starting with Aristotle, all major state and social philosophers – in particular those with a conservative or liberal outlook – have concluded that subordinating all social objectives to one single goal, regardless of what it may be, will ultimately destroy the very ability of society to achieve any goals at all, produce performance and get results – indeed, its very ability to function.

Chapter 5

What Is a Healthy Business? Assessing Corporate Performance

If corporate management is to focus on the company and its prosperity, health and viability – rather than a set of interest groups, however they may be defined – then criteria need to be defined against which the company, its performance and its success are to be measured. This question is important for both the supervisory and the executive body, and for all top and middle management levels.

The key question has to be: *What is a healthy company, and what needs to be monitored if its health is to be assessed?* The answer will influence – indeed, *define* – the entire range of tasks of the corporate supervisory body. As a consequence, it also determines the tasks of all other corporate bodies and of the company as a whole. It further determines what and how much information the supervisory body needs, what executives need to focus on, and how – from what perspective – financial controllers have to do their job and produce their reports for the supervisory body.

Applying a set of variables to assess the health and success of a company involves a considerable expansion of the supervisory body's traditional retrospective function, which has largely relied on accounting figures. The variables and fields of assessment concern all supervisory tasks. They should form the "cockpit"[25] for both the executive and the supervisory body. In essence they provide the basis for exercising corporate governance, and the *only* possibility to avoid the pitfalls of both the stakeholder and the shareholder theory.

---

25 In my latest book, *Corporate Policy and Governance. How Organizations Self-Organize*, Frankfurt/New York (Volume 2 of the series "Management: Mastering Complexity") I refer to these variables as "Central Performance Control" (short CPC) for the sake of linguistic clarity.

One of the gravest mistakes in measuring corporate performance is to exclude everything that cannot be measured in the ordinary sense – just *because* it cannot be measured. In most cases, that is the deeper reason for why people tend to cling to the financial variables that are easy to quantify, thus seeming to provide safety, objectivity, accuracy, and reliability. Upon closer analysis one will find that financial parameters are anything but safe, objective, accurate, and reliable.

In today's corporate governance, the dominant instrument for controlling and assessing a company and its business success is still the accounting function. However, despite all the improvements achieved in this field, it does *not* suffice to ascertain and evaluate business success.

How and based on what can one determine whether a business is healthy? What are the key variables that provide the necessary information to assess a company and its business dealings reliably and comprehensively? What are the factors one must take into account in order to recognize looming trouble in time to take countermeasures?

There are six key variables which, individually and in combination, permit an early and reliable assessment. The best tool by far for their qualification and empirical validation is the scientific research program PIMS.[26] It must be ensured that financial controllers pay attention to these variables, that they determine and monitor them and report on them in an appropriate manner. *In addition* to these variables, many more things must be known. Without these six key variables, however, there will be a systematic risk of *wrong assessment* and *misdirection*.

The six variables also permit bridging the gap between *short-term* and *long-term* assessment.

Market Position

The first key variable is the *market position* of the company overall and each of its business units.

---

26 See Malik, Fredmund: *Management. The Essence of the Craft.* (Volume 1 of the series "Management: Mastering Complexity"), Frankfurt/New York, 2010, as well as Buzzel, Robert D./Gale, Bradley, T.: *The PIMS Principles. Linking Strategy to Performance*, New York, 1987.

It took a long time for the significance of market position to become sufficiently known and accepted. Still, there are many people who find it difficult to grasp or to accept, arguing that it was, for instance, only relevant for major corporations or less relevant for their particular industry. Also, in the standard literature on business administration, market position is not given the space it deserves.

A *continuous improvement* in market position, or *at least holding* a *defendable* market position, is the first key variable for assessing business success. Market position is a key factor for success – for *any* kind of company of *any* size and in *any* industry.

But even in organizations where this has been realized, the efforts made to systematically define, determine and continually monitor this variable are often insufficient. Even there, market position often is not a standard item on the agenda at executive and supervisory board meetings. Dealing with this variable is left to planning and staff departments – although it is the *first* to belong on the radar screens of *top-level management bodies*.

Market position is a *complex* variable, and thus not easy to define. In most cases, it cannot be quantified in one single ratio. Naturally, the company's market share, or the market shares of its divisions, and above all the *relative* market shares have to be included.

But market position as such is much more than quantifiable market share. It also includes public awareness and image, customer satisfaction, customer value indices, and presence in individual segments.

As a matter of fact, the starting point must be the following questions: "What determines market position specifically for us? What is included, what is not? How can we best determine and assess it?" One should never expect to get ready-made answers, for instance from text books. On the contrary, thoroughly examining these precise questions is one of the primary tasks of top-level management boards.

Is the market position improving in the *right* markets, with the *right* customer groups, in the *right* distribution channels? Take, for instance, pharmaceutical companies. Some enjoy excellent market positions with physicians in higher age groups, while the younger doctors tend to prescribe competitors' products. Others have a strong presence in pharmacies but not in hospitals.

Furthermore, it is important to have a clear position on *substitution products*. For commercial banks, a good position in the field of commercial loans has always been considered essential. In the US, however, commercial loans have lost much of their significance over the past 15 years – more so than anyone would have thought possible. Even medium-sized companies now draw their funds from the market, not from bank loans.

Knowing the *substitution channels* is equally important. Nothing has changed more in recent years than distribution channels. Almost all specialized trade segments are suffering massive erosion, have been replaced by other trade forms, or had to restructure. None of these things appears in official statistics or in the national product. Traditional economic analyses do not cover these factors.

There are no theories or methods to determine even the market position of a company. Every organization needs to do this work for its *individual situation*, also thinking through what the elements are which adequately describe and depict its position.

Innovation Performance

The second variable is the *innovation performance* of a company. It is the most reliable *early warning signal* for assessing *long-term* success. Companies that stop innovating are on the slide – long before this is reflected in their accounting figures. It can take years before this downward development is detected by the traditional tools – and then it will usually be too late for corrections.

One typical case is the Sears Roebuck corporation: by all conceivable criteria it was a clear success story for 60 years, before it ran into deep trouble from which it is now slowly recovering. In the 1970s, the company had shown clear signs of weaknesses with regard to its innovation performance. It took 15 years until the truth was fully revealed. But it had been visible early on for anyone paying attention to innovativeness.

The story is the same as with market position. There are no standard answers to the question on innovation performance. The *question* is the *same* for all industries and companies, but the *answers* are *different* in every single case.

One of the key ratios expressing innovation performance is the *innovation rate*: what percentage of sales is contributed by products or services with a maximum age of three to five years? The correct value of this rate must be determined individually, but it should never be below 10 percent.

On the other hand, innovation rates in excess of 30 percent usually have negative effects on mid to long-term returns.

Another key variable for innovation performance is the ratio of *successful start-ups versus flops*. Yet another is *time to market* – the time required from the original idea to the point when the new product is launched in the market. These ratios must be monitored over time, and contrasted with those of the competition.

But innovation performance does not only refer to market-related innovation. In addition, the innovativeness *within* the company also has to be "assessed" and monitored, in order to be able to judge whether the company innovates too much or too little. Too little internal innovation means that the business is slowly wasting away; too much means hectic, pointless actions, and lots of hustle and bustle instead of effectiveness. The significance and interpretation of such variables is linked to difficult and high-risk decisions. Monitoring innovativeness is not about simple measurements.

Productivities

A third area of performance assessment is *productivity*, or more precisely: productivities. Over the past 100 years, only one kind of productivity used to be measured: that of *labor*. It is still important but *no longer sufficient*. Increasingly, other productivity ratios are required in addition – in particular those of *capital*, *time*, and *knowledge*.

Labor Productivity

Labor productivity is the classic productivity ratio par excellence. It has been around for over 100 years, and its improvement is one of the great success stories of economics, as I have explained before.[27] Nevertheless, the measure most widely known and used is sales per capita. It is also the most ineffective.

---

27 See part I, chapter 5.

The starting point must be *value-added*[28] per capita. But although this ratio is easy to determine, in most companies it is not regularly monitored and discussed at the top management level. In addition, it is also important to determine the labor productivities for different categories of work, or "workers" – that is to say, the value-added per blue-collar worker, per sales rep, per laboratory worker, per staff employee, per administrative employee, and so on.

Moreover, labor productivity will have to be improved. In the past years, due to the recession, major shortfalls have become visible. Now, in the past three to four years, labor productivity in Germany – as an average cutting across all sectors of the economy – has been raised by 15 to 20 percent. This is quite an achievement, and individual organizations have been even more successful. Still, it is not enough. There is much more to be done, regardless of all the social consequences this will have.

But the fact remains: labor productivity is no longer the central arena for productivity increase. We will continue to have this problem, but it will not be the most important one. Other forms of productivity are much more critical.

Capital Productivity

In the past years, capital productivity has outranked labor productivity in terms of importance. And it is the easiest and fastest to improve. Money knows no fatigue, needs no motivation, is not unionized, and works 24/7. It is also the only truly global resource. It speaks all languages, and it can travel to in Frankfurt today, to New York tomorrow, and to Tokyo the day after. It is all the more surprising that there are still organizations that pay little attention to this productivity ratio. There can hardly be any other reason for the vast differences in capital productivity between companies in one and the same industry. General Electric, for instance, long had about twice the capital productivity of Westinghouse, and considerably more than Siemens.

Measuring the productivity of money and capital needs to start by

---

28 Value added here equals sales minus goods and services bought in. This is not the same as the "economic value added" which is widely used today but would be but largely meaningless in this context.

determining the *value-added* per currency unit invested. This – relatively rough – initial ratio must then be refined: value-added per currency unit in the different current and non-current assets, referring to the money still passing through, but also value added per currency unit entailed in the main expenditures and revenues. The best, although somewhat radical way to improve money and capital productivity is to charge subsidiaries a relatively high interest rate and keep them short on cash. The managers of corporate entities must be kept moaning and groaning under the pressure of funds being scarce and expensive, and this should be a point of complaint at every management meeting and a standard topic at every meeting on budgets and business results. Nothing teaches people the ABC of economics as quickly and effectively as scare and expensive money, and nothing contaminates their thinking as badly and quickly as having access to large amounts of cheap money. It is ultimately the only means of establishing economic and entrepreneurial thinking in an organization. Only when pressured by high capital cost do managers deal with the laws of general economics and business economics, and only this way do they really learn these things.

Time Productivity

The first two kinds of productivity, of labor and of money, are the best known. Most people know much less about the productivity of time, and least about that of knowledge. There is plenty of work to be done in both areas.

One of the few truly variable figures in a company is time. The same thing can be done slowly or quickly. Time is one of the absolutely critical dimensions of what is going on in the market, and it is therefore important – also for the supervisory body – to know whether the company is getting faster, stagnating, or slowing down. The importance of this issue has been recognized for development and throughput times where considerable improvements have been achieved in part. Also, things like the responsiveness of customer service or the speed at which complaints are handled have become an issue. But that is not enough.

All processes in an organization need to be systematically examined as to their time productivity, and improved as needed. One of the most important ratios will be the time productivity of the single employee group that has been growing at the fastest rate: the *brainworkers*. However, only very few companies have begun to measure their brainworkers' time productivity. There is hardly another area where differences between top performance, mediocrity, and poor performance are greater.

Most brainworkers have not even begun recording the time they need for different tasks, which would be a basic prerequisite for productivity improvements. They are still in the dark about their productivity. Many are even proud of this and convinced that it cannot be measured, arguing that the *quality* and *complexity* of mental work are what matters.

No question, quality is important. But *first off,* there is a considerable number of brainworkers who *can be compared to each other*. For instance, I do not see any reason why the effort going into a market analysis for Italy should not be comparable to the one required to perform an analysis for Spain, provided that both observe the same standards for what the analysis should entail. Nor do I see any reason why the planning work required for a new hotel building and for a new office building should not be compared, at least in part, for instance with regard to crucial variables such as cubic contents, floor space, contract price, and so on.

Second, even for basically *very different* kinds of brainwork there can be important leads if the times required are systematically monitored over an extended period of time and for larger numbers. For instance, newspaper editors paying attention to these things over several years will be able to make a rough estimate of how long they take to write an editorial, even if it is on a very different topic each time. Experienced orchestra conductors can surely tell how much time they need, more or less, to rehearse even very different symphonies. Experienced managers know how long it takes them to prepare important meetings or negotiations, and they block this time on their agendas; and scientists who have learnt to monitor these things are also able to say approximate how much time they need to write a printable manuscript, and what their daily output is in terms of pages of a well-written article.

Needless to say, one will always operate with *ranges* and *approximate* figures. But in the course of a longer period of time there will be *regularities, typical characteristics* and *unusual ones*; there will be *patterns* and *convergences*. Quite certainly, one will be able to tell whether productivity is *improving* or *deteriorating*, although not down to the decimal values – which is not necessary anyway.

Knowledge Productivity

Knowledge productivity is still not very well understood. If the hypothesis is right which I laid out in part I, chapter 5, then knowledge will be the most important economic resource. In many industries, this is already the case. If management is the transformation of knowledge into value, we should be able to measure the productivity of *knowledge* and its *use*, and thus the productivity of *management*. It is entirely possible to determine in special cases what percentage of the knowledge basically available is being used and made use of, for instance, by a team set up to solve a certain problem. It is thus also possible to compare the work done by several teams, even though only roughly. Another, relatively simple, possibility is to measure, say, the value-added per university graduate employed (and the same for the other educational levels represented). If this ratio does not improve over time, the conclusion is that while the organization in question is facing the high cost associated with employing university graduates, it is probably not getting the full benefit of their superior knowledge.

There is much more work to be done in the field of measuring knowledge productivity, and we will have to make do with rough approximations for a while yet. But we have to start working on these issues today if we want to have the problem under control tomorrow. Each and every organization would be well advised not to wait for scientists to solve the problem, but to start working on it themselves, even if initial results may be unsatisfactory. Those who don't could be in for a rude awakening – once they realize that their competitors have taken the lead and they might not be able to catch up.

Total Factor Productivity

All *partial productivities* – all productivities of *key resources* – must continually be improved. Which leads us to the determination of the *total factor productivity*. Both the aggregate ratio and its components must continuously be improved. Not all companies will be able to keep *growing* in the future, but all will be able to keep getting *better*.

One *single* productivity component *alone* is no longer enough to assess any advances made in productivity, for it is easily possible for a company to *increase* its labor productivity while simultaneously *decreasing* its capital productivity. The times are over when it was considered a basic law of economics that any increases in labor productivity gained by investing more capital would automatically result in cost decreases. This is one of the main reasons for the serious difficulties some sectors are in, such as health care or parts of the computer industry.

Attractiveness to Good People

The fourth measure of health and success of a company is its ability to *attract and retain good people*. As trivial as the old phrase about people being an organization's most important resource may sound, it is still true and significant, and although it should be a matter of course, many managers still fail to act accordingly.

The usual key figures such as *staff turnover rates* or *absenteeism* are doubtlessly important; but while they provide important information, they are not what is essential. What matters is not *how many* people leave and join the company, but *what kind of* people. It is a serious warning sign if really good people start leaving, or if an organization finds it hard to find the right people and spark their interest.

Staff turnover per se involves *just costs*. They, too, are a serious issue, in particular when they exceed the level typical of the industry in question. But fluctuation among the *real performers*, the top-quality people, does another, much more serious kind of damage. It hampers the *performance* of an organization and is a *signal* which all other employees pay attention to. It is a warning sign relating to the *trust* placed in the organization's management, in the organization itself and in its future. Seeing good people leave causes others to start wondering. It also raises doubts, with immediate consequences for people's motivation, determination, and faith in the company.

When, on top of everything, management plays down such occurrences with flimsy excuses – which often happens – its *credibility will soon be lost*. When occurrences like these cannot be avoided, it is important at least to face up to them and make it clear that they are taken seriously, and that measures are taken to prevent them from recurring. This is a prime opportunity to show *leadership* visibly and effectively.

So when this warning signal occurs, the matter must be thoroughly analyzed. Not only should the turnover rates as such be determined; rather, analyses should extend to the level of individual *names*. For a series of reasons it is extremely important to have exit interviews with key people and find out what their motives are, even if the fact that they are leaving cannot be reversed. These exit interviews tend to be unpleasant affairs, as they often reveal bitter truths about the company and about oneself – the person interviewing. But they are necessary, even if the impulse to avoid them is strong.

Every top-level executive and each of the members of the supervisory body are well advised to regularly request a list of the people leaving the firm – no matter at what level. It must be ensured that the managers at each level look into these matters and keep records. The most significant cases must be investigated personally, in order to find the truth and obtain clarity about the situation. This is one of the most effective ways to learn the truly important things about the culture and working climate at one's organization.

I also do not advise against carrying out occasional staff surveys, although I am somewhat skeptical with regard to their value. I have my doubts as to whether employees will really tell the truth, even if surveys are kept anonymous. In any case, their statements cannot be true to reality in the sense of being objective, but often people do not even stick to reality by their own, subjective standards. It is generally known that the answers to such surveys are often used to express opposition. People want to teach management "a lesson". There may be good reasons for that, but it is difficult if not impossible to interpret such answers correctly. The moment of truth – if it ever happens – will be when in the course of an exit interview the individual asks: *"Do you really want to know why I am leaving?"*

Liquidity and Cash Flow

With the next measuring field I am entering more familiar terrain. Of the numbers that management receives from the accounting department, two are particularly important: *cash flow* and *liquidity*.[29] Sales revenues, total

---

29 See Siegwart, Hans: *Der Cash-Flow als finanz- und ertragswirtschaftliche Lenkungsgröße*, 3rd revised and amended edition, Stuttgart/Zurich, 1994.

order value, costs and profits are certainly important. However, an old adage says that a company can survive for quite a while *without making profits*, as long as there are cash flows and liquidity – but it does not work the other way round. When losses occur, a company will first get rid of *bad business*, which is doubtlessly right and will often help to improve the bottom line quickly. In the event of a liquidity squeeze, however, it will have to part with the *best* performing business units, as this will be the only way to secure a fast inflow of funds. In most cases it is also a guarantee of greater difficulties to follow. Cash flow and liquidity are just as important for a business as oil pressure and oil level are in a car. Any warning signs require *immediate* action.

It is important, also and particularly for the supervisory body, to make sure that any maneuvers aimed at increasing profit – for instance, by expanding the sales base – are not pursued at the expense of liquidity. One will often find that management "purchases" higher sales instead of "earning" them, for instance by giving discounts, granting advance financing to customers, offering to take over interest rates, and the like. Markets and customers, however, which are "purchased" in this way are not stable. They will be lost as soon as a competitor offers even better terms. The US automotive industry had to learn this lesson the hard way in the early 1990s.

Profitability

The last of the six measuring variables is the *profitability* of each of the individual businesses, and of the company as a whole. Most companies have a sophisticated set of tools with numerous indicators for this. I will therefore confine myself to commenting on just a few points. *First*, all extraordinary and/or non-recurrent revenues and expenses must be *excluded* from the calculation of a business's profitability, and *second*, profitability must be determined *before* overhead is allocated. *Third*, effects of inflation or deflation have been taken into account. In any case, it is important to work with *purchasing-power-adjusted* values in addition to nominal ones.

Furthermore, it should be determined *how* the profitability came about. The total operating profit, as is generally known, equals margin multiplied by capital turnover rate. Many companies have a tendency to maximize their *margins*. This, however, is an open invitation to the competition to start attacking, and thus a strategy whose consequences should be carefully considered. In most cases, a much easier and less risky approach, though not a quicker one, to improve total profit is to change the capital turnover rate – for instance, by reducing fixed reserves or by using the existing capital to serve a larger business volume.

Two further aspects are essential here. First, in order to reliably assess the profitability of a business it is imperative to know the *interest rates* charged to the different business units, divisions, or subsidiaries for the capital tied up in them. *Costs of capital* and *total costs of money management* are factors which are more important than most managers care to admit. Most financial managers are aware of this, of course, but many others are not.

Above all, they are not aware of the fact that the total costs of money management are *much higher* than just the interest to be paid, or the cost of capital in the narrower sense. Broadly speaking, the total cost of money management equals about *twice* the capital market interest in a normal interest situation. In an extraordinary interest situation, with rates well above 10 percent, this rough approximation will no longer apply; it will then be reduced to about half or one-third. It is therefore important and extremely valuable in "educational" terms to charge *high interest rates* to the individual business units, as I already mentioned when talking about the productivity of money.

As a second and final point, I would like to return to an idea I outlined in an earlier chapter. This is where it will find its *application in practice*. It is that of orientation by the *profit minimum* rather than the profit maximum. The key question relevant here is: *"What is the minimum profit – or cash flow – that this company needs in order to remain in business tomorrow?"* The rationale behind it can be found in the chapter mentioned, and does not need to be repeated here. I would, however, like to call the reader's attention to the fact that the question about the minimum profit required is by no means an expression of an unambitious, minimalizing, or – worse still – an anti-profit attitude. As a matter of fact, the attitude behind it is much more ambitious and demanding and leads to much higher performance standards than the question about the profit maximum. Above all, it triggers a discussion about future issues.

Finally, let me point out that a profit statement linked to a certain point in time and its assessment are largely meaningless. Experienced practitioners are aware of this. But even a comparison of several points in time is not sufficient. It is best to monitor profits, in the form of moving averages, over a period of 36 to 48 months, preferably not only as absolute numbers but as indices. Only the changes and trends expressed in these figures will contain truly relevant information.

In addition, it is advisable to have an occasional look at the total returns on total assets over extended time periods – such as 10, 15, or 20 years – across the entire company. In doing that, one will repeatedly face the problem of limited comparability, as the company will have changed its business activities during this period, or undergone several total restructuring efforts. Despite all these difficulties, comparability still exists, or rather, it may not even be that important a concern. At that precise time, the company had a total result and a total investment. It is important to know whether the ability to use resources productively has increased or decreased overall, and the method I am suggesting here makes this quite clear.

Precision of Measuring Variables

Many managers believe that only very precise and detailed "measuring" provides information. But every experienced practitioner knows this is wrong. Even relatively rough data can contain a lot of information. Proportionalities, relationships between different data, and above all, trends over time matter much more than precision – which in economics is a rarity anyway.

This is why I use the word "measuring", but only in inverted commas. As I said at the beginning of this chapter, in economics we cannot expect the kind of precision we are accustomed to from scientific or technical measurements. In economics, *interpretation, assessment* and *judgment* will always be at least as important as measurements, even if the future brings advances in this area. It is therefore important that managers systematically improve, train, and enhance their power of judgment.

A judgment can never be made based on *one single* piece of data or data point. One has to be able to make *comparisons*, in particular comparisons with regard to structure and *over time*. The usual budget and target/actual comparisons are therefore *not* sufficient to form an opinion regarding the health and success of a company.

As I explained in the section on profit, it is best to depict key indicators as *moving averages* over a period of 36 to 48 months, both as absolute numbers and index ratios. These values and the changes in them provide relevant information.

Having the Right Discussions

An appropriate controlling and reporting of the key CPC variables of corporate success discussed here will lead to *radical* changes in the quality and relevance of executive and supervisory board meetings. Their members' attention will be directed to the right things.

The value of addressing these questions, however, manifests itself long *before* these variables can be reported on. As soon as one begins working on these issues, one will find that no two experts in the company or in scientific circles will agree on what the best, most important, and most reliable factors, variables, and definitions are for the six areas described.

The opinions of experts from marketing, accounting, manufacturing, and R&D will greatly diverge. There will be plenty of debate – and this is one of the *most valuable* things that management bodies can initiate. Even if, at the end of prolonged rounds of discussion, there is still no consensus among all involved – which cannot be expected anyway – they will all know *much more* about the company than before. They will understand the nature of the business much better. Employees will have become more competent and more valuable; their thinking, their attention, and ultimately their actions will have become more *relevant* because they will have dealt with the *right* and most *important* things.

At the same time, there will be noticeably fewer of the far less important discussions about motivation, leadership style, working climate, or the grand philosophy of corporate culture.

Biological Thinking in Management Is the Future

The reader has probably noticed that I sometimes use terms from biology and medicine, such as health, survival and viability. Some words of explanation may be in order here.

First, business practitioners themselves – and, it seems to me, in particular the most *competent* and *experienced* ones – use such terms when they talk about a company, referring to more than what is reflected in the accounting figures. They use accounting terms to describe what can be recorded with accounting tools. But once the discussion is about *more* and *different*, perhaps even more important things to do with the company, they often intuitively use terms from biology.

They are well aware that a healthy *balance sheet* does not necessarily signify a healthy *company*. There are – or rather, were – companies reporting excellent results over many consecutive years, companies that withstood even the most sophisticated balance sheet and cash flow analysis – and which were still terminally ill and perished in the end. Examples include the Swiss watch industry of the early 1970s and, earlier still, the European office machinery industry up until the mid-1960s. The same thing later happened in the automotive industry, in computers and consumer electronics, in the New Economy and in the financial sector. These companies used to be jewels of the industrial landscape. Still, the disasters were inevitable. However, not even the slightest warning signal was detectable by using accounting tools, and even with the state of the art reached in accounting today, it would not be possible. So there must be a reason why some practitioners prefer using biological terminology, and I see no reason not to use it in this book. The question is not whether a word belongs to the terminology of a specific scientific discipline or subject, but whether it helps to understand something better.

The variables suggested here *define* what a healthy company is. If all variables described are in a healthy constellation and keep improving, or at least are not deteriorating, quite a lot has been accomplished for the company. It is still no reason to be careless but the most important things are under control.

Second, I believe that in the future we will learn more about the management of business enterprises, or indeed of any other kind of organization in a society, from the *biological* sciences than we will from the economic sciences. I consider it to be a fundamental deficiency of the economic sciences that they still define themselves in a way that became common about 200 years ago: by what is referred to as the "delimitation of academic disciplines". When today's university emerged, the individual subjects had to be organized and delimitated from each other. This is how the disciplines were formed. And while this kind of organization of scientific work contributed to scientific progress, it has been a constant problem and has often led to stagnation and to science being irrelevant. Albert Einstein has been quoted as saying that God has no knowledge of physics. Surely his intention was not to commit a sacrilege – rather, he wanted to express that the world – nature – is an entity, rather than being structured by academic disciplines. At the university or in a laboratory, it is possible to delimitate, to isolate, and to reduce to just a few aspects. In reality, however, all things come together.

What the economic sciences deal with is not *the* economic system but certain aspects of it. In truth, economists do not talk and conduct research about the economic system but about what they consider the most important economic aspects. But the economic system includes *much more.* Above all, it includes the entire human being, not only an academic abstraction called *homo oeconomicus,* and it is embedded, inseparably, in society.

This is particularly evident in the case of business enterprises and their management. Business administration does not deal with *the* business enterprise but – as any textbook will make clear to you – only the "economic side" of a business enterprise. There is no doubt that this is important; the question is whether it is sufficient. The entrepreneur, no matter whether he is an employee or an owner, and the management bodies of an enterprise need to focus on the enterprise as a whole, with all its relevant aspects.

This kind of wholistic view can basically only be found in *biology* and in the so-called *system sciences,* two disciplines that are closely related. Biology deals with the living organism as a whole, the system sciences always deal with an entire system.[30] This is why, as I explained before,

---

30 Vester, Frederic: *Die Kunst, vernetzt zu denken,* Munich, 2007; Malik, Fredmund: *Strategie des Managements komplexer Systeme. Ein Beitrag zur Management-Kybernetik evolutionärer Systeme,* Berne/Stuttgart, 1984 (9th edition, 2006); Blüchel, Kurt G./Malik, Fredmund: *Faszination Bionik. Die Intelligenz der Schöpfung,* Munich, 2006.

we will learn more from these fields of science than from the dissecting approach of the classically delimitated disciplines.

I am not saying that a business enterprise *is* a living organism. This view can be encountered occasionally, but of course it is not correct. We must be careful not to resort to platitudinous and superficial analogies. But a less superficial question would be this: *Suppose the business enterprise was a living organism – what could we learn from biology?*

Third, I would like to introduce another thought which may seem a bit peculiar at this point but could soon play a major role in competition. The transformation I describe in part I, chapter 3 is largely driven by the progress made in information sciences and electronics. This is why it is often said that we are moving towards an *information society* and that this involves a so-called *paradigm shift* – namely, the shift from an economic system based on the *mechanics* model to one based on the *informatics* model.

While this is certainly not wrong, it is not what is essential. Indeed, we are going through a paradigm shift – but what kind? Informatics and electronics are just as *mechanistic* by nature as mechanics itself. What is more, informatics is the very *culmination* of mechanics and of a mechanistic way of thinking. The "mouse double-click" is a visible symbol of it. Informatics and electronics lead us to the perfect machine, where even two phenomena well known to all engineers no longer exist: friction and wear. We do want computers to work perfectly and reliably. Informatics as such, however, will not lead us out of the current mechanistic paradigm.

But something *else* will first be triggered by informatics: the real step towards a new paradigm will not be completed until we use informatics to shape society's organizations, above all the business enterprises, according to the *model of biological organisms* or – put in more general terms – according to the *model of viable systems*. Only then will all those qualities and capabilities move into the realm of possibility which we rightly find impressive in living organisms: their flexibility, their adaptability, their ability to learn, their self-regulation and self-organization, and, last but not least, their perfect efficiency. In other words, the step to be taken will be from the *model of mechanics* to the *model of biology* – and informatics can and will be the enabling link.

These considerations may seem neither understandable nor relevant to hard-boiled shareholder value proponents; but it could turn out to be useful for top-level corporate managers to give some more thought to this aspect. For if a rival company succeeded in achieving the qualities and capabilities of a highly developed living organism, instead of the considerable sluggishness of even the best companies, this would constitute a serious problem for all its competitors. First attempts are being made, although they still appear to be quite inadequate. At least the terms exist – such as the learning organization, the network structure, and so on. The reason I consider the present attempts and papers to be still inadequate is that they are quite naive and, in particular, that they fail to use the enormous state of knowledge reached in the biological sciences, the system sciences, and cybernetics.[31]

---

31 The best readings available on the subject are the works by the management cybernetician Stafford Beer, whom I have mentioned before, on the viable systems model, which is one of the greatest innovations in management theory. Unfortunately his work is unknown to most. Beer, Stafford: *The Heart of Enterprise*, London, 1979 and 1994; Beer, Stafford: *Brain of the Firm. The Managerial Cybernetics of Organization*, Chichester, 1972 and 1994.

Part II

Chapter 1

The Architecture of Top Management

Despite extensive efforts and a host of publications and discussions on the subject, including the creation of corporate governance codes, some essential requirements to correct (in terms of content) corporate management have yet to be fulfilled. Practically all the corporate crises, scandals and affairs that have occurred in the ten years or so since the original version of this book was first published, and which involved gigantic capital destruction and excesses of enrichment,[32] are owed to misguided corporate governance.

However, what has been even more detrimental to practice is the constitutional inability of today's corporate governance to deal with complexity. The architecture and functionality of governance as well as its management bodies have to be aligned to the highly complex systems of the 21st century, and to their unpredictable and incomprehensible nature. They have to be capable of mastering complexity and of using it to the benefit of their particular organization. The key design criterion for corporate governance must be an increase in functionality and functional reliability, rather than an increase in economic value. The words of this short chapter has been left almost unchanged, so that readers will be able to see what the state of affairs was in 1997.

A brief recapitulation:

In part I, chapter 1, I expressed the view that the supervisory body should take an *active role* in corporate management. Chapter 2 of part I contains a discussion of the main mistakes made in the recent past, mis-

---

32 As has been mentioned previously, these excesses were committed by a minority of managers. Still, their media presence has dangerously distorted economic reality, and thus been potentially explosive.

takes which must be attributed directly to top management and which could have been avoided if the corporate management had been competent and professional. The *material damage* directly resulting from it, in the form of losses and waste of resources, could probably be calculated or at least estimated. The amount of capital and resources destroyed has been considerable. The *indirect damage*, however, has probably been greater, although it cannot be calculated. There has been a dramatic loss of profits and above all of world market positions, or a failure to expand them. There have been attractive opportunities, in particular since around 1990, since the recession in Japan which started that year and is still ongoing has forced Japanese firms onto the defensive. These opportunities have been missed – a mistake which in itself would be reason enough to demand improvements in business management.

But there are further, even more important reasons. In chapter 3 of part I, I explained that the biggest tests for management are still ahead of us, as the economy and society are in a *process of profound change* and we are in the midst of a period in which management must meet the highest standards.

I then demonstrated in chapters 4 and 5 of part I that there is a useful, though perhaps not fully developed, *theory of corporate governance*, and that the most important *variables for assessing* businesses and their health can be derived from it.

In this context, however, it must be noted that while the most recent development in business economics – the orientation toward shareholder value – does indicate a fundamental change in top management thinking, unfortunately it does so in the *wrong* direction. As a consequence of this trend, there is now a risk of long-term performance being harmed by short-term and superficial successes, which further exacerbates the problem. Thus the diagnosis is that a substantial number of companies are not being directed but *misdirected*. The potential consequences of this error could go to the very foundations of a democratic society under rule of law. The state of the economy is all the more important, as the business enterprise is basically the *only* societal institution which essentially can or at least could act.

Whatever the state of each single business – some are forging ahead while others are lagging behind – it would be easy to introduce a usable corporate constitution everywhere within six months and to base all action on it. What are the prerequisites?

1. A functioning top management structure must consist of *two bodies* with a carefully planned division of labor, supplemented and supported by an *auditing authority*. The single-tier model is constitutionally not functional, although it can function in practice if it is in the hands of the right people, which, however, cannot be assumed in principle. In the practice of well-managed businesses, and where the law allows it, it has *de facto* developed into a two-tier system,[33] so it does have the advantage of allowing for very *flexible* two-tier solutions. The two-tier system is preferable, but only where supervision is not viewed as mere control, and certainly not as retrospective control. In Germany, therefore, far more than just the statutory minimum will have to be satisfied. But, as stated before, even the German situation allows for the two top-level bodies to be set up in such a way that, in theory, they can meet *all* needs.

2. In principle, the division of duties between the two top-level corporate bodies can and must be *the same* everywhere, although the details may vary depending on the human resource situation. The *tasks* and *responsibilities* of the two top bodies as well as their *modus operandi* must be documented in writing, either in the articles of association themselves or, preferably, in separate documents legitimized by the articles of association. At the same time, a decision has to be made as to how the auditing authority should be organized. If this step requires changes to the company's articles of incorporation, and thus shareholder meetings to approve them, the whole procedure may take longer than the six months stated above. The practical application of a new corporate constitution, however, can in most cases start before the formalities have been completed.

It is with deliberation that I am speaking of *tasks* and *responsibilities* here, not of *rights* and *duties*. It is obvious that tasks are always

33 In England, the practice of having two-tier systems distinguishing between the two top-level bodies of supervision and executive, Chairman and CEO, has gained widespread acceptance over the past years. 95 percent of all English businesses have introduced this solution which, according to general opinion, permits better governance and performance. In the US only 15 percent of all businesses have adopted it (*The Economist*, May 24, 2008). In Switzerland, the separation is recommended in the Corporate Governance Code but is only being implemented half-heartedly. Germany adopted the two-tier system as early as 1936.

accompanied by rights and duties, but they must be derived from the tasks and not vice versa.

3. Based on these elements of the company constitution, the second step is to clarify the *material* questions of *corporate governance*. The results also have to be recorded in writing and constitute another document guiding the work of the top management.

4. Following and based on these regulations, the members of the supervisory and executive bodies have to be *committed* to exercising their mandates in accordance with the documents mentioned. The best solution is to have this obligation stipulated in a special agreement, which would require first clarifying a few legal questions as to who has the authority to conclude an agreement of this kind. However, even if this formal agreement should not work out for some reason, or should appear unnecessary or inappropriate, the top management team can nonetheless agree to be *de facto* bound by and comply with the company constitution.

5. Up to this point, the individual steps have been almost completely *irrespective* of the industry and business focus of the company. In this step, the *allocation of responsibilities* and *rules of procedure* for the executive body have to be adapted as is appropriate. In doing so, the industry and business need to be taken into account, although a substantial proportion of the executive body's organization is still independent of it, in particular the part that determines the effectiveness and quality of business management.

6. As a final step, I would recommend introducing a systematic process of reviewing and, if necessary, redefining the *purpose* and *mission* of the company – or what might be called *"the theory of the business"*.[34] These are the foundations of and inputs to corporate strategy.

The following graph shows the basic model of my general management system, which is described at length in my book on corporate policy.[35]

---

34 This topic is dealt with in detail in volumes 1 and 2 of my book series "Management: Mastering Complexity".

35 Malik, Fredmund: *Corporate Policy and Governance. How Organizations Self-Organize*, Frankfurt/New York, 2011. See also www.malik-management. com.

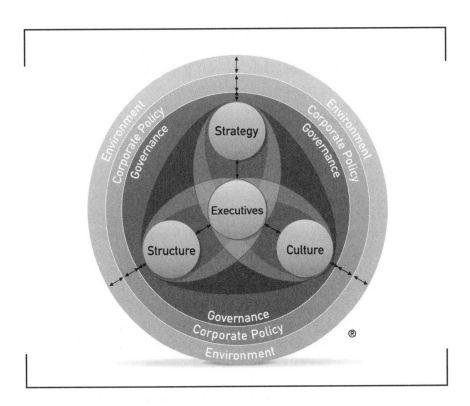

Chapter 2

Designing the Supervisory Body

The supervisory body's tasks are basically independent of the particular legal framework. Legal provisions may make it easier or harder to fulfill these tasks; they may stipulate a certain framework of conditions or procedures for their completion in the individual case. However, the legal system is not what primarily *defines* the tasks, nor are they exhaustively described by it.[36]

The tasks of the supervisory body are derived from *two* sources: *first*, from the *purpose* of the company and the function required to fulfill that purpose; *second*, from the fact that organizations are managed by *human beings*.

The purpose of the organization is to create satisfied customers or, to put it in more general terms: to transform societal resources into customer value. The fact that organizations are managed by people is the main reason why an effective supervisory body is required. The management of an organization, in particular of a major corporation facing global competition, requires a center – the executive body – with considerable power. Power, however, can only be legitimated if someone is held responsible for it. Power corrupts people, as everyone knows, and absolute power corrupts them absolutely. Therefore, power may never become absolute – it must be held in check. If there is one thing history has proved, it is that full self-control is an illusion.[37]

---

36 Even the corporate governance codes do not, or not sufficiently, describe the purpose and tasks. They usually contain formal provisions, but hardly any substance.

37 Some may object here that the owner-investor has always controlled himself. As a matter of fact, while he is not controlled by a supervisory function, he is controlled by the customer and, above all, by his capital liability, which is largely non-existent in the case of corporate management bodies.

Executive bodies have and should be given a considerable amount of power. They need it to perform their business management tasks. But at the same time, a countervailing power is necessary to turn that power, which may reach the limits of what is humanly reasonable and bearable, into a power that is controlled and accounted for.

Tasks of the Supervisory Body

In order to effectively supervise a business, *five functions* are required. In principle they can be fulfilled fairly effectively under any legal system, although procedural aspects may differ in detail. The basis for fulfilling these five supervisory functions and their object consists of the purpose of the company and the variables indicating its health and functionality which were described in the previous chapter.

1. Retrospective Function

Determining results and assessing their quality are a first set of tasks for the supervisory body, and assigned to it under all legal systems. The crucial questions, however, are what this task refers to and how it should be carried out. For the reasons laid out in chapter 4 of part I, this function is not limited to the ascertaining and assessing business results, balance sheet and profit and loss accounting.

In order to be able to form an opinion, the absolute *minimum* that has to be known and discussed are the six areas of the Central Performance Complex, within both the company as a whole and each of its key business areas:

- *Market position* and its development over time
- *Innovation performance*,
- *Productivity* and its development, referring to the most important productive resources: capital, human resources, time, and knowledge;
- Ability to attract, retain, and effectively deploy *good people;*
- *Liquidity* and *cash flow*, their development and, above all, their quality – and

- *Profitability*, along with its development and intrinsic quality.

The last two factors are the only ones that regularly appear on the agendas of supervisory board meetings. In all likelihood, *two additional factors* will have to be included in the future (in some industries they already have been): the results achieved in assuming *ecological* and *social* responsibility[38] in the broadest sense.

2. Foresight Function

As mentioned before, retrospective and even concurrent control works, if at all, only in a stable and economically friendly environment. A world marked by turbulences, discontinuities, and fundamental change requires more than that: *prospective, proactive control.*[39]

Even though this may appear more difficult than would be desirable, it is necessary for supervisory bodies interested in pursuing their task to thoroughly deal with the *strategies, structures*, and *systems* of a company, as well as with its *corporate culture,* and to be involved in relevant decision processes and have the last say in them. It is necessary to examine whether executive bodies are dealing with the *right issues* and setting the *right priorities*, whether they do this thoroughly and carefully enough; what *infrastructure* is available to them in order to recognize *trends* and *trend reversals* early on, whether this infrastructure might be exaggerated or insufficient, and what its performance and effectiveness are.

In addition to present and past successes, another factor for prospective assessment is the company's success *potential*, such as technological innovation and substitution. This assessment must be based not only on investment plans submitted but also on the future-oriented *awareness categories* of the executive bodies themselves – the managers' radar, so to speak –,

---

38 Recent trends have effectively pointed in this direction: today, corporate citizenship and corporate responsibility are standard in corporate governance documents.

39 This is one of the fundamental laws of cybernetics, and one of the indispensable conditions for the functionality of systems. For the rationale, examples, and solutions, see Malik, Fredmund: *Corporate Policy and Governance. How Organizations Self-Organize*, Frankfurt/New York, 2011 (Volume 2 of the series "Management: Mastering Complexity").

because an investment plan submitted too late usually is also a misdirected investment project. Further, it will have to be examined whether and to what extent any *fads, false doctrines,* or *charlatanisms* are tolerated or even actively encouraged in the company, which would ultimately result in a waste of time and in *"mind contamination"*. To do this, it is necessary occasionally to examine *staff development* and *education programs* with regard to their content, not only with regard to the budgets involved.

3. Top Executive Selection, Management, Evaluation, Compensation, and Replacement

Since this is another task explicitly assigned to the supervisory body under the (German) Stock Corporation Act, which also provides one of the most powerful levers, one should think it is fulfilled well. Alas, in most cases, reality paints a different picture.

The way in which staff decisions are made is by no means fixed and straightforward (see also part II, chapter 6). There is neither clarity nor consensus on the criteria for the *selection* of top-level executive managers and the *assessment* of their managerial performance. In most cases, there is not even such a thing as real assessment.

The smallest issue, at least in German-speaking countries, has been the way in which top managers' *income is determined* – but that, too, is beginning to change for the worse.[40] In the United States it has all gotten out of proportion, which will cause ever more and greater problems for the US economy.

A highly questionable element, however, are the "golden parachutes" – the severance and pension benefits – usually entailed in top executives' employment contracts. These terms are anything but conducive to top-quality performance, in that they eliminate virtually all risks and are usually subject to inadequate assessment criteria.

A particular problem, both in Germany and Austria, is the *replacement of board members*. Conventional wisdom holds that this is a rela-

---

40 When this book was written, a tendency towards excesses was already beginning to show, although it was not clear how far this trend would go. Related developments were sparked off by the post-merger adaptation of Daimler-Benz top management income levels to those of Chrysler top executives.

tively easy matter, provided that contractual claims are met. This is a misjudgment. According to the relevant legal provisions and court rulings, board members can only be replaced on substantial grounds, and this clause is interpreted very restrictively. Even *"unbridgeable differences between the executive and the supervisory boards with regard to fundamental questions of corporate policy do not, on principle, provide substantial grounds for replacement, as long as the executive board remains within the realm of the discretionary power it is entitled to under §76 of the German Stock Corporation Act, i. e., its discretionary decision is justifiable."*[41] So if push came to shove, the supervisory board would have to convene a general meeting and obtain a vote of no confidence against the executive board. There are conceivable situations in which a board member, having been demoted, can sue for reinstatement.

In the context of the supervisory function described in this book, in particular any "unbridgeable differences on fundamental questions of corporate policy" would be the crucial *casus belli* requiring clear leadership. In cases like this, one would basically have to part "in mutual agreement", which typically does not only involve considerable cost but also sends the wrong signals. The replacement of executive board members is one of the points that make a revision of the relevant German legal provision seem urgently desirable.

Contrary to widespread opinion, executive bodies need to be *managed*, not only controlled. Of course, they have to be managed by other criteria and in other ways than "ordinary" managers do, but the fact is they need to be managed. In particular, it must be ensured that executive bodies actually fulfill their obligation to set a *good example*, both internally and externally, rather than just talking about it.

"Setting an example" may be an old-fashioned concept. But the fact remains that not only business enterprises but society as a whole cannot function in the long run if the people who have to fulfill top-level management tasks set a *bad example*. Nothing is lost more quickly than *trust* and *credibility* – particularly in a media-dominated world – and nothing contaminates society, its organizations and their performance as permanently as such loss.

---

41 Hoffmann-Becking, Michael (ed.): *Münchener Handbuch des Gesellschaftsrechts* ("Munich Handbook on Company Law"), volume 4: *Aktiengesellschaft* ("Stock Corporation"), Munich, 1988, 141 (emphases correspond to original).

A regime of terror, excessive privileges, ostentatious luxury, intrigues, arrogance, incompetence, fraud for personal gain, excessive compensation, even "minor" irregularities at the top will sooner or later render an organization *unmanageable*. Even the best-intended measures and programs will then remain without effect; on the contrary, they will be regarded as particularly cruel forms of cynicism. These are essential causes of social division, hostility, bitterness, and pain in the workforce, of collapsing motivation and of class societies forming within an organization, for the people at each organizational level will emulate the "example" set by those at the top. Consequences outside the organization include an anti-business attitude, aggressiveness, militant behavior of the unions, and ultimately even political movements demanding an overregulation of the business sector.

For this and other reasons, it will therefore be necessary – more often than can be observed at present – to remove managers from their positions, to hold them accountable, and to honor and enforce responsibilities and liabilities, and to do all these things without offering "golden handshakes" and safety nets. This is one of the few effective ways sustainably to improve decision quality, management effectiveness, and the corporate culture. It is also the only way to uphold the societal credibility of business.

4. Organization of the Executive Body, Allocation of Responsibilities, and Rules of Procedure

It is the supervisory body's task to organize the executive function, allocate its *responsibilities*, and determine its *rules of procedure*. Together with task No. 3, this is the *strongest lever* for influencing the overall management of the company. In countries where corporate management is based on the American board system, and thus on a single-tier structure, this is quite obvious, although it is not always handled professionally.

But even under German stock corporation law and with the country's two-tier governance system, this task is the supervisory board's responsibility and cannot be withdrawn from it according to the current state of theory and jurisprudence.[42] With regard to the content of an executive

---

42 See Hoffmann-Becking, Michael (ed.): *Münchener Handbuch des Gesellschaftsrechts*, volume 4: Aktiengesellschaft, Munich, 1988, p. 175 et seq.

body's rules of procedure, the stock corporation law contains no stipulations on this matter. Consequently, this instrument can be put to extensive use.

The relevant literature[43] contains some indicators suggesting that any changes to the allocation of responsibilities could cause problems if they collide with any of the clauses in executive board members' contracts. The conclusion is that the allocation of responsibilities must provide a basis for the employment contracts, not vice versa. Thus, the significance of this supervisory task is all the greater. Key points to be considered when determining the allocation responsibilities and rules of procedure will be dealt with in part II, chapter 3.

5. Shaping Relations to Stakeholder Groups

The corporation has *de facto* long grown beyond its immediate economic function and become one of the key factors of social, economic, ecological, and political *stability*, as well as the societal entity which is perhaps most essential for the adaptability of society as a whole. As a consequence, it no longer has *one* constituency – the owners – but a great *number* and *variety* of them. Whether that is desirable or advantageous from a regulatory point of view remains to be seen. It is a fact. Even if the stakeholder theory is not suitable as a guideline for good management – as I explained in part I, chapter 4 – it is an undeniable fact that corporations face numerous, often starkly contradictory demands.

It must therefore be one of the tasks of a supervisory body to deal with these diverse constituencies, in particular with the question as to whether these legitimate or factual demands and interests can and should be satisfied, and if so, to what extent it has to be done, and how. This takes time, intense contacts with the individual constituencies and their representatives, and considerable skills of communication and explanation. These decisions, at least on basic issues, cannot be left to functions such as PR and Corporate Communications, even though these will play a major role in their implementation. The supervisory body cannot perform this task alone but should do so in collabora-

---

43 See Hoffmann-Becking, Michael (ed.): *Münchener Handbuch des Gesellschaftsrechts*, volume 4: Aktiengesellschaft, Munich, 1988, p. 175 et seq.

tion with the executive body. At the very least, corresponding tasks and regulations must be contained in the rules of procedure for the executive body.

So much for the *key tasks* of the supervisory body. It has become clear, I think, that effective corporate supervision is much more than just control. Even the term "supervision" is not really appropriate. The fact that there is no perfectly fitting term for this bundle of tasks of a supervisory body is probably an indication that the question of effective management is still largely unsolved, both with regard to form and substance.[44]

Size and Internal Organization of the Supervisory Body

Size

The size, internal organization, and ability to work of the supervisory body are closely related. In the past, there seemed to be a trend towards an expansion of the supervisory body. There was much too little consideration on the question of what the optimal number of supervisory board members could be. In many cases, supervisory bodies were artificially bloated for reasons of prestige, good personal relations, countervailing powers, etc.

Meanwhile, some changes are going on. There is a noticeable tendency to *downsize*, even if consideration towards the individuals concerned makes this hard to accomplish. The size of a body is a factor absolutely critical to its effectiveness. Virtually all factors speak in favor of a *smaller* supervisory body.

Practice and, in part, the law are in opposition. In particular in Germany, we need to distinguish between codetermined and non-codetermined companies. Non-codetermined corporations need a minimum of three supervisory board members; if there is a larger number of them this number must be a multiple of three. Codetermined companies need a minimum of 12 supervisory board members up to an overall headcount of

---

44 The term "corporate governance" has come into widespread use by way of quasi-imperialist expansion, which, however, has obscured rather than clarified things. As for the rationale, see the new preface and introduction.

10,000; of 16 up to a headcount of 20,000, and of 20 supervisory board members (as a maximum size) if they exceed that headcount.[45]

Swiss law knows no such regulations. Here, the board of directors can consist of just one person. In practice, its size differs greatly. On average, the number of members of a board of directors is 12 in the industrial and 15 in the services sector.[46] There are large corporations where the board of directors comprises but five members, while the largest boards are 20 to 30 strong.[47]

How about the issue of size from the point of view of effectiveness? A group comprising more than 10 people is *in itself* – that is, in its entirety – not really capable of working. It will either be ineffective or it will form an internal structure, or it has to be given one. There is no valid reason for supervisory bodies of mammoth proportions, as are so often found, except for making them *de facto* ineffective or providing a few people with ultimately uncontrollable power.

The excessive size of a supervisory body, to the extent that it hampers its working effectiveness, can always be justified with numerous arguments –

---

45 Maximums do not have to be exhausted; smaller numbers would greatly enhance effectiveness.

46 Glaus, Bruno U.: *Unternehmungsüberwachung durch schweizerische Verwaltungsräte,* Zurich, 1990.

47 This has changed for the better, but not for the best. At the big Swiss corporations, the boards of directors have around twelve members, which I still consider too many. It becomes evident when looking at the communication needs. With twelve board members, there are 132 communication relations in the group. If there are an additional five committees with four members each, this translates into 60 additional relationships, so that a total of 200 relationships have to be managed. The timing and organization of board meetings is insufficient by nature for coping with such potential complexity. Although a "small number" is recommended under the Swiss Corporate Governance Code, the Swiss supervisory bodies curtail their own effectiveness through their unnecessarily large size. Even very well-intended corporate governance codes cannot make up for that. In them, the problem is not even dealt with and seems to have gone unnoticed. In Germany, effectiveness is curtailed by the codetermination laws in place, which is not in the interest either of the company or of its workforce. Remarkably, in both the German and the Swiss corporate governance codes there is no recommendation with regard to the size of the supervisory body, although this would be one of the most effective measures to increase corporate governance effectiveness.

such as consideration of the different relationships, reasons of representation or image, or providing for family members or veteran politicians. These reasons may have their weight in individual cases, but they have nothing to do with the working effectiveness of corporate governance.

The bigger a supervisory body, the more unwieldy it becomes in almost every respect; there will be less discipline and more absenteeism, as neither the individual member nor his or her absence is really noticed. The individual member does not count for very much, an ever greater number of people makes ever less active contributions, and the inevitable consequences are demonstrable ineffectiveness and the emergence of all kinds of variations, from small groups to coalitions, alliances, and the like. A large body will soon cease to be a supervisory body, instead becoming a *political* apparatus in the most negative sense. As a consequence, it will then need an internal structure – consisting of committees – but actually its work could just as well be done by a smaller body.[48]

If we assume the chairman of the supervisory board to have two votes, which would make sense for many reasons and would be legally permissible, the supervisory body must have an *even number* of members, including its chairman, as otherwise the chairman's right to exercising the deciding vote would be ineffective. Therefore, the *optimum number* is either *six* or *eight* people. With *ten* members, the supervisory board would be just capable of working. Anything above that number is not reasonable, in my view, in terms of effectiveness.

Of course there will always be individual cases where even a larger supervisory body can unfold its full effectiveness. That, however, will usually be due to the particular professionalism of its members, which cannot be assumed as a given, even if members are selected with greatest care.

In Germany, the optimum size of the supervisory body cannot be achieved due to codetermination regulations for large-scale corporations. This is not helpful in enhancing supervisory effectiveness. Boards have a choice between installing committees and having plenary sessions which are bound to be unwieldy. The de facto division of large supervisory bodies in two factions, representing the capital and the employee sides respectively, is one of the greatest obstacles to effective supervision.

---

48 The standard committees stipulated or recommended by corporate governance codes do not represent progress but actually decrease the functionality and accountability of supervision.

On the other hand, a group of fewer than six people will develop *too much intimacy*. Even with deliberate efforts to maintain a focus on facts, these will always be people with their specific behaviors. Inevitably there will be personal relationships, both positive and negative, which always have a dysfunctional effect, in particular when the supervisory body faces serious challenges.

If, for whatever reasons, the supervisory body needs to have a size exceeding the numbers stated, there will be no other choice but to establish committees. They have their advantages and disadvantages.

Internal Organization – Chairman's Committee and Working Committees

In a small supervisory body of up to six people, it is advisable to form neither working committees nor a chairman's committee. While they do not much to improve effectiveness, they tend to be viewed as discriminatory by those supervisory board members who are not represented in any of them. In order to avoid that, *each* board member would have to work on a committee, which would make for some rather peculiar structures. A supervisory body this small only needs a *chairman* plus one, possibly (in exceptional cases) two *deputies*. They should however, not act like a *chairman's committee*. With six people overall, virtually everything can be handled in the plenary. Instead of establishing committees, it is much better to assign special *tasks* or *missions* to the individual board members as the situation may demand.

The same is basically true for supervisory bodies comprising eight or ten people, although in these cases a *chairman's committee* comprising three people – the chairman himself and two deputies – should be established and entrusted with certain responsibilities, above all the preparation of personnel and financial decisions. The chairman's committee should not have any power of decision – except for cases of crisis – and if it does in particular cases, the chairman's deciding vote should not be valid within the committee.

Whenever a supervisory body exceeds the size described here, the formation of additional committees besides the chairman's committee will be *inevitable*. Hence the question is by what criteria and for what subject areas these committees should be established. From the management perspective, what immediately comes to mind are the areas of *personnel, finance,* and *strategy* – in this order of priority.

In the final analysis, the only way to control a company is via personnel and finance decisions. For while the supervisory body should have some strategic knowledge and will ultimately have to share responsibility for the organization's particular strategy, it is not responsible for developing it. If a choice has to be made between personnel and finance as an additional assignment for a committee, I would recommend focusing on *personnel issues.*

If human resources permit, almost any conceivable subject area form the broad range of top management tasks is basically suitable for establishing a working committee. It is impossible to make any recommendations in this regard as they will depend on the necessities in the individual case.

One thing, however, which is at least as important as defining thematic focal points is to ensure that committees work *efficiently.* They need a clear mission, direction, a specific working approach; it must be ensured that their work is documented and that they report to the supervisory body as a whole. Furthermore, it should be ensured that committees are *disbanded* once they have completed their tasks.

Composition

Needless to say, the composition of the supervisory body is of the utmost importance in the context of the tasks outlined. In most cases there are no specific legal requirements to be met. Exceptions include the *employee representation* required in some countries, the *incompatibility* in some countries of serving on both the executive and the supervisory body at the same time, and finally the ban on *interlocking relationships* under the German Stock Corporation Act. Apart from these exceptions, any person of full legal capacity can basically be elected a supervisory board member. In practice, however, some customs and criteria have emerged in the context of supervisory board elections which have largely done anything but contribute to the effectiveness of corporate supervision.

An opinion frequently expressed is that the functionality and effectiveness of corporate supervision depend on the *personalities* on the supervisory board. Well, this implies too much and yet too little. It is right and it is wrong.

It is obviously right in the sense that a supervisory body needs people who are up to the demanding task, an insight which is as correct as it is trivial, even though it is not always observed. The view regarding personality is, however, wrong in the sense that the functionality of the supervisory body must never depend on accidental factors existing in even the most careful selection, but on compliance with the *constitutional* conditions described in chapter 1 of part II.

As a matter of principle, the design of corporate supervision should follow the same rules that apply for the functionality of the authorities of a constitutional government. As important as it may be that they be staffed with the most suitable personalities, and that everything be done to ensure this, there is never a guarantee that these efforts will succeed. And precisely in the event of failure there must be binding constitutional provisions to at least minimize the damage done to the company, even if the personal component does not work well.

Depending on the individual case, there will be numerous factors to be considered in appointing the supervisory body, ranging from the reputation of a person in public to family considerations. The two most important selection criteria, however, are the person's *expertise* and *independence*.

Expertise

It goes without saying that some knowledge *of the subject matter* at hand is important. Further indispensable prerequisites for an effective execution of the supervisory function include business experience, or experience gained in another area of society, and probably also a substantial degree of life experience in general.

It is *not* necessary, however, for supervisory board members to have first-hand industry experience. Industry-specific knowledge can be acquired. Nor are comprehensive general skills required. Despite the often-heard call for generalists, genuine and competent generalists are very rare. But since a supervisory body always consists of several people, it is more important to ensure an adequate composition, a *combination* of individual skills which are important for the institution supervised. It is often better to combine a person's particular strengths in an area which is important to the company with the strengths of other people, than to pursue an unspecific, hence often noncommittal generalist approach.

A matter of utmost importance, however, is to ensure that *each* and every member of the supervisory body is clear as to what the tasks at hand are and tackles them with all *conscientiousness*. Working effectively during the time allotted to meetings, which is usually much too short, requires that *all* members of the supervisory body be familiar with the cornerstones of corporate governance, the variables used to assess the company, and the basic principles of correctly developed corporate strategy, structure, and culture. These things are unrelated to the industry a company operates in. If the body's work begins by having to define, communicate, and find consensus on basic matters, it will be an extremely laborious and time-consuming affair.

I have frequently observed that people with *executive* functions in their own companies tend to bring the corresponding way of thinking into the supervisory bodies of other organizations. It cannot be taken for granted that even high-ranking executives are able to "change hats". But that is precisely what is necessary, as otherwise there will be a mix of attitudes and subject matters which can be dangerous for the organization. When in doubt, it is up to the chairman to establish clarity and ensure that no one acts "out of line".

Independence

The criterion of *independence* – except for any interests resulting from *ownership* – is even more important than expertise. A member of the supervisory body must not be affected in his interests by the organization supervised. Conversely, the company must not be dependent on the interests of the supervisory board member.

It says a lot, in my view, that this criterion is not even mentioned in Bleicher's representative survey[49] – neither in the questions nor in the answers given. The same applies to the very comprehensive and detailed analysis by Wunderer[50] of the chairman of the board of directors. By contrast,

---

49 Bleicher, Knut: *Der Aufsichtsrat im Wandel*, Gütersloh, 1987.
50 Wunderer, Felix R.: *Der Verwaltungsrats-Präsident*, Zurich, 1995.

"independence" is consistently referred to as the most important criterion by US sources.[51]

Corporate supervision cannot be exercised effectively if there is so much as a hint of interwoven interests. A supervisory board member needs *clout* to execute his tasks, particularly in difficult and sensitive situations. This is only possible if the person has *credibility* and *power of conviction.* And it is required in particular when it comes to making decisions that cannot be guided by factual arguments alone. Actually, it is only necessary in situations of this kind – but then it is *truly important.* They occur fairly often in supervisory bodies; indeed, they are the rule rather than the exception. But even factual arguments lose all power of persuasion if there are real or perceived conflicts of interest. The logical conclusion from this criterion is that there are a number of *rules of exclusion* which – this much has to be admitted – force very difficult decisions.

Hence it is much easier to say who should *not* have a seat on a supervisory body than to say who should. A positive decision on whom to elect can ultimately be taken only for the individual case, while negative decisions – whom not to elect – can be generalized.

The following negative list may seem extreme, and there may be reasons to make allowances for individuals; yet it cannot and should not be ignored. The most serious consequence stemming from this list is that the composition of supervisory bodies will be *more difficult* and will require careful preparation, as the circle of people coming into question will be narrowed. This is not necessarily a disadvantage but it will involve *more* preparatory work and lead to the formation of *smaller* boards.

Rules of Exclusion

As a matter of *principle*, the following persons do *not* belong to a supervisory body.

1. Active and former members of the executive board of the *same* company
2. Persons who have an *active* business relationship with the company (customers, suppliers, attorneys, consultants, accountants, etc.)

---

51 NACD Report on Director Professionalism, Washington, 1996.

3. Representatives of the company's *principal bank*, except for cases in which they represent true ownership interests
4. Persons with *numerous mandates*
5. Persons who have *no time* for the function.

This negative list warrants some comments. It violates a series of unwritten laws of business practice, and of usages for which there may be weighty reasons. In part it also collides with vested rights and power positions, which is why my suggestion may provoke reactions which are not entirely fact-based.

Of course, applying the criterion of expertise *alone* would result in another list. However, as mentioned above, I consider the independence criterion to be *even more important*. The members of a supervisory body may have to perform unpleasant tasks, so in several aspects their independence has to be equal to or approach that of a judge, as otherwise they would not be able to exercise their function effectively. As long as a company is doing well, operating in a favorable business environment and in a prospering economy, and so on, independence does not matter much. Under such circumstances, the only unpleasant task of a supervisory body will probably be to enquire from time to time whether the company could not generate even better results than it does at the moment. This may be perceived as annoying, but not really as unpleasant, and certainly not as threatening.

A supervisory body is put to the ultimate test when there are *genuine* problems to be solved, no matter what the cause. Massive change needs, restructuring of the business, serious disagreements over the right decisions in matters threatening the organization's existence, opposition to the executive body, and far-reaching personnel decision are just some examples of situations in which, above and beyond the expertise of a supervisory board member, his independence is of vital importance, as is his freedom – not only formal but also factual and, above all, psychological – to *form and express his own opinions*. There should be no need for any "superhuman" courage or "martyrdom" in order to be an effective member to a supervisory body.

Active and Former Members to the Executive Board

a) The membership in the supervisory body of active executive managers of the *same* company is only possible in countries with a single-tier governance structure. In Germany it is legally prohibited. I consider the German system to be superior in this respect. It is not a good idea, as a rule, for people to have a part in controlling their own performance. In fact, it is inhumane or corrupting – and it does not work. Whatever they say or do, they can never really escape from the perception of bias.

In my view, it gets particularly bad when executive managers are in the majority within the supervisory body, as is possible under Swiss law. In circumstances such as these, it will be increasingly difficult to persuade competent outside personalities to serve on the board of directors: first, because they will always have a lack of information compared to insiders; second, because they would be in a losing position in case of a vote – which represents the typical situation of someone in the role of a puppet or figurehead.

b) There are always other ways to get active executive managers involved in the work of their company's supervisory body, or in this case, that of the board of directors. For instance, they can and should participate in the meetings, either for the full duration or for selected agenda items. They report, request, and actively participate in the discussion. If both sides work together well, this kind of involvement of the executive body will be the rule rather than an exception. Still there has to be a possibility for the supervisory body to meet alone, at the exclusion of any executive managers, in order to discuss, consult, and make decisions. And it should be practiced in reality, in order to prevent any vested rights (or interests perceived that way) to be established, which could turn out to be a burden to the sensitive relationship and collaboration once the case arises in which the supervisory body demands to meet exclusively.

c) Even *former* executive board members – and this is perhaps the most delicate or hotly contested rule of exclusion – should not become members of the supervisory body of *the same* organization.[52] As valuable as their experience may be – the Japanese approach is much better in this context: establishing an advisory council for these "elder statesmen" or keeping their capabilities available to the company by way of consulting agree-

---

52 While it used to be common for the majority – almost two-thirds – of former CEOs to become supervisory board members, the ratio has dropped to about one-fifth of all cases. This is clearly a step forward, and it is surprising only that it took so long to reach this level. The German Corporate Governance Code now includes this rule, too.

ments. The higher the number of former executive board members in the supervisory body, the more difficult it will be to bring about necessary changes in the company.

If the era of the former CEO was positive for the organization, he will now, as a supervisory board member or even chairman, benefit from the whole weight of his former success, and consequently it will be extremely difficult for the new CEO to implement any changes.

If the era of the former CEO was not particularly successful, there is no reason to appoint him to the supervisory body, and if it is done anyway, he will be bound to perceive any changes as direct or indirect accusation against his former administration. Either way he will be biased.

I am fully aware that there have been cases where the major move from CEO function to chairmanship has turned out well. And there are some *strong* reasons in its favor. It is one of the most difficult and risky decisions, and this is definitely the point at which people will be most tempted to deviate from the basic rule.

On the whole and in principle, however, I think it is better not to switch from the executive function to the supervisory one. The way must be clear for a new management. The successor(s) must be able to do the job in their own way, without any unrelated considerations.

Persons in an Active Business Relationship

Persons maintaining an active business relationship with the company, or representing organizations that do so, will continually be faced with the issue of conflicts of interest, actual or potential, existing or perceived. Of course, the circle of persons listed under points 2 and 3 is, as such, highly valuable and welcome to supervisory bodies. The minimum requirement, however, is that there be no significant commercial relations with the company for the duration of the mandate.

A compromise solution might be that the persons concerned abstain from voting when decisions of a delicate nature are to be taken, or that they withdraw from proceedings altogether when such agenda items come up. The rules of procedure have to include provisions permitting both the chairman and each of the members to enforce this if need be.

Apart from the issue of perceived bias, the aim is to ensure that the company is free to take advantage of competition in the market, regardless of any relations to and without consideration of supervisory board members. Specifically, according to current and long-standing practice, this concerns the *representatives of principal banks*. The same arguments apply here, except for cases where the banks represent *genuine* ownership interests.

Persons Who Have No Time

Although the folly of accumulating mandates has largely been recognized as such and the number of offices per person has been limited by law, these limits are still too high.

It is conceivable that there are people with such pronounced expertise and experience, and a working approach (and/or a corresponding infrastructure) so perfect as to be able to effectively fill ten mandates as an ordinary member and another five as chairman, as is permitted under the German Stock Corporation Act.[53] If there are such people they are definitely exceptions, even among the handful of top people who could reasonably be assumed to possess such capabilities. But even if someone is capable of coping with this workload, the danger of conflicting interests – real or perceived – is all the greater. Moreover, there will also be a collision of appointments. These people will have to make unpleasant decisions of prioritization, which will not make them look very good and actually constitute an unreasonable demand. All of these things make the supervisory job even more difficult.

Even with a maximum of competence and working effectiveness, one will constantly have to deal with the unspoken question as to whether it is truly possible to know each of five large corporations – which for reasons of competition will have to be situated in different industries – well enough to get involved in decisions on make-or-break matters, and to do so in good faith. Corporations of this kind may be active in several dozen of business areas. Usually all of the corresponding divisions are sizable businesses in their own right; all operate in different markets with different competitive situations, in different countries and with different technologies.

How much of a genius does a person have to be, then, to sufficiently survey, understand and assess everything, even on the level of abstraction

---

53 Even five mandates, as stipulated in the German Governance Code, are usually too many in my opinion.

associated with a supervisory function? All other members of the supervisory body, and in particular the executive managers, will always have nagging doubts, which will not really help that person's credibility and power of conviction.

The key problem – and in my view this would be the ultimate criterion in making such a decision – will only arise in case of *difficulties*, which will usually appear on several fronts at the same time. In that case such a person will no longer be very useful as he will have no time to deal with the matters at hand. The accumulation of offices is a typical consequence of long-lasting economic prosperity, stability and continuity, a consequence of the times when neither executive nor supervisory bodies faced major challenges.

To sum up, the composition of a supervisory body has to be determined with a view to its *difficult* situations, both in the negative and in the positive sense. It is imperative to consider situations requiring the group's *full* commitment and *undivided* attention. This is when the body is truly needed. It is impossible to tell whether and when such situations occur and what they will look like. Perhaps they are never going to happen; perhaps they will come quickly and surprisingly. In view of the profound changes which business and society are undergoing, it is very likely that we have to reckon with the latter for the coming decades.

Whether they are crises or opportunities does not really matter. In both cases, neither the executive nor the supervisory body will face "business as usual". Instead, they will have to make difficult and usually very prompt decisions. A greater number of meetings will be required, and they will have to be scheduled quickly. The members of the supervisory body will have to be available instantly, and they will need the kind of profound knowledge of the company which is underestimated much too often in favor of a noncommittal generalist approach.

Due to the significance of the supervisory body's personal composition, allow me to add a few words on the positive question – that is, when and why someone should be elected. In my introductory comments I said that this decision can only be made with regard to the individual. This is certainly true. Still, I do want to issue an urgent warning regarding a widespread error. It concerns the search for the *universal genius*. Unfortunately, there are many publications describing requirements for the members of the supervisory body which are simply *impossible to fulfill*. Incidentally, the same is true of the executive body and of management in general. It is relatively easy to compile a catalog of criteria for the *ideal* candidate – the list of qualities and capabilities will always be very *impressive* and plausible. Alas, it has the disadvantage that there will be *nobody* who meets all criteria. Such catalogs are works of fiction – often academic ones. When occasionally I speak of having "highest expectations" with regard to the supervisory and executive bodies, I always mean "highest realistic expectations".

What is needed are not people who are "good", "well-reputed" and so on in a *general* sense, but people who have *specific* strengths based on which they can deliver a *tangible* contribution to the company. Thus, the ideal does not consist in an "ideal catalog of requirements"; rather, the ideal would be to be able, in every corporate situation, to put precisely those people on the supervisory board who would offer the greatest expertise *for that situation.*

While this obviously has its natural limits, it can be considered to a certain extent by defining the period of office accordingly and by giving this topic particular thought at each new appointment (see also following section). A company which is growing rapidly and powerfully needs another kind of supervisory body than a company in crisis. A company operating on a regional basis needs supervisory expertise which differs from what a company needs which is globally present or about to go global. More details on personnel selection and decisions are given in part II, chapter 6.

Period of Office and Age Limit

In Germany, there is no minimum period of office, only a maximum one which is, in practice, regularly set at five.[54] In Switzerland, the period of office for members of the supervisory body is three years at least and six years at most. Both legal systems permit an unlimited number of reelections. From the perspective of effectiveness of corporate supervision, determining the period of office is anything else but a minor issue. On the one hand, the members of a corporate supervisory body need a certain *minimum time* to familiarize themselves with matters and demonstrate that they can add value.[55] On the other hand, it should be possible to part with

---

54 Hoffmann-Becking, Michael (ed.): *Münchener Handbuch des Gesellschaftsrechts,* volume 4: *Aktiengesellschaft,* Munich, 1988, p. 175 et seq.

55 While the one-year tenure that has become customary helps increase flexibility

people who have proven to be incapable or unsuitable in a fairly uncomplicated and decent manner. Besides, unlimited reelection can bring about a *situation of interests* – namely, in being reelected –, particularly if the remuneration is high.

In essence, there are *two* dilemmas when establishing the period of office for both the supervisory and the executive body: on the one hand, balancing *flexibility* with regard to the group's composition against the aim of *continuity*, on the other hand, finding the optimum trade-off between short-term performance pressure and long-term orientation. It seems there is no ideal solution, in particular when bearing both management bodies in mind. And surely there is more than one answer to each of these questions. Every institution needs to find the solution most suitable to its specific needs, considering all relevant circumstances. After weighing up the pros and cons, I tend to prefer more flexibility and performance pressure, since I believe that their potentially negative effects are easier to compensate than those of the opposite constellation.

The best solution, in my view, seems to be a term of office of *three years* combined with the possibility of being *reelected once, perhaps twice.* Within the space of three years it is possible to form an informed opinion as to whether a person does or does not add value to a supervisory body. Also, it is enough time to familiarize oneself even with a complex corporation and to demonstrate one's capabilities. If a person does not perform, the mandate can be terminated after three years simply by not renewing it. This allows everyone involved to save face. It also permits flexible replacements when the organization, due to major shifts in its situation, needs another combination of strengths in its supervisory body. In view of the rapid change in the world of business, this kind of flexibility seems particularly important to me.

On the other hand, a person who has proven to be capable can serve another term. With the possibility for just one reelection, there can be no major interest situation. During the second term of office, it will be totally nonexistent, which permits full independence and liberty of action.

The downside of this suggestion is that after six years – or nine, respectively – the group must get by without the contribution of a truly capable member. This may be regrettable; however, there are other capable peo-

---

in replacing individual persons, it is not very conducive to factual effectiveness. This effect, however, is offset by the reelection option.

ple, and new minds can bring in new ideas. Apart from other benefits, this solution also has the advantage of preventing permanent inside connections and alliances.

An exception may be permissible for the chairman. It is sometimes advantageous to have a capable chairman serving two terms. For cases like this, a double reelection could be permitted. In concrete terms, this means that, if someone has served one term of office as an ordinary member to the supervisory body, which will regularly be the case, and if this person served as chairman during his second period of office, he could be reelected once more – as chairman, but not as ordinary member. A total of nine years should suffice even for the most capable of people to fully exploit their capabilities and then hand back the mandate. If the decision is made to allow an ordinary member to be reelected twice, the regulations for the chairman need to be adapted accordingly.

As regards the age limit, I would recommend a generous solution. I see no reason for setting a limit. *First*, and contrary to popular opinion, there is no correlation between age and ability. There are individuals of advanced years, in their late seventies or eighties, who are remarkably efficient. In cases of doubt, most things will be settled by the solutions described regarding the term of office and reelection. However, someone in his seventies should not be allowed to become chairman, since this involves an enormous workload and a great deal of stress. This function is surely better placed in the hands of younger people.

Compensation of the Supervisory Body and the Principal Agent Theory

The work of the supervisory body as proposed in this book is just that: *work*, *plenty* of it and quite *hard* work. It takes up a great deal of time – far more than is accounted for by the number and duration of meetings.

An ordinary member of the supervisory body of a complexly structured corporation will have to expect to devote fifteen to twenty working days to his job, if he intends to perform his task conscientiously. The compensation should take this into account. No one should have to feel bad about demanding good performance, strong commitment, and the necessary time of the members of the supervisory body, and they, in turn, should not have to feel bad about making that kind of commitment. There is *no* reason why a member of a corporate supervisory body should be paid less than an excellent consultant, a top lawyer, or – *pro rata temporis* – a member of the executive board. On the other hand, the remuneration should not be so high as to create an economic dependency for the individual member. This decision can only be made for the individual case, taking into account these principles; usually it will not be too difficult, though.

The *chairman* of a supervisory body has to commit far more time and energy than an ordinary member. If it is a *large* corporation – and if the quality standards suggested here are applied – his office will be comparable or close to a *full-time* assignment. But even in the case of a smaller, dynamic organization he will need a minimum of 25 to 50 percent of his (ordinary) annual working time to do his job well. His remuneration should reflect that. The costs incurred by corporate supervision under these circumstances, including the necessary infrastructure, are quite moderate compared to the remaining expenditures accruing in large corporations, and in particular to the risks associated with a potential failure of the supervisory body.

In view of the previous development of corporate governance, the relatively best solution will be for all members of the supervisory body – irrespective of a potential equity stake – to receive a remuneration which is fixed, equal among all, and adequate for the demanding task, but includes *no variable* component that depends on the company's financial result. The chairman's pay as well as that of the chairman's committee members, if applicable, should be higher, in line with the additional work involved, but should also be fixed.

This is the solution most conducive to impartial opinion and decision-making which exclusively serves the interests of the company. The members of the supervisory body should not be tempted to let their decisions be influenced, if only implicitly, by personal financial motives. This should be obvious also to the outside world.

For each person's specific contribution there will be a separate contract to be approved not by the general shareholders meeting but by the supervisory body in plenary. Obviously, the individuals concerned have no vote in this decision.

It is an illusion to think that financial incentives could help ensure the alignment of supervisory and executive bodies with the company's interests. The only thing achieved this way is an alignment with short-term monetary interests. A functionally correct alignment can only be ensured by permanent ownership, with very restrictive conditions for divestiture.[56]

At the same time, however, it is also recommendable to abandon the premises of the principal-agent theory which says that managers are potential fraudsters betraying owners. While the principal-agent issue does exist, it is exaggerated by a theory which does not take into account that in thousands of years this problem has been solved in many ways, even if there have been occasional slip-ups. The fact is that the problem of mutual trust and unilateral breach of trust has no intra-economic solution; it does, however, have numerous solutions once you abandon the rigid and unrealistic premises of a purely economic perspective.

The problem of trust and breach of trust may not have a *universal* solution, but it has so many possible solutions for the specific case that, by and large, commercial enterprises and many other organizations of society work quite well. When they don't, the problems can rarely be found where the principal-agent theory would presume it to be.

Likewise, nor do we need the so-called stewardship theory which is based on the opposite premise: that the goals of assigned managers and those of the assigning owners are congruent in principle.

It is preferable not to adopt such premises, which are theoretical in the worst sense – that is, fiction – but to shape a solution that fits the particular situation, which is usually quite easy.

Management of the Supervisory Body

A high-quality composition is a necessary but not a sufficient condition for an effective corporate supervisory body. Another essential aspect is the quality and professionalism of *management* of the supervisory body.

The competent execution of the tasks listed at the beginning of this chapter requires thorough preparation on the members' parts, as well as professional meeting management – in terms of how meetings are prepared, conducted, and followed up on.

---

56 Here, I would like to remind readers of the basic principle saying *"If you can't sell you have to care."* See part I, chapter 4, as well as part II, chapter 5.

Number and Duration of Meetings

Empirical research[57] has revealed that the average *frequency of meetings* is 3.8 per year in Germany and 4.45 in Switzerland.[58] What matters more than averages, however, are the figures occurring most frequently, which are not always indicated in empirical analyses. For Germany, Bleicher[59] reports that roughly half of all supervisory bodies convene four times a year, an additional quarter of them meets three times per year. Another source states that larger corporations usually confine themselves to three meetings per annum.[60] US American boards have a much higher frequency of eight to nine meetings per year, which in Switzerland is equaled only by committees within the board of directors.

Three meetings per year are *definitely not enough.*[61] One meeting has to be set aside for dealing with the previous year's business results and preparing the next general meeting. The *second* is required for dealing with and agreeing on operative planning, as well as the budgets submitted for the upcoming fiscal year. Both issues are absolutely essential, but have little to do with effective supervision.

The widespread and thus usually intense scrutiny of the results of the previous business year is little more than a ritual. It represents an *analysis of history.* There is nothing more to be done about the facts of business; all that is left to do is to present them to the public in a positive light. I do not mean to belittle the significance of this meeting about the annual results and report. In itself, and related to the specific subject, it is

---

57 Bleicher, Knut: *Der Aufsichtsrat im Wandel*, Gütersloh, 1987; Glaus, Bruno U.: *Unternehmungsüberwachung durch schweizerische Verwaltungsräte*, Zurich, 1990.

58 These numbers are outdated since a legal minimum of four meetings per year has since been introduced. For Switzerland, there are no legal provisions governing this issue. The Swiss Code of Best Practice recommends having a minimum of four meetings "as a rule", and additional meetings "whenever necessary" (Section 14).

59 Bleicher, Knut: *Der Aufsichtsrat im Wandel*, Gütersloh, 1987; Glaus, Bruno U.: *Unternehmungsüberwachung durch schweizerische Verwaltungsräte*, Zurich, 1990, pp. 41 et seq.

60 Hoffmann-Becking, Michael (ed.): *Münchener Handbuch des Gesellschaftsrechts*, volume 4: *Aktiengesellschaft*, Munich, 1988, p. 289.

61 Current legislation reflects the same view.

obviously important in that its purpose is to ensure that accounting and reporting rules are observed. Any errors or omissions will lead to immediate accountability. Still, the fulfillment of this supervisory task has little or nothing to do with the health, robustness, and viability of a company – apart from certain lessons learnt and the consequences that may have been drawn from past experience. As has been mentioned several times before, once the point is reached where warning signals and unfortunate developments are reflected in business results, it is too late for corrections. The information required to assess the fundamental, long-term development of a company cannot even be found in the annual report.

The meeting that deals with the plans and budgets for the following year is much more important. There will still be time to take countermeasures and to bring about new and better decisions if required. But even in this meeting, a long-term and strategic perspective will usually be missing. So there will be just one meeting left to deal with truly important and fundamental issues. This is clearly not enough, at least not in complex organizations, even if it is one of those very rare meetings that span several days.

For all these reasons, anything under four meetings per year will be inadequate; much rather there will have to be six of them – in *normal* times, that is, and with a *normal* course of business. The precise number has to be subject to the *complexity* of the business. In a homogeneous, transparent and thus rather straightforward business, four meetings per year plus an occasional fifth may be enough. In a complex corporation engaged in numerous, very diverse fields of business and operating a series of divisions across a range of geographies, as many as six meetings may not be sufficient even in normal times. At Mitsubishi, the body corresponding to what would be a supervisory board in Europe is reported to meet twice a month for about four hours.

Times of crisis, turnaround situations, and the confrontation with profound changes in the markets, competitive situations, and technologies: All these things require a much higher number of meetings – apart from the effort required for meeting preparation – if the job is to be done well.

A smaller number of plenary meetings of the supervisory body can be compensated for by having the individual committees – if there are any – meet more frequently. Although I am fundamentally opposed to holding too many meetings in an organization – and all the more to rampant "conferencitis" – I feel that for the *supervisory body* it is generally recommendable to keep the number of meetings at the *upper limit* of the frequencies mentioned.

With only three to four meetings per year, the danger of failing to fulfill the supervisory function, or of fulfilling it poorly, will drastically increase.

The situation gets even more problematic when it comes to determining the *duration of meetings* of the supervisory body.[62] For Germany, an average duration of three hours is recommended; for Switzerland it is approximately four hours.[63] Again, statistical measures would be much more useful than average values, since it clearly makes a difference whether, e. g., the meetings dealing with routine matters last a mere two hours – and justifiably so – whereas much more time is allotted to the one or two meetings when truly important matters are on the agenda.

All in all, I consider the duration of meetings to be *much too short*. From a practical point of view, a distinction must be made between the official and the actual duration, and between gross (presence) and net duration (working time). Even with an excellent organization, timely invitations, and tight management of the meetings, there will be considerable time losses due to breaks, conversations over lunch, late arrivals and early departures of at least some of the participants, and the like. Although there are no studies available on this, I am sure that the *real net working time* is well below the empirically recorded figures. In such *short* meetings, however, it is impossible to discuss truly *important* things in sufficient detail and *thoroughly* enough. The opposite view, which is widespread, is illusory and/or a sign of managerial incompetence.

Except for meetings dealing with rules and formalities – as mentioned – there is *every reason* why meetings should regularly be set to last *a whole day* – provided that the supervisory body's effectiveness, thoroughness, and credibility are considered a priority – and there are many reasons why there should be a *two-day* meeting at least once a year, possibly including a part of the weekend.

Only then can it be ensured that matters are dealt with *thoroughly* and *conclusively*. Only then can one be fairly certain that the members of the supervisory body get adequately *prepared*. Even without major experience – and with it, all the more – it is easily possible to "improvise" one's way through a three to four-hour meeting. Improvising for a whole day is much more difficult. So this is the only way to make optimal use of partici-

---

62 Bleicher, Knut: *Der Aufsichtsrat im Wandel*, Gütersloh, 1987, pp. 45 et seq.

63 Glaus, Bruno U.: *Unternehmungsüberwachung durch schweizerische Verwaltungsräte*, Zurich, 1990, p. 127

pants' time, both in the interest of the company and in their own. Usually meetings also require people to travel. It is much more effective therefore to invest the travel time necessary in a thorough and effective, if somewhat longer meeting, than having to spend the same amount of time and effort for short and superficial, and thus ultimately inefficient meetings.

Almost always, the only obstacles to this way of handling the supervisory function are participants who have *numerous mandates* or an otherwise *heavy workload*, and who in relevant surveys regularly call for even shorter meetings[64] – for reasons which are entirely understandable but irrelevant to the company in question. *Anyone unable to make the time should not be engaged in corporate supervision and should not be accepted as a member to a supervisory body.*

One should not forget that longer meetings also require much more thorough preparation on the part of *executive managers*, and a carefully set-up agenda. No chairman of a supervisory body can afford to call high-caliber people to an all-day meeting, just to bore them with incidentals and annoy them with poor presentations. So the pressure is on *both sides* and it is extremely *valuable*.

Attendance

As far as attendance is concerned, I am only aware of one empirical figure, which is for Switzerland: here, attendance is at an exemplary 92 percent. Whether this ratio can be generalized remains an open question.

In any case, poor attendance – for whatever reason – is a surefire way of triggering three negative developments: *first,* the undermining of authority and credibility of the supervisory body, *second,* the inability to take decisions, or irrelevance of decisions taken, and instability of any (apparent) consensus reached, and *third,* the exponential increase in complexity of its task, as there will be a permanent need for further information and coordination.

Apart from exceptional situations, full attendance is a must, and there are only two ways of ensuring it. *First,* the meeting dates must be set *well in advance; second,* members with chronic attendance problems have to be *expelled* from the group.

---

64 Bleicher, Knut: *Der Aufsichtsrat im Wandel*, Gütersloh, 1987, p. 45.

Members of supervisory bodies are usually very busy people with crowded schedules. Therefore, unless meetings are scheduled twelve to eighteen months in advance, full attendance can hardly be expected, or there will be a permanent need for individual members to change their schedules. This is a surefire way of making oneself unpopular and giving an impression of incompetence. When in doubt, it is always better to schedule an *additional* one or two meeting dates. Canceling meetings which prove not to be necessary is easy. Setting additional meeting dates, which usually has to happen at very short notice, is almost impossible with schedules already busy.

Meeting Cycle

The frequency of meetings is not the only factor that matters; it is far more important to align the meetings of the supervisory body with the rhythm of the business. Empirical studies have nothing to say about this. A prominent management topic in recent years was time-based management, but it was largely applied to *operational* business. A company cannot move at a faster rate than its management bodies make decisions, and they do that at meetings. Thus, the *meeting cycle* is essential in *setting the pace* of an organization on the time axis. Just like a musical piece, a symphony, has its rhythm and tempo, so does an organization. It is largely dependent on market events and needs to be aligned with them. Of course, the meeting cycle of the supervisory body must be coordinated with that of the executive body or bodies, and possibly also with the cycles of major business-related activities, such as strategically important projects, which create a need for major decisions.

It is no exaggeration to compare the orchestration of all corporate bodies with the work of a composer having to coordinate all instrumental parts. In simple, small companies it can be done "in passing". In large and complex corporations it may require a considerable amount of infrastructure.

Follow-Up and Follow-Through

According to what can be found in official documents, the Pearl Harbor disaster is owed to a circumstance which in itself may seem a bit ridiculous, which is why it is not taken seriously in many organizations and therefore causes the much-bemoaned *lack of implementation skills*: it is systematic follow-through.

The infrastructure of the general staff at Pearl Harbor failed to monitor the alert orders that were actually issued, and did not ensure they were received and executed by the local units in Hawaii. This disaster led to a complete and profound reorganization of the War Department to ensure that this kind of failure would not repeat itself.

Decisions to be taken by the supervisory body and assignments given to the executive bodies must not be lost from sight. Both require a *systematic* process of monitoring, following up, and implementation control. This is an essential contribution to overcoming the widespread implementation weaknesses in large corporations.

If this should sound too "military", you may be confusing an indispensable functional principle with its external manifestation. It is not military style that I am proposing here, but *reliability of function and implementation*. To this end, the supervisory body needs an infrastructure which may be small but must be efficient. Hardly anything else can ruin the authority, credibility, and effectiveness of a supervisory body as permanently as insufficient or altogether lacking control of pending tasks. The circle between the issuance and the execution of an assignment must be "watertight". Otherwise there is a clear risk of exposing oneself to ridicule. The members of the executive body, but also of the supervisory body, need to know that the implementation of everything decided will be tightly monitored. It is the only way to be taken seriously.

Setting the Agenda

If a supervisory body really intends to manage, as far as the law permits and in the sense described in this book, it will have to do so by gaining *thematic leadership*, or else it will not manage but be managed. Much too often, all the chairman puts on the agenda are rules and formalities, while everything else is dependent on and determined by the executive board. What this means is that the supervisory body leaves all leadership to the executive body and allows itself to be forced onto the defensive.

It goes without saying that the executive body has to be consulted in setting the agenda, but it should not have full responsibility for it, as is often the case. Since it is the chairman's duty to prepare the supervisory body's meetings, he is also formally responsible for setting the agenda. This gives him a powerful lever for influencing the fortunes of the company. If he is smart he will not pursue this task on his own but, at an early stage, consult with the remaining members of the supervisory body as well as with the executive management, in order to be able to form an opinion as to who considers what to be the key *issues*, and for what reasons. In the final analysis, however, it is his *personal* management task to set the agenda. This way he will ensure not only management *of* the supervisory body but also management *by* the supervisory body of the company. Needless to say, the individual members' rights of input to the agenda remain unaffected by this. In any event, pending matters each meeting should start with a discussion of pending matters.

Under German law, the supervisory board has no right of initiative, let alone a right to issue directives to the executive board. Nonetheless, this kind of direction via shaping the agenda is possible, as long as there is a minimum of cooperation between the two governing bodies. In any case, once a point is reached where all interaction and collaboration between the two bodies involves a great deal of legal technicalities, this is an indicator of an alarming development which usually requires personnel changes to prevent the company from becoming unmanageable.

Information Balance of the Supervisory Body and Indiscretion

In order to be able to perform the tasks described, the supervisory body needs to have adequate information. How and where can it be obtained? Its main source is the executive body, which can either be generous and frank with information or pass it on restrictively and filtered – which occasionally gives supervisory bodies a welcome opportunity to claim that they did not know anything. Some do not *want* to be informed.

Is it enough to have an executive body which communicates openly and generously? I doubt it. The supervisory body must be able to – and indeed has to – obtain its own information, and do so from independent sources. This brings us to one of the most sensitive issues: how to gain access to all the information needed to perform the job – without snooping, scheming, or undermining the executive board's authority, and in full awareness of any co-responsibility that might *de facto* arise from this knowledge.

In Germany, the supervisory board has to "turn to the executive board" for information; the members are not permitted to get in direct touch with, say, managers outside the executive board. It does, however, have considerable possibilities of requesting additional reports, conduct examinations, etc.[65]

I suppose the best is to stick with the following procedure: In coordination with the executive board, and with its consent whenever possible (in any event it has to be informed), individual supervisory board members are commissioned to get a picture of the situation and report to the supervisory board. In some cases it will be necessary to report to the executive board as well. Apart from that, there are numerous options available for gathering individual information. They do, however, require dedicating some extra time. In the final analysis, it is all a *question of trust*, namely of *justified trust*.

In practice, what this means is:

a) Mutual tasks and responsibilities must be discussed; they must be known and made unmistakably clear, as well as recorded in writing and mutually accepted. These form the *constitutional basis*, as it were, for the work and collaboration of the two bodies. Anyone unwilling or unable to accept them does not belong in either of the two bodies. This is why – as mentioned in chapter 1 of part II – I speak of tasks and responsibilities here, not of rights and duties.

b) Work and collaboration must be based on *mutual trust*, and each of the two bodies has to contribute towards achieving this. The key to it, or the secret behind it, is clarity and candor (although in Germany this may be impeded by codetermination laws, which do not serve the interests of the company).

c) A suitable method to improve the state of information, the base for an assessment, but also the supervisory board members' understanding of the way the company works is to get them involved (in an advisory role) in projects that are of central importance for the entire company. In Switzerland, this is legally possible and often practiced by companies with a sophisticated management. While there are some disadvantages to this approach, it does enhance the involvement of the supervisory board.

---

65 See Hoffmann-Becking, Michael (ed.): *Münchener Handbuch des Gesellschaftsrechts*, volume 4: *Aktiengesellschaft*, Munich, 1988, pp. 197 et seq.

Another question in this regard is how the supervisory body treats the information it is given. One of the most serious problems is indiscretion. A supervisory body leaking information cannot and will not function well until the leaks are sealed. Otherwise, the function of forming opinions and decisions will constantly be undermined by indiscretion; and within a short time, the whole group will be contaminated by distrust and intrigue. Everything will be dominated by the interests of groups or even individuals, rather than those of the company. As a result, the only issues that can be discussed at meetings will be those which cannot be affected by indiscretion, which are precisely those that are basically irrelevant.

Occasionally, leaks can be detected by applying intelligence methods, as far as they are legal, for instance by systematically feeding misinformation to people under suspicion in order to find the source of indiscretion.

Evaluation of the Supervisory Body

A body which has to perform duties and bear responsibility, and on whose activity the prosperity and success, but also the failure of the company depend to a considerable degree – and which may even be held liable itself – needs to reflect on its working approach and its effectiveness on a regular basis. There is no reason, therefore, why there should not be an evaluation of the supervisory body, except for the fact that it is unusual and can occasionally reveal unpleasant truths.

The company's bylaws should therefore stipulate – as a mandatory item – the regular evaluation of the supervisory body, to be performed either by the body itself, one of its committees, or an auditing authority. There are many ways to do this, from an open discussion to a formalized, anonymous self-assessment process to a specific management audit.

What matters much more than the technical details is the *effect* of a regular, systematic, and serious evaluation. The supervisory body should basically agree to apply the same principles and standards for itself which it demands of the executive body and the company overall. Performance, results, productivity, quality, and effectiveness are criteria that are just as relevant for the supervisory body as they are for everyone else. Key questions in this respect are these: *How well did we do our job in the previous fiscal year? What were our most essential contributions to the prosperity of this company? What can we improve, and what do we need to change about the way we work?*

I believe it is important that it is *known* throughout the organization that the supervisory body, too, faces up to the logic of doing business, the pressure to perform, and the evaluation of results. There are cases in the US – although they are still relatively rare – where a dedicated governance committee of the management board is responsible for evaluating the whole board and presenting the results to the shareholders meeting. I imagine that this can be much more effective than a dividend raise, particularly over the long term and in difficult situations. It is like offering shareholders a *dividend of trust.*

Management Audit

Every sizeable business, and especially every decentralized business, needs an audit, irrespective of how well equipped finance and accounting, controlling etc. are and how well they function. The year-end audit in connection with the annual report is not enough. The time interval is too long and the audit too restrictive and predictable.

People in Switzerland have largely accepted this fact. But whenever I have proposed this idea to managers elsewhere over the past few years, their response was almost always silence, incomprehension, or resentment – with the exception of the banking and insurance sector.[66] While this may be understandable on a human level, the demand for auditing follows a compelling logic when it comes to performance, effectiveness, and responsibility, or in general the functioning of a system. With an effective audit system, I suppose that the vast majority, perhaps all of the grossest scandals and affairs that took place in the past years could have been avoided.

To a large extent, decentralized organizations can only function *based on trust.* It is not possible to regulate or check everything. As important as trust is, however, it is still important to make a clear distinction between *blind trust* and *justified trust.* It is one of the paradoxes of the trust phenomenon that trust is greatest when it is not *needed* – that is to say, when

---

66 This subject is not addressed in Bleicher's analysis of the German situation.

one can be reasonably sure that nothing can get out of control. This has nothing to do with Lenin's famous dictum about trust being good and control being better. It is all about designing a system that *cannot* be abused or undermined:[67] the kind of control that Lenin referred to will then be superfluous. In system designed by these principles, there will be no attempt at abuse because it would be futile and everyone knows it.

Hence, companies need an audit which, irrespective of the year-end one, is continuously performed. It does not matter whether it is carried out by external or internal people. Both solutions have their advantages and disadvantages. What matters is that they serve the purpose. The very knowledge in an organization that there is an ongoing audit helps prevent abuse. So there is no need for a large and expensive apparatus. Unannounced random checks are enough. Modern statistics is one of those areas of science where there has been enormous progress over the past years. As a result, even a small number of random checks suffice to achieve a fairly good level of certainty.

The important thing is that, *first*, auditors can access all parts of the company without forewarning – basically, nobody may be excluded – and, *second*, that the audit includes all processes. The subject of the audit is not just the financial and accounting figures; indeed, not only figures or quantitative aspects at all. On principle, everything must be subject to auditing. The system called "enterprise" and its functioning are the subject of the audit – which is why it has to be set up as a comprehensive *business and management audit*.

The executive bodies are most likely to accept the notion of an audit if the auditors report to them. That is better than nothing. But from a corporate governance point of view, the auditors need to report to the *supervisory body at minimum*. In my view, it would be even better if they were accountable to a dedicated shareholder committee established by the general meeting, a kind of *control committee*, and reported either exclusively to that committee or – to avoid embarrassing situations – to the executive bodies, the supervisory body, and the control committee *simultaneously*.

Both approaches would have the advantage that the evaluation of the supervisory body's functioning would be included in an independent,

---

67 Designing a system in the way described here requires management based on the laws of cybernetics. See my book *Corporate Policy and Governance. How Organizations Self-Organize*, Frankfurt/New York, 2011.

impersonal, impartial, and thus – as far as humanly possible – objective assessment. In order to prevent the auditors from being influenced, it would be best to commission an external organization which would perform the audit in accordance with professional standards. However, as has been mentioned before, internal solutions are also feasible and have their advantages.

Of course it is possible to view such an audit exclusively from a negative standpoint, criticizing the fact that it is an opportunity for snooping, spying, restricting freedoms, establishing a "Big Brother" system, and so on. On the other hand, however, it is possible – and in my view, imperative – to look at it from a *constitutional* perspective. A well-functioning corporate supervision, combined with an impersonal audit, then provides essential *conditions* for *decentralizing* companies sufficiently for them to stand their ground in a complex global business environment and use all their local expertise and skills: operational and executive managers can be given a maximum of *competences* and *freedom*, as well as the corresponding *power* so they can perform their tasks effectively. With the approach suggested the company can be certain that their power will be both *responsible* and *accounted for*.

The Chairman of the Supervisory Body

It is the duty and responsibility of the chairman to ensure that the supervisory body operates correctly and effectively. Considering that professional quality is the yardstick, managing a supervisory body is one of the most difficult tasks of all. It requires a combination of skills, experience and knowledge rarely found even in managers. Despite the tough requirements, it is nonetheless a task that can be carried out professionally if a few rather simple ground rules are applied.

The chairman of the supervisory body has to work with people he cannot choose, or only to a very limited extent. If the right decisions were made when staffing the supervisory body, the chairman will encounter *strong* and thus also difficult personalities with rough edges, people who are professionals like himself. All of them will watch his actions and notice every single mistake. If there are weak people in the group, the chairman's task will not get easier, as he will still have to lead the supervisory body to effectiveness and results.

It depends on the chairman what the relationship between the supervisory and the executive bodies are like. He is the person with the most frequent and intense contacts to executive managers. It depends on his actions and behavior whether there is a reasonable working relationship between the two bodies or one determined by statutes and formalities.

From a mere *legal* perspective the task is not that difficult. Complying with legal provisions and formalities is relatively easy. Everything else, however, is a task determined by *personal authority* and true *leadership* (see also part II, chapter 4).

The chairman of the supervisory body has to establish a *foundation of trust* between the members of the supervisory body on the one hand and the supervisory and executive bodies on the other. Distrust between these two bodies and within them would be poison for their ability to work productively. The chairman needs to be attentive to any signs of it, examine them more closely, and eliminate the causes. All involved need to know where they stand with him. His interests and the standards guiding his actions need to be known by and transparent to everyone – and his interests must not be of a personal nature. Rather, he must quite literally represent the interests of the company. His maxim has to be: *What is right – for this company?* He must not yield to the temptation to indulge in political maneuvering or let himself be entangled in intrigues. It goes without saying that he must never initiate any intrigues himself. Apart from factual authority, perhaps the most important element he needs is *personal integrity*.

The chairman has to ensure a disciplined working approach in the supervisory and executive bodies. He may have to settle serious conflicts. To do this, he needs a considerable amount of toughness, straightforwardness and assertiveness, but also empathy. Another responsibility of his is to ensure that the work of both the supervisory and the executive body is performed with appropriate thoroughness, accuracy and diligence. He determines the issues to be dealt with by setting the meeting agendas; it is his responsibility to ensure an appropriate breadth and depth of discussion, professional reporting and precise assessment of the situation, and it is up to him to determine *how* decisions are taken – plus he has major influence on *what* decisions are taken.

As a chairman, one can hardly operate on instructions, directives or orders given to those involved or in a top management context. Rather, the position requires natural leadership, both inherent in one's personality and resulting from one's behavior. The chairman of a supervisory board has to be a captain without "playing the boss". While he has an information advantage compared to the remaining members of the supervisory body, he must never use it, as this would immediately cause distrust and create the impression that he is manipulating his peers, or perhaps even being "chummy" with the executive board. Compared to the executive body, however, he will almost always *lag behind* in terms of information. He will never be able to know as much as, for instance, the executive officers do about the details of the business and the connections between them. A considerable share of the truly important information cannot be found in the official reports, but can only be obtained through personal contacts.

In this context, the signals sent out by the chairman of the supervisory board are crucial for the culture of the overall organization. It will be largely up to him which values are regarded as really important, how good morale is in the company, and whether or not there is mental corruption. It is also up to him to set standards for how people are treated, based on his own personal conduct.

It depends on him whether there will be the kind of decency in the organization which ought to be shown to every human being, regardless of how harsh business life can be otherwise; whether there will be the minimum of mutual respect required to work together; whether objectivity or emotions will prevail. Above all, it will be up to him whether the probably most important principle of good management is known, understood, and followed in the company: the importance of focusing on people's *strengths*, not their *weaknesses*.

It begins with the members of the supervisory body. Even with a most careful selection the individuals in the supervisory body will have not only strengths but also many weaknesses. It is no use to the chairman or the body to get worked up about these weaknesses. There is only one way of achieving results: by making use of what people are *capable of.*

The same is true when it comes to working with the executive board. There will and there have to be discussions about the quality and performance of each of its members. These will obviously also include their weaknesses. This topic is inevitable and should be dealt with at the very start of the discussion – never at the *end*. Once the weaknesses have been thrashed out, there has to be someone to say something along the lines of: *Now we know all the weaknesses of our executive officers and what they are not good at. But what are they good at?*

People are on a company's payroll because of their strengths, not their weaknesses. And they will only be useful for the company based on their strengths. It is an almost commonplace experience that everyone in a supervisory body knows very well what all the members of the management board are *not* capable of. But if questions are asked about their strengths, the answer is embarrassed silence.

It is up to the chairman of the supervisory board to instill this way of thinking in the members of the executive board, so that they, in turn, carry it into the organization. Over and over again, the chairman will have to use his hopefully numerous contacts to teach the top managers small lessons – subcutaneously, as it were – about good corporate governance and the standards of professional management. Top managers generally do not attend trainings any more, and they hardly have the time to read sophisticated specialist literature. It is the chairman of the supervisory body who will have to keep educating them on the job, so to speak, and developing them – and if possible, to do so without their noticing it.

In *codetermined* companies, one of his most difficult tasks will be working with the representatives of the workforce. No matter whether one is in favor or against codetermination and its specific manifestations – they are a reality which has to be accepted and dealt with. There are companies where the climate between the shareholders' and the employees' representatives is severely damaged or has been destroyed, where distrust, mutual hostilities and accusations prevail and there are insurmountable conflicts of interest. Under such circumstances, whatever their reasons, working together is impossible. As a result, the company concerned will not have any control or supervision, let alone any kind of management by the supervisory body. The top management structure will collapse, and all leadership will be with the executive body, which will then have to cope with severe hindrances. Agendas will *de facto* be swept clean; meetings of either group will be used primarily for discussing how the other party can be set up, duped, outsmarted, or paralyzed. There will be hardly any discretion (irrespective of legal provisions) and in essence it seems senseless keeping on. Everyone will focus on defending essential power positions.

But there are also cases in which – usually due to the prudent leadership by a competent chairman – the governing bodies have managed to establish a collaboration which may not be based on great sympathies but is constructive, fact-based, and in the best interest of the company. People have learnt to understand and respect each other's positions, even if they cannot fully accept them. They know each other's basic interests, views and political-ideological positions – but they understand how to turn them into opportunities. *They integrate them in the interest and to the benefit of the company.*

The keys to that – and this may sound idealistic or even corny – are: openness, decency, integrity, and reliability on the chairman's part – even in those situations when he does not necessarily encounter the same attitude on the opposing side.

He must keep his promises, and he must only make promises he can keep. There is no other way but to take the workers' representatives seriously, to respect and diligently observe, perhaps even over-fulfill their rights as members of the supervisory body, to meet their information needs as far as possible – going beyond what is legally obligatory – and to treat them as full members of the supervisory body.

I am not saying that one will always be richly "rewarded" for acting like this. But it is the only chance to achieve a reasonable collaboration – provided this is possible at all. It is the only way to build a trust base. This does not mean, of course, that each and every demand of the workers' representatives has to be met. All of the above does not eliminate the need for tough negotiations and debate. But it is the only way in which they can be carried on in a reasonable fashion.

The chairman will have to continually invest enormous efforts in defining and expressing the *interests* of the company; but he must not stop there. Workers' representatives in virtually every company have probably heard more than their share of pretty words. The chairman must let his *actions* speak, and place them *exclusively* in the service of the company, not of individual groups. In this precise context, a thorough understanding of corporate governance, as outlined in part I, chapter 4, is key. This is the point where it becomes very obvious how much a business enterprise is also – for better or for worse – a political and social institution, perhaps even a moral one.[68]

If the tasks of a chairman in a large organization are to be performed

---

68 Aside from corruption, there is no way of getting workers' representatives on a supervisory board to work in the interest of the shareholders alone. On the other hand, they vehemently defend their own stakeholder groups, the employees. The only way of preventing or mitigating this potential stalemate situation is by strictly focusing corporate governance on the company and its functionality, and to do so consistently and uncompromisingly.

effectively, they practically add up to a full-time or almost full-time job requiring an adequate infrastructure. In countries which have some form of board system, this fact has been recognized and is increasingly handled that way. In countries with a two-tier system, however, the full assignment of a supervisory board chairman is still an *absolute exception*.[69] Which explains much of the *factual ineffectiveness* of corporate supervision.

In my view, the aspects dealt with in this chapter are the most essential for the effectiveness of a supervisory body. To sum up, a supervisory body will ideally consist of six to ten people meeting the highest standards in terms of expertise and character, competently managed by a full-time chairman supported by an adequate infrastructure (office, assistant), performing their duties – as described in the first section of this chapter – with diligence, thoroughness, and care, taking sufficient time for the task and concentrating their energies on the company, taking due consideration of the responsibilities and the integrity of the executive body, applying high standards to their performance, using a maximum of objectiveness, and working exclusively in the interest of the company, its functionality, and its prosperity. Furthermore, the supervisory body will ideally be supported by an auditing function.

A crucial aspect, which will bring us to the topic of the next chapter, is the fact that even the best supervisory body cannot meet its obligations if the executive body does not function well. As I said before, it is one of the tasks of the supervisory body – perhaps its most important – to shape and organize the executive body. This topic is addressed in the next chapter.

---

69 Bleicher, Knut: *Der Aufsichtsrat im Wandel*, Gütersloh, 1987, p. 64.

Chapter 3

Design of the Executive Body

This chapter was written from the point of view of the supervisory body and its conceptional tasks. It therefore does not, by any means, contain everything to be said about the functionality of the executive body, only the few important aspects on which the supervisory body should keep an eye. Addressing the topic from the perspective of the members of the executive body would require a separate book.[70]

As I have said several times before, top management has to be considered in its entirety. No matter what the basic model stipulated by legislation, de facto there will always be a certain division of labor between the immediate management task and its supervision. At least it is recommendable. Depending on how the executive body is designed and structured and what working approach it pursues, corporate supervision will be more or less effective, perhaps even impossible.

Now one of the essential tasks of the supervisory body is to design the executive body and its internal allocation of duties. Even under German law, the *allocation of duties* within the executive body and its *rules of procedure* – in short, *its organization* – are the responsibility of the supervisory body. The executive board may not be empowered to organize itself, not even by including clauses to this effect in the company's articles of association.

Hence, it is in the hands of the supervisory body, even under the rather rigid provisions of German law, to ensure the functionality of the executive body by designing it accordingly. Apart from the composition of the executive board and the practical collaboration between the two bodies, this is the *most effective* way to ensure competent management of the corporation.

---

70 See volume 2 of my book series "Management: Mastering Complexity".

Quite remarkably, this task is *never* even mentioned by the respondents to Bleicher's representative empirical survey on the German situation.[71] It should be noted here, however, that the task was not included in the list of tasks presented to the persons interviewed. In one-tier solutions, such as in Switzerland, it is very clear that this is one of the board of directors' *most essential* tasks.

Tasks of the Executive Body

I do not wish to repeat the usual list of business management powers; they can be found in many other sources. They do, however, not say very much about the "material", content-related quality of management, or help to ensure that the company is not merely managed, but managed *well*, and that its executive bodies deal with the right things in due time and thoroughly enough.

An occasional argument is that this is covered by the general duty of commercial prudence. This term, however, can be understood to mean many things, and once its meaning becomes the subject of dispute, perhaps even a legal one, it is too late. Apart from that, a company can go bankrupt in spite of observing all rules of commercial prudence. So the legal duty of prudence is not enough.

Structuring the executive body[72] is one of the *most difficult* management and organization issues. Theoretical knowledge in this area is not very rich, so in practice people help themselves by applying some standard forms and combinations. Even today, the division into *functional* board departments can be found quite frequently. Depending on the structure of the corporation, however, which often has to meet several organizational criteria at once, one will find numerous forms of multiple responsibilities borne by the individual members of the executive body, which does not make the job any easier; moreover, it cannot be ensured in this way that the truly important tasks receive appropriate attention.

---

71 See Bleicher, Knut: *Der Aufsichtsrat im Wandel*, Gütersloh, 1987, pp. 13 et seq. and appendix.

72 For more on this subject, see Malik, Fredmund: *Corporate Policy and Governance. How Organizations Self-Organize*, Frankfurt/New York, 2011, part IV.

Irrespective of whether the executive body is structured by functions, products or divisions, geography, business lines, or as a matrix – it *always* has to fulfill the following tasks (the execution of which has to be monitored by the supervisory body).[73]

1. Thinking through and determining the business's purpose and mission, and developing a strategy.
2. Defining standards and criteria:
3. Developing and maintaining human resources:
4. Thinking through and defining the institution's overall structure:
5. Maintaining the company's key relationships to outside parties.
6. Representing the institution
7. Being prepared for situations of crisis.

There are many more tasks to be fulfilled in an organization, from research and development to marketing, from production to finance. It goes without saying that the members of the executive body will be involved in those tasks as well. Usually they head the respective divisions or departments; yet the management of divisions is *not* really a top management task, although it is often perceived that way. In essence, heading a division is an *operational* management task. True top management tasks, as evident from the list, are of a different nature.

And it is due to the fact that top executives usually carry responsibility for a division, be it a functional, business, or regional one – and the more so if it is a multiple responsibility – that the *true* top management tasks are usually executed *rather poorly*. They are performed *in passing*, or *delegated* to others, such as consultants, or—even worse—not done *at all*. For all these reasons, it is one of the crucial tasks of the supervisory body to ensure that top management tasks are given appropriate attention, and that they are perceived and handled as *principal* rather than minor matters.

It cannot be the purpose of this chapter to list the top management tasks in detail. The following points will have to suffice.

---

73 See also Drucker, Peter F.: *Management*, London 1973.

1. Thinking Through and Determining the Business's Purpose and Mission, Developing a Strategy

The key question has to be: *What is the purpose of this company – what should and shouldn't it be?* The term "vision",[74] which I have commented on in other sections, has become fashionable in the German-speaking world over the past ten years or so. Truly competent people rarely use it, though. I would advise every member of top management, be it supervisory or executive, to be very cautious and alert when people talk about vision. In most cases the word is meaningless and therefore superfluous. In the worst of cases it is even dangerous, as numerous examples in recent European and American business history have shown.

Spontaneously, one may tend to point to the articles of association (or corporation or partnership) thinking that the purpose of the business is defined there. And indeed these documents contain a clause on purpose. It is, however, mostly phrased in such general terms that it is useless as a basis for strategy. This is why it is one of the key tasks of top management to define the business mission.[75]

Based on a clear and precise understanding of the business purpose and business mission, a *strategy* has to be developed. After roughly 20 years of expert discussion on the subject of strategy, one should think that the development of a strategy, in terms of both substance and methodology, must now be a natural part of any manager's toolkit. That is not the case. On the contrary, it is remarkable how few executive officers have any significant knowledge of the matter; much less do they master it – let alone brilliantly. The most obvious proof for this rather unpopular observation is the staggering number of consultants still hired for strategy development, as well as the far too many business failures owed to strategic ignorance.[76]

Members of corporate headquarters, management boards, and the like have to master the craft of strategy just as pilots have to be able to deter-

---

74 See my book *Uncluttered Management Thinking. 46 Concepts of Masterful Management*. Frankfurt/New York, 2011.

75 This topic is dealt with in detail in volumes 1 and 2 of my book series "Management: Mastering Complexity".

76 Due to the predominance of shareholder value as the only reference variable, purely operational aspects have increasingly replaced strategic ones in the context of corporate management.

mine the course of their flight. All the more so, as it is possible today to determine very clearly what the key elements of a strategy are, and hence for the key questions to be answered. There are clear standards for distinguishing a good from a bad strategy. Although I cannot go into the details here, the following aspects are worth emphasizing:

The *basis* of a corporate strategy must, *first*, be a precise *assessment of the current situation of the company*, covering the most important developments in the economy and in society, the specifics of the particular industry, and the immediate competition and potential substitution. Chapter 3 of part II provides a basis for this. A situation analysis first and foremost requires *sober realism*; it is also hard work. I am not saying that top managers have to do everything themselves, but they do have to deal with the subject to an adequate extent. It is not enough just to have a situation analysis prepared and then presented, be it by staff employees or external consultants.

A *second* essential element is the clear distinction between the requirements of the *current* business and of *tomorrow's* business. This requires a precise understanding of *innovation dynamics* and *innovation management*. In this context, the key ability is to strike a good *balance* between *today* and *tomorrow*. The supervisory body needs to pay special attention to this capability. Having managers at the top of a company who find this hard to do is dangerous.

After all, it is the crucial top management skill to *simultaneously* keep several dimensions in view and in control. There is hardly a manager who would have problems if he could *fully* concentrate on the current business and its success, without having to consider the future. Almost anyone could do that. And nobody would have difficulties if he had to focus on the future only and could disregard the current business. These are the easier tasks. But they do not exist at the top level.

A *third* element of a strategy – immediately related to the balance between the current and the future business – is the *allocation of resources*. This is usually associated with investment decisions. While they are *part* of it, there is much *more* to this. The key resources of a company do not only consist of money – they include human resources, knowledge, time, and attention.

These, more or less, are the things to be considered in connection with the first top management task. Each member of the supervisory body would be well advised to deal with these issues and study the relevant content, which has only been roughly sketched out here, in order, *first*, to be able to ask the right questions, *second, to* be a competent discussion partner to the executive managers, and *third*, to be able to respond to warning signs referring to the quality of execution of this task.

2. Defining Standards and Criteria

The second top management task concerns, in the broadest sense, what has been referred to as *corporate culture* since the early 1980s. In part I, chapter 2, I have said a few things in this regard, so I can be rather brief at this point.

The executive top management has to manage by giving a *personal example* and being a *role model*. There is *no other way* of managing. Whatever the members of the executive body do not exemplify by their actions will not be done. It does not matter what the top managers say, announce, propagate, or try to implement through large-scale programs. If they do not practice what they preach, people in the organization will focus on their *actions*. They will provide the benchmarks.

The top executives have to call people's attention to the gap between what the organization *is* and what it *could be*, and give a living example of the latter. In the final analysis, they make it visible by the way in which they meet their responsibilities.

The members of the supervisory body cannot be too attentive to these things, nor can they be too demanding and strict with regard to the standards they apply to top management conduct. Every little deviation will be noticed: by the entire workforce, the managers at all levels – who, in turn, get their bearings from the top management conduct – and perhaps also by the media and the public. In situations like these, all eyes are on the supervisory body: *Are the people "up there" going to do something about this, or is this how they want things to be…?*

3. Developing and Maintaining Human Resources

The third task of the executive top management concerns the company's *human capital*. Verbally, virtually all managers agree that organizations cannot be better than their people or, indeed, their weakest members.

Unfortunately, their actions often belie their words. Much too often, related tasks are left to the human resources department, although they are really one of the central responsibilities of the executive body and cannot simply be delegated. When I speak of human resources I am talking about the *entire* workforce. Of particular importance, however, are the *managers* at all levels as well as the *experts* as bearers of knowledge. Getting the age structure right, identifying high-potentials, ensuring a systematic evaluation and career design are all elements of the human resources task. The managers of *tomorrow* have to be developed and trained *today*. It has to be ensured that they adopt the right value systems, that they are tried and tested extensively before being assigned major management tasks, and that they can gather the right experiences.

The most important decisions to be taken in a company are *not* those concerning investments and finance. As important as they no doubt are, there are even more important ones – above all, the *personnel decisions*. Even the best investment decisions will remain without effect if the personnel base of the company is eroding and decaying, whether in terms of people skills or in terms of morale. *All* personnel decisions in the company are important, but first and foremost those concerning senior management positions. *Personnel* decisions are the *most significant* signal for what management truly wants, for the values it represents, and thus for its credibility.

It is all the more remarkable that about two-thirds of all personnel decisions are bad or just about acceptable. No more than one-third meet the standards of good management. Due to its importance, this subject is dealt with in a separate chapter of this book.

4. Thinking Through and Defining the Company's Overall Structure

Only the executive body can determine the basic structure and organization that the *company* needs in order to perform and be competitive. To avoid misunderstandings, let me emphasize here that the supervisory body is responsible for the organization of the *executive body*, not for that of the *company*. Questions pertaining to the company structure can only be addressed by managers who are continuously and immediately involved in the business. While the supervisory body should have a part in the *decision* itself – indeed, participate rather intensively, possibly through a dedicated committee or a member to whom the subject is assigned – it does not have to participate in preparing this decision or in developing an appropriate structure.

Again, the situation is similar to what has been said about strategy. The task of developing an appropriate organization structure cannot be left to *others*. As a top manager, one has to deal with the matter personally. Organizational knowledge is the perhaps *most underdeveloped* skill among managers. Only few are familiar with the key issues of organizing, and only the best are able to answer them. This is also the reason why, among other things, they avoid implementing a matrix organization because it is so difficult to make it work.

Nowhere is top management's dependence on external experts greater than in this area. At the same time, there is probably hardly another factor – apart from human resources – that is as crucial for future *competitiveness* as a company's organizational structure. In part I, chapter 5, I briefly pointed this out. Today this subject is closely linked to questions of information technology and telecommunications, which, in addition to posing technical and organizational challenges, also require a major share of the funds to be invested, with very uncertain or at least incalculable returns.

5. Maintaining Key Relationships

This is also one of the tasks of the supervisory body. The redundancy in the work of both management bodies is intentional. In essence it requires a carefully designed division of labor between the executive and the supervisory function. Occasionally some relations, for instance to the world of politics, are better left in the hands of members of the supervisory body than in those of the executive officers; others, in particular those with customers, belong on their own agenda. By no means can or should the supervisory body perform this increasingly important task alone. Most of it should be the executive officers' responsibility.

Hence it is largely up to the executive body to maintain, cultivate and shape key relations with key groups. The latter include customers, suppliers, financiers, the media, politicians, and the public. These relations determine much of the company's performance capacity. In some industries they are vital, in others they may be somewhat less significant – but they are never completely unimportant.

The supervisory body cannot simply leave it to the executive officers to decide how they wish to perform this task: it has to ensure, first, that they do perform it and do so thoroughly enough; second, that they perform it properly. Economic history is full of examples in which imprudent behavior, sometimes even foolishness, a lack of sensitivity, or an inability to correctly assess the public's reactions has led to situations that threatened companies' existence and caused enormous damage. Factory accidents, tanker disasters, bribery cases and the like have provided dramatic evidence of right and wrong management conduct. The disasters or affairs themselves may be regarded inevitable in a world of fallible human beings. Imprudent behavior, however, is avoidable.

6. Representing the Institution

The sixth task is linked to the fifth but not identical to it. It is about the *general* representation of the company towards the worlds of business, politics, arts, and sciences. Invitations, receptions, events of any kind, supervision of and participation in delegations, up to and including state visits – all these things create active and passive obligations which in most, if not all cases have to be met by the top management.

There is no need for lengthy explanations here, as this task is usually executed well. Of course, there are top managers who throughout their lives hate having representative duties and never feel at ease with them. Some also lack style and manners. Most mangers, however, are quite good at these things once they have developed a taste for them. On the supervisory body's part, it is important to ensure that nothing is exaggerated and everything is done with sensitivity and good judgment, that things are kept in proportion, and that there is no excessive flaunting of luxury – particularly relative to employees' standard of living – unless there are very good reasons.

7. Being Prepared for Crises and Special Opportunities

Last but not least, the executive body's tasks include serving as a stand-by authority for crises and opportunity. When everything else fails, the members of the executive body will function as a reserve in mastering the crisis at hand. Likewise, they will be needed when a special opportunity, such as a potential acquisition, suddenly presents itself. In situations like these, the members of the supervisory board may be able to provide valuable help. Most of the work, however, will have to be done by the executive body.

Effectiveness of the Executive Body

There are more things to be considered with regard to the functionality of the executive body, irrespective of the specific organization and division of tasks. They concern the quality and effectiveness of management much more than they do questions of formal organization.

Avoiding Dissipation

Even for managers at the top executive levels it is anything but self-evident to have an effective work approach and to know and apply the principles of human and organizational effectiveness. A supervisory body can never simply presume its top managers to have an effective working method. Most top executives work hard, of course; long working hours are the order of the day, not counting representative duties. *Hard* work, is not the same as *effective* work.

The biggest problem at the top is the danger of *dissipating* one's energies and *fragmenting* one's strengths. Over 40 years ago, the Swedish management scientist Sune Carlson,[77] in his studies on top management work, found that none of the twelve top managers he studied were able to work on the same matter for more than 20 minutes without being interrupted. Not much has changed since then, apart from the few managers who deliberately and systematically worked to improve their working methods. They are *not* in the majority. In virtually all cases, the dissipation of energies in top management is transferred to the organization. As a result, effectiveness is replaced by hectic, and results by much hustle and bustle.

Precisely *because* top managers have to do so *much* and such a *vari-*

---

77 Carlson, Sune: *Executive Behaviour*, Stockholm, 1952.

ety of things, they need a precise and disciplined working approach. The secret of successful managers is in their *concentration on a few things*, on a few carefully selected topics, possibly even a single one. There is no other way to achieve effectiveness and results.

As soon as the supervisory body notices that this principle is being violated systematically and has been over an extended period of time, there is an urgent need for action. Exactly what should be done has to be decided for the individual case. It may be a one-on-one conversation, occasionally also a discussion in the supervisory body plenary, with the top managers present; in some cases it may even suffice to recommend a good book on the issue or make a well-placed humorous or sarcastic remark, or perhaps it is possible to have a few words with the manager concerned over one of the far too numerous business lunches or dinners or during a joint business trip. Whichever way it is done, if there are weaknesses in this area they *must* be communicated.

Staying in Touch with "Real Life"

One of the key questions in organizing the executive body is: *Should top managers perform operational tasks?* In addressing this question, one is likely to get entangled in endless discussions. From my personal experience and having studied countless current real-life cases and biographies, all I can say is: *All of the top people who have had true impact insisted on taking on an operational task which they executed personally.*

There are two reasons for this. They are valid in particular for the heads of executive bodies and for chief executive officers in corporations. And they are both simple and compelling. *One*, people at the top of corporations are far away from the realities of doing business, from the market, the customers, and the competition. Without any operational tasks, in a matter of one or two years even the best people lose what is perhaps the most important thing, the very reason why they are paid more than other people are: their *good judgment.* Only an operational task will force them to personally deal with the *real* reality, again and again. Otherwise they will inevitably come to depend on others' reports about reality. Nowadays, with all the technology at hand, such reports are easy to get. The question is whether they are *true.*

Too often, the reality of business is passed to the top-level people in the company through a number of filters: employees, staff people, secretarial services, consultants. Do they all report the truth? No – not because they are incapable of doing so, but because they are structurally unable to. They can only tell *their* reality as they perceive it to be. So in the best case, these reports are the product of selective perception. In the worst case they have been manipulated. Many first think about what the boss might want to hear today – and that is what they tell him.

The second reason for taking on an operational task is that it helps to be and remain a *competent discussion partner* for one's associates and colleagues. Once you are completely out of touch with reality you will be easier to manipulate. People can lead you up the garden path and you won't know it. Your only resort is *distrust*. This is quite frequent particularly in the top echelons of business. Distrust, however, is poisonous for any working climate and any corporate culture. Another resort is *abstract philosophizing* – which explains several of the great disasters of recent years.

The supervisory body should therefore make sure that the company's top managers not only perform *management tasks* but also, to a certain extent, *operational ones*. The share of time invested in them does not have to be, and usually cannot be, very large. Without a *certain* share of operational work – for instance, 20 percent – before long, the whole executive body will be nothing but *puppets* that have no first-hand knowledge of the realities of life. Poor decisions will become more frequent because the members will lose their power of judgment; instead, they will talk in abstract philosophical terms and make grand speeches, and substance will increasingly be replaced by form and style.

Now the question is what kind of operational activities top managers should take on. As I said earlier, it does not necessarily have to be – indeed, should not be – the management of departments. I am aware of the fact that in smaller firms many compromises will have to be made and it may well be impossible to avoid managing a department. Larger companies, however, will have sufficient human resources, even when they are economizing, not to have to make any foolish compromises here.

When top managers are put in charge of a department, it is important to ensure – if they are promoted from within the organization – that they give up their previous assignments. In particular the head of the executive body should relinquish his original department so as not to foster suspicions that he is using his power to give this department and his previous activities top priority within the company.

Almost routinely, a financial manager appointed CEO will start managing the company from a financial perspective, a technician from a technical one, and a marketing manager will get it in trim for marketing. Top management, however, means considering *all* the different dimensions and coordinating them for the success of the company. This is what top management is about. By contrast, if a manager holds on to his previous domain he will always have appearances against him, no matter how much he may strive to take all entrepreneurial aspects into proper account. People around him will always assume that he is doing what he is doing not because it is right but because it springs from his *"déformation professionelle"*.

Operational assignments in the sense referred to here can, above all, be cross-functional tasks, in particular as they tend to slip through the cracks of organizations. Examples include the responsibility for major innovations, which the head of the executive body could reserve for himself, or for acquisitions (which is very recommendable) or for filling key management positions in the corporation. Alternatively, he could decide to make the development of junior managers or the decision on new business locations his special concern. Tasks of this kind will enable and also force him to maintain and develop a *feel for the realities* of the business.

There are more battles to be fought and developments to be nipped in the bud. They include personality cults, bloated infrastructures such as staff departments and secretariats, but also "extra structures" such as the excessive and often senseless use of external consultants. Biases for luxury and feudalism, arrogance and complacency must be curbed early on; also, the supervisory body needs to fight against management fads, grand theories and hollow phrases – in short: against the "contamination of minds and brains". Furthermore, it is important to ensure that executive managers do not spend all their time in the office, but walk out and see first-hand what is really happening in the company, in the markets, at the customers and competitors.

Term of Office

The term of contract for the members of the executive body is a major architectural element influencing the body's functionality and effectiveness. As in the case of the supervisory body, there is probably no ideal solution. All variants have their advantages and disadvantages.[78]

Relatively short periods of office, for instance, three years, put executive managers under a pressure to perform that is basically desirable. They have to deliver quick results if they want to be reappointed. It also puts the supervisory body under pressure to permanently look for good people. Nobody can sit back and relax. But these advantages come with a price: shorter terms of contract result in short-term thinking and acting, frequently also in hectic and hustling and bustling. Strategies and projects, which require continuity and long-term thinking to be successful, will be less likely to be given priority.

Long terms of contract spanning five years and above have the opposite effects: the long-term orientation of the executive body – which is basically desirable and often necessary – involves the danger of declining performance pressure with its typical effects: results tend to be put off until later and a certain take-it-easy attitude starts spreading.

Another aspect to be considered when determining the term of office is the particular timing of the industry. There are industries, like microelectronics or telecommunications, where three years is an eternity in view of the pace of change in the markets and technologies. In other industries, promising strategies require long periods; examples include utilities, aircraft construction, and parts of the insurance industry.

As a result, there is no single right answer to the question on the term of office of the executive body. This is probably the reason why the "golden mean" – the five-year term – is chosen so often. It is, however, not always the best way to go. The ideal solution would probably be to restore the situation that has always been the reality for a true entrepreneur: basically being in office for an unlimited period of time, thus also being able to (and indeed having to) extend his focus even to successor generations, but at the same time facing the possibility of being "unseated" by the market at any time – without receiving severance benefits but, on the contrary, facing the risk of bankruptcy.

In other words, it would be best to commit the members of the execu-

---

78 While the excessive increase in CEO turnover that took place between 1995 and 2005 seems to be flattening out now, the performance-related turnover rate still seems to be considered positive. "Performance" in this context is financial performance, of course, not performance in terms of prosperity.

tive body – and, in a broader sense, this also applies to other key positions in the company – for an *indefinite* period of time while reserving the option to let them go or moving them to another position if things do not work out. For the corresponding decisions by the supervisory body, including the associated cost, an adequate procedure – a due and fair process – should be defined and made mandatory.

Due to the long-standing practices most organizations will not be able or willing to do away with fixed-term contracts. In accordance with my considerations regarding the term of office of the supervisory body (part II, chapter 2) I tend to suggest *short* contract periods of, say, three years combined with the option of unlimited re-appointments until the age limit is reached. All the arguments I listed there apply here, too; the two dilemmas have to be dealt with: flexibility versus continuity and short-term versus long-term orientation. In either case, it seems both possible *and* easier to make up for the disadvantages of flexibility and a short-term orientation. This is only seemingly in contradiction to my basic proposal to ensure long-term orientation of the overall management, which I expressed in part I, chapters 4 and 5.

As mentioned before, short contract periods lead to the desired performance pressure and an undesirable short-term orientation. It is, however, easier for the supervisory body to counter the resulting behaviors than, in the opposite case, having to constantly spur on the members of the executive body if long contract periods do result in low performance pressure and excessive leisureliness.

A focus on short-term results does not necessarily imply that these results have to be of a financial nature. I have explained at length why this would be wrong thinking. It can be prevented by the *way* in which the supervisory body executes its leadership: by ensuring that the right variables are monitored and the principles of correct corporate governance – correct in terms of both, form and substance – are observed. In addition it is possible, and indeed advisable, to signal (but not to guarantee!) to the members of the executive body in good time that their contracts will probably be extended unless they will make serious mistakes during the time before their reappointment.

One advantage of short contract periods is that employment can be terminated by non-renewal, without having to terminate the contract, which in a top management context is preferable for reasons of appearance and spares those involved from having to explain too much. A *second* advantage, which is particularly important in times of fast-paced change, is that the executive body can flexibly be adapted to changed conditions. Again, the same applies which has been said for the supervisory body, but to an even greater extent: it is not enough just to have "good" people in the executive body, but people with precisely those specific strengths that the company needs to master the specific situation.

Situations can change quickly, and in the course of a greater transformation they definitely will, which makes every contract renewal a window of opportunity for rethinking what the best possible combination of strengths might be. In this way, business organizations can regain the flexibility they have lost as a result of both long contract periods and the vested-rights and play-it-safe mentalities frequently found even at the top. I believe this would be an important signal of credibility vis-à-vis the workforce, the unions, and certain parts of the political world. Companies have no right to demand flexibility of people if they are unwilling to show some themselves.

I am aware that many of my suggestions resemble attempts to square a circle. But this, precisely, is one of the characteristics of corporate governance and of the collaboration between the two governing bodies. I am equally aware that some of my suggestions narrow the range of potential candidates for executive top management positions. In my view, that is not a disadvantage. In times of roaring booms, and thus of a supplier market for top management talent, one will have to make temporary concessions. That, however, should not be a reason to justify a permanent and systematic erosion of the principles of right and effective corporate governance.

Whatever the specific solutions will ultimately look like, the suggestions I have presented here – combined with my considerations regarding the liability of managers (part II, chapter 5) and on the selection of candidates (part II, chapter 6) – would point the way toward a revitalization of true entrepreneurship.

The Executive Body as a Team

Executive top management is usually *team work*. The tasks to be performed are so diverse that one person alone cannot be expected to fulfill them competently and comprehensively. A one-person top management either represents a *risk* to the company, or it is a *fiction*. By all appearances, there may be one person in the top position; on closer inspection, however, it often turns out that the work is actually done by a team – particularly in organizations where everything seems to work very well.

"Team" is a term that is quickly said and is well-worn; forming a team and making it work is difficult. This is especially true of top management teams. Most top managers are not easy to deal with anyway. In particular when they are very capable, they are also very strong *individuals* and often *individualists*. They are – hopefully – strong personalities, which is why they are often difficult and rough around the edges. And they should be.

There is yet another thing that top managers – as much as they may differ from each other as human beings and personalities – usually have in common: most of them are true *power freaks*. So in order to avoid the phenomena inevitably found in the top echelons, such as struggles for power and rank, scheming, "top dog" attitudes, ego trips, image neuroses, and the like, it is important to closely watch how top management teams work together. For them to work well, *three conditions* and *six ground rules* must be observed.

Three Conditions

The first condition is obvious and generally agreed on, although far from being observed everywhere. The second is more controversial, and the third is rejected by most. The conditions are:

- Extreme discipline,
- Putting aside personal relations, and
- Absolutely disregarding the "chemistry" factor.

The *first* condition, discipline, is important for any team. There is actually a clear *criterion* for the transition from a *group* to a *team*: The team begins when members decide to forgo the luxury of group dynamics, instead replacing it with discipline. Here, top management teams have to meet the highest standards, and in general there is broad agreement with regard to this condition.

The *second* condition is not generally accepted. This is precisely why it is important. Personal relationships, sympathies, friendships and, in extreme cases, cronyism are poison for any management team. Its work must be dominated by *fact-based relationships*. Agreeing to a certain decision must not be a matter of doing a friend or colleague a favor, but be aimed exclusively at reaching the decision that is factually right – possibly even struggling for it – irrespective of personal relations. It is therefore always advisable for members of top management bodies – and even more for the chairmen – to keep an equal distance vis-à-vis all other members. Even slight biases in perception can cause serious difficulties.

The *third* of the three conditions is connected to the second but not identical to it. (Note that the "chemistry" can be right even though people do not maintain a friendship or go on vacations together.) The third condition is rejected by almost all ordinary executives, often very emotionally, and it is not accepted – or at the very least, it is viewed skeptically – by most top managers. Truly *experienced* managers, however, share my view. Since this condition is so hotly contested, it warrants some explanatory comments.

Of course it is a good thing for a team if the "chemistry" between the members is right, and it is doubtless more pleasant working with people if the emotional basis and relationship among all is sound. This much has to be admitted. Under these circumstances, however, when the personal level is right, there will be not be any problems anyhow. But the condition discussed here and the rules associated with it are particularly important when the "chemistry", for whatever reason, is *not* right. This is the point where a top management team has to be *able to function nevertheless*. A top team cannot be allowed to function *because* of "chemistry" alone, but must instead be able to work constructively *despite a lack of it*.

The members of an executive body – even the chairman – usually cannot choose their colleagues as they are appointed by the supervisory body. If the "chemistry" is right things are certainly easier – but it cannot be considered a *condition* for top teams. Likewise, if the chemistry is wrong it must not be used as an excuse for poor cooperation.

When I explain this view in speeches and seminars, participants often tell me that these things are "really difficult". Which is certainly true. Simple problems do not require top managers. Ordinary people can solve them. Compliance with the conditions and rules for the effectiveness of top management teams may sometimes challenge the members to the limits of what people are capable of doing and enduring. Anyone unable to withstand these pressures has no business being in a top-level position.

The three conditions described here do not, as is occasionally presumed, imply the absence of human kindness, friendliness, and even humor at the top echelons. Fortunately, these things are not mutually exclusive.

Six Ground Rules

The ground rules for the effective functioning of a top management team are simple, but observing them is not always easy. Compliance with team rules is not guaranteed to make a company successful. *Disregarding* them, however, is a *guarantee* for the company's failure or at least its running into serious problems. These rules are independent of the actual organization structure, and they are independent of what kind of responsibility is required legally. The collective responsibility laid down in German law does not say anything about the way an executive body comprising several people actually works. To be functional and effective, a team must observe the following rules:[79]

a) Every member of a top management team has the last say in his or her sphere of responsibility. He speaks on behalf of the whole team and thus secures its commitment to collective decisions.

Each individual team member represents, in his area of responsibility, the authority of the entire executive body. This means that there may be no such thing as an employee's "appeal" against a decision taken by a member of the top team, directed to another member. If this was permitted it would be a sure and quick way of having the company infested with intrigues. It would be an open invitation to undermine the authority of the entire team. For very special cases, the possibility of recourse to the overall body or its chairman may be established.

b) No one takes a decision in an area outside his own area of responsibility.

The second rule is the counterpart of the first. The members' areas of responsibility must be mutually respected. If an executive member is approached by an employee and confronted with a matter in someone

---

79 See also Drucker, Peter F.: *Management*, London, 1973.

else's responsibility, he will refer the employee to the executive member responsible or ensure the matter is dealt with there. In any case, he may not make the decision himself.

Violations of these two rules will not only create enormous confusion in an organization, ultimately paralyzing its effectiveness, they also lead to power struggles. I would like to expand the second rule a bit: not only does it mean that a member will not take any decisions in another members' area of responsibility – he does not even express an opinion in this regard *outside the team*.

c) Outside the team there will be no judgment of other team members.

The members of a team do not have to like each other. There may be instances in which they find it hard to accept one another, and there may also occasional situations in which they cannot even respect each other, which doubtlessly means that a dangerous point has been reached. Whatever the case may be – there must be *no agitation* whatsoever. Note that this rule applies to members' behavior *outside the team*. Inside the executive body, there may be fierce debates; they will and they should take place – with all due objectivity. That is hardly avoidable when it comes to making crucial decisions for the company. In outward communications, however, nobody should express any personal opinions about their colleagues, and nobody should make *qualifying comments* about others – not even praise them.

d) A team is not a committee; it therefore needs a team leader or chairman. He has to have the right to cast the deciding vote in case of a stalemate.

Contrary to widespread opinion, a well-functioning team is not a group of equals with equal rights, even if the legal system formally requires it. Teams have nothing to do with *democracy*. What matters is *effectiveness*. Everyone is a member of the team because he or she has to make a distinct contribution. This is why functioning teams do have an inner structure and a management.[80]

---

80 Under German law, the head of the executive board cannot be a CEO in the Anglo-Saxon sense. According to §77 of the German Stock Corporation Act, the executive board in a German stock corporation acts as a collective body.

The leader of a team must ensure that the team performs its tasks and observes the rules for the team's functionality. In addition, he is the key person in situations where the team is paralyzing itself and threatens to become incapable of acting. For cases like these, the team leader needs to have the authority to solve a stalemate situation. Ideally he will never have to use his right to the ultimate decision. If he has to use it very frequently, it is a symptom of fundamental problems within the team. Yet it is needed for situations of crisis.

In order for decisions to be taken, several formulas are possible and customary, including decisions by simple majority, or by qualified majority, or the principle of unanimity. For the top executive body *unanimity* seems preferable, although it has its disadvantages. In a case of crisis, however, it is important, above all, to ensure the team's decision-making ability.

Although votes must be possible on principle, they should remain the exception. The head of the executive body must make every effort to establish *consensus* – but not the superficial kind that can be observed so often, and which only conceals problems instead of solving them. It is important, therefore, that the head of the team is skilled in dealing with *dissent*. Sustainable consensus – the kind that will hold even through difficult phases of decision implementation – only arises from disagreement which is openly voiced.

If polling does become necessary because consensus cannot be reached, it is indispensable that the minority will back the majority decision and support it with loyalty. They have to do everything possible to contribute to the timely implementation of the decision. Neither active nor passive opposition is admissible. Misconduct of that kind, even if subtle and only insinuated, undermines the executive body's authority and effectiveness to an almost irreversible extent. If someone is definitely unable to support a decision, there is no other option but to ask that person to resign.

e) Certain decisions must be left to the team as a whole.

The first rule says that every member of the team has the last say in his or her sphere of responsibility, that he speaks on behalf of and thus commits the whole team. This is an important – and, in my view, indispensable – rule to ensure a company's ability to act quickly. In itself, however, this rule could lead to abuse, which is why a corrective is needed. Certain decisions must *not* be taken *alone by anyone*. They require *everybody's* consent.

Typical cases include acquisitions or alliances, large-scale innovations, the establishing or closing down of whole lines of business, or personnel decisions concerning key positions. The nature of such cases which the team reserves the right to decide collectively must be defined in the executive body's rules of procedure. At the same time, there must be a general clause according to which *in cases of doubt* the team, not an individual member, has to make a decision. The supervisory body's rights of approval, or co-decision, remain unaffected in any case.

f) Each team member is obliged to keep the other members informed about what is going on in his or her area of responsibility.

This rule is another corrective to rule No. 1. When there are *autonomous decisions* in each sphere of responsibility, there must also be *comprehensive information* given to all other team members.

It is the supervisory body's task to ensure functionality of the executive body by establishing its organization and introducing the conditions and rules for effective functioning. The supervisory body has to monitor the execution of the top-level tasks and functional rules, and to sanction any deviations immediately and unequivocally. Even minor deviations cannot be tolerated. The principle is to prevent them before they even take hold.

The tools for regulating these things are the schedule of responsibilities and the bylaws. Admittedly, developing and formulating these regulations is a demanding endeavor which requires the joint efforts of lawyers and management experts. It is a matter of getting the substance right *and* of phrasing it accurately.

Executive Pay

As one of the consequences of the corporate governance currently practiced, managerial salaries have become a hot topic. The executive pay excesses in the management of US, German, and Swiss companies have hit the headlines and become the talk of the day. Only in Asia, particularly in Japan, the virtue of self-restraint seems to exist to this date.

The focus on shareholder value and monetary value increase have led to a general tendency to value everything in monetary terms, first and foremost the performance of top executives. The inevitable result was excessive money-mindedness among executives, which is hard to resist even for those that are far from assessing their work or viewing their management task in monetary terms.

Note that I am not speaking of *greed*, as the word expresses a moral judgment which may make for good copy in the media but not illuminate the matter as such. Still, the context of current corporate governance has made it easier than ever for the money-driven type of psychological personality to get ahead, as precisely this characteristic is widely regarded as a positively qualifying criterion. Due to the introduction of Economic Value Added (EVA) as a one-dimensional measure of corporate success, performance and performance evaluation have been mechanistically tied to this exclusively monetary variable.

It is an altogether different story with family-managed enterprises, even the larger ones, where money-mindedness is generally an exclusion criterion for top-level positions.

People are quick to discuss managerial income in ethical categories. It is not an ethical issue, however, but a question of how the productive systems of society – the business organizations – function. Consequently, these questions can be discussed as being completely system-immanent. Neither philosophical nor moral or political-ideological arguments are needed. Even where managers' pay is at clearly unjustifiable levels, its a question not of ethics but of the supervisory body's failure to make corrective personnel decisions. I deal with this issue in part I, chapter 2.

Transforming corporate governance codes into rules of general etiquette, as is often done, is completely unnecessary and fails both the purpose of and functional requirements to corporate governance.

Pseudo-Justification by the Market

"If we don't pay the highest salaries we won't get the best managers. The market calls for the highest pay." Arguments like these are often used to justify extraordinary managerial income. Are the most expensive managers really the best? Is there a connection between income levels and leadership qualities? Does the market really bring the best people into the best positions?

As long as the stock market boomed and before scandals became visible, it may have been justifiable to argue along these lines, although there has long been reasonable doubt and criticism even before the recent occurrences – which was expressed, among others, by such respected and experienced minds as the doyen of management theory, Peter F. Drucker. After the scandals came to light, the argument can no longer hold.

No doubt good people must be paid well. Conversely, however, well-paid people do not necessarily deliver good performance. Why should it be impossible for cheaper people to do an even better job than expensive ones? If some corporations with excessively paid top managers, such as Enron or Worldcom, had been spared these people, not only would they have saved a lot of money but they would probably still exist; and the shareholders of a leading German automobile manufacturer would have lost less money. No one could have managed these companies worse than those big earners did. A ruined company or a bankruptcy can be had for less.

It is an unsubstantiated supposition that a top income will create great performance, let alone top performance. Once again, the logic of the market was turned upside down: while great performance justifies a high income, the opposite is not true.

At the beginning of the 20th century, the American tycoon John P. Morgan, one of the greatest believers in capitalism, initiated a study in his business empire. He wanted to know what the differences were between his successful businesses and the less successful ones. It turned out that there was only one point where the former differed from the latter: it was the difference between the salary levels in each company. In successful ones, it was no more than 30 percent from one level to the next; in less successful ones it had gotten out of control. J.P. Morgan then introduced that same ratio everywhere.

Today, almost more than 100 years later, we can be a bit more generous with these proportions, especially in case of success. And absolute top performance should be rewarded with an absolute top bonus.

A New Beginning for Managerial Income

It is time to stop trying to repair systems that never have worked and never will work. It is in the most vital interest of the top executives themselves.

Even the most sophisticated reforms undertaken now, in order to salvage the remainders of stock option programs, for instance, will not solve the problem. There is no effective arithmetic-mechanical system of determining the right compensation for the complex tasks at the top level. No such system will do justice to the rapid change of conditions under which it is supposed to function. Most of these conditions have not even been considered by the inventors of those systems.

No arithmetic system will work for rising and falling stock prices alike, for boom phases and in recessions, for business as usual and in turn-around cases, for acquisitions as well as divestitures. There is no system that, by using mechanical calculation, could take proper account of the essential dimensions of corporate management – operative and strategic, short and long-term, today and tomorrow.

What is the alternative? There is only one: an autonomous decision by the supervisory body, freely taking into consideration all relevant circumstances. This solution is far from being ideal – but it is the best there is, once it has generally been acknowledged that the ideal is an illusion and cannot be implemented. There is no arithmetic-mechanical system that would work here. This idea has to be abandoned once and for all. In over 30 years I have not seen any such system work. They are fair weather systems.

This alternative gives back to the supervisory body its most important function: to determine and evaluate the company's overall performance, the way it is achieved, and the executive's contribution to it. Under the influence of pseudo-rational arguments, this function had been ceded to rigid mechanics. No doubt this is one of the most difficult tasks in the context of management and control. But it is also the most important and noble one. This is how the supervisory body fulfils its *core task*; this is where its true significance lies. Without the competent and responsible fulfillment of this task there will be no corporate governance.

The solution is simple and straightforward.[81] To recognize it, however, one needs to abandon some of the dogmas of the past 15 years, in particular some misguided theories on business administration and economics, and give up the notion that top management performance can be measured in money. Only then will the members of an executive body be able to present realistically and comprehensively what they have really

---

81 See also part II, chapter 5.

achieved and under what circumstances, instead of having to reduce their achievements to monetary figures. This solution is clearly better for both the executive and the supervisory body.

1. Managerial income levels must be decoupled from financial figures and the stock exchange.
2. There must be no arithmetic-mechanical relation between someone's pay and the targets he is given.
3. Managers should be paid *from*, not *for* the profits they achieved in the current business year.
4. They should be paid for their contribution to future prosperity and to the competitiveness of the company. Contrary to general opinion, this contribution can certainly be determined with sufficient objectivity and accuracy.
5. Specifically, this contribution can be assessed using the first CPC variables I described in part I, chapter 5 – that is, the improvement achieved in market position, innovativeness, productivity, and attractiveness to good people.

The implications may seem unusual in light of current practice, but they are beneficial to the functioning of the company and indispensable for its health. Current practice in this area is anything but "best practice" – it is just "common practice". Moreover, it is fair-weather practice and thus totally counterproductive in times of economic downturn. Moreover, it does not do justice to the actual performance of corporate management, which has to be much greater in difficult times than can be reflected in the financial results alone.

With the approach suggested here, top management performance is not derived from monetary variables, which can partly be manipulated and partly depend on coincidental circumstances in the economy and the stock markets. Rather, the executive body's performance has to be described, substantiated and explained in terms of the CPC variables mentioned. The supervisory body, for its part, must deal with the overall situation of the company and its managers intensely enough to be able to fulfill its task competently. This will require some work, but the supervisory body is appointed and paid for it. In companies with a sophisticated management system it has always been that way.

The most frequent counter-arguments are easily refuted:

1. One argument is that the supervisory body is not in a position to fulfill this task because it is too far removed from day-to-day reality. Wherever that is the case, it will have to move closer to it.
2. Another argument is that the supervisory body does not have the competencies. In that case it is time to appoint competent people to it.
3. A third argument is that managers would make less money.
   On the contrary, incomes could even be higher. Above all, this approach leads to a fairer correlation between performance and pay, as a turnaround task will be rewarded with bonuses even if the company's annual result is negative. Getting a company out of a loss situation caused by predecessors' mismanagement is an achievement which warrants an attractive compensation – something that is impossible under the current monetary-mechanistic systems, which is why they would have to be bypassed in that case.
4. Some say the decision is of a subjective nature.
   That is correct but irrelevant. Every judicial decision is subjective because it is taken by a thinking, considering, judging person or group of people. The important point is that the decision must not be *arbitrary*. Subjectivity is often mistaken for arbitrariness. In terms of procedure, it is possible to exclude arbitrary decisions, as has been demonstrated by judicial practice over the past centuries.
5. Managers would not know in advance what they will have earned at the end of the year.
   Correct. This was and is exactly the situation every entrepreneur is in. His income is never known in advance, as business results are rarely predictable. So when somebody has an entrepreneurial task and the responsibility that comes with it, he will have to deal with this situation.

The compensation itself can be paid either in cash or in stocks or options. In the case of option programs, however (at least if they cover a major share of the manager's income) it is important to ensure that they can play both ways – profit and loss – as they would otherwise fail their purpose in multiple ways.

Chapter 4

Management or Leadership

Neither top management body will be able to avoid the topic of leadership and leaders. Where, if not at the top of a company, should there be leadership? The supervisory body is responsible for filling top executive positions with the best people available. Should they be managers or leaders? Is there a difference – and if so, what is it? Current leadership theories are not much use in terms of providing transparency; they even give rise to many a false doctrine. Once the errors have been recognized and eliminated, however, it certainly is possible to define clearly what leadership consists of and how it is created. Besides other things, we must first of all distinguish between *great* and *true* leaders.

Errors and Misconceptions

In this chapter, as well as in part II, chapter 6, the reader may notice that I mention names more frequently than I usually do. For some, there may be too many American examples, and too many from politics and the military. The reason is not that there are no suitable examples from the business sectors in other countries, including the German-speaking world. Neither do I have an exaggerated preference for the political and military sectors or Anglo-Saxon history.

The reason is simple. The history of political and military leaders has been *documented* much better than that of business leaders. It has always met with much more interest on the part of historians and biographers. This is true especially of the recent history of the United States, where politics and military were a public matter and, particularly during the two World Wars, not much could be hidden from a free press which insisted on its democratic rights. As a result, much more is known about the persons I discuss below than about other people who might also be suitable examples. Hardly anything has been documented as carefully as, for instance, the actions of American generals during the Second World War – as opposed to Germany, where much remained unrecorded due to the political system, and a lot of significant material was lost in the turmoil of war.

There is a wealth of papers, congresses and training programs dealing with the topic of this chapter. Leadership is turning into a *fashionable fad* and, as always happens with fads, the *substance* is *thin*. There is hardly anything that has been thought through, researched well, or really challenged, not to speak of a lack of sound arguments, let alone evidence.

With a series of other fads, such as chaos management,[82] empowerment, or New Age, the associated superficiality does no harm simply because they are nothing but fashionable topics that will disappear as quickly as they have come up.

With leadership it is a different story. Every company needs to deal with it. At the same time it is a *delicate* issue, as we know from history. Significantly, in German-speaking country the words "Führerschaft" and in particular "Führer" are generally avoided and replaced by their English translations. The general assumption seems to be that the English terms do not come laden with historical baggage or other unwanted connotations. "Leader" seems unproblematic in a way that "Führer" definitely is not.

It is all the more important to handle the subject with great *care*. As a fashionable fad, it could be expected either to degenerate into intellectual scrap or to become dangerous. Anyone faced with the topic of leadership in his job should be familiar with some trends, errors, and misconceptions and consider them in his decisions.

1. Almost all of the literature written in the past years is *devoid of historical context*. It gives the impression that the topic has only just been discovered and that there was never such a thing as leaders and leadership before.

Well, that is not the case. It may be true that our present time and its problems have a particular need for leadership. But it is certainly *not the*

---

82 To avoid a misunderstanding: *Mathematical-physical* chaos theory certainly is a step forward. But what has been made of it by transferring parts to the management world is unacceptable. See also part I, chapter 2.

first time that questions of leadership have ever been addressed. The last instance was a mere 50 years ago – and it exemplifies the whole range of ways in which this topic can be discussed.

2. A major part of recent literature is *one-dimensional*. It talks about leadership in *business*, as if there were no other areas in which leaders and leadership are important, such as the churches and religious orders, or military organizations, or politics. In these areas, the debate has made much more progress and reached a higher level than it has in business. I do not mean to imply that leadership theories can or should be transferred from there into the business sector. However, dealing with work that has been done in those areas will be inevitable. It cannot simply be ignored.

3. Leadership is consistently regarded as something that is *absolute*. People search for the "absolute" of leadership and presume it to reside in certain *personality traits*. There is no such thing as traits which clearly define leadership, as I will explain later. At this point I want to emphasize something else: Leadership is not absolute but relative, depending on the *situation*, and it can only be understood and explained based on a given situation.

The same person can exercise leadership in one situation and fail in another. One example is Winston Churchill. It took the situation of the Second World War to turn Churchill into a great leader. After his early success he went on to lead a politically meaningless life as a backbencher in British Parliament. In those times he was closer to being a loser than a leader.

It is the situation and the specific action taken in this situation that generates leadership. Without the situation, the action referred to as *leadership* would be neither necessary nor possible, nor would it make any sense. In order to find the secret of leadership, it is necessary to ask: *What was it, about or in the specific situation the person was in, that made him a leader or enabled him become one?*

In this context, another factor is significant which is constantly disregarded: People generally believe that leadership is something very *rare* and *unusual*, which is why they search for the "mysterious" qualities of the "rare" leaders. Contrary to this widespread view, leadership behavior is something that occurs quite frequently. In most cases, however, the situation in which someone exercises leadership is not particularly remarkable or worth reporting. For instance, the media will not take an interest if it is an everyday situation. Someone who rescues a child from a river or a burning house, or who calls and provides help to the victims of a traffic accident, shows all the essential leadership characteristics. Whether he is a hero is another question, but he is a leader. There will hardly be much more than a brief report in the local paper, though. It is the sensational, particularly newsworthy situation and the special action in that situation which causes leadership to be perceived as such and to be publicly noticed. Since *situations* like these – not the leadership behavior – are rather rare, the general conclusion is that leadership, too, is something rare and unusual.

4. A leadership theory worth dealing with has to achieve the following *at minimum* and *in any case*: It has to address the issue of how to distinguish between *leaders* and *misleaders*. A good leadership theory has to *enable*, even *force* people to make that distinction. It has to provide clear criteria for identifying and excluding the misleaders.

Many authors seem not to see the problem, let alone offer solutions for it. They spin their yarn about some or other qualities and characteristics that people must supposedly have in order to be leaders. They fantasize about enthusiasm, inspiration, grand visions, and glorious triumphs. I consider that to be romantic twaddle – at best. Some seem to never have made it out of the early childhood stage. They have got stuck in the fantasy world Cowboys-and-Indians – a bit of Leatherstocking here, a splash of Wild West there, a dash of young Siegfried ... needless to say, all of it now global and Web-based.

But that is not how things work. It will be necessary to say at the very least what the *commonalities* and, above all, the *differences*, are between Churchill and Hitler, or Truman and Stalin. And it will be necessary to analyze what, beyond the fact that they were remarkable in *historical* terms, constituted the *leadership* of people such as Kennedy, Adenauer, de Gaulle, Thomas à Becket, Loyola, Calvin, József Mindszenty, or Zhou Enlai.

5. One thing that is particularly striking is the pronounced tendency of most authors dealing with leadership to create a *stark contrast* between management and leadership. In order to depict the significance of leadership as being very *great*, they make that of management as *small* as possible.

According to them, *managers* would be mere administrators, operators, and executors, who stick to what they have and what they know, focus on the present, work with rules and controls, and basically are nothing but boring bureaucrats – while *leaders* are depicted as innovators, exciting visionaries, and brave pioneers. Everyone is free to portray things that way. The question is what is gained by it.

I suggest something else: if we hope to recognize, analyze, and perhaps – if at all possible – teach what is essential about leadership, we need to start with the *most positive* image of management possible and ask ourselves what leadership means *above and beyond* it. Otherwise, everything *bad* will be referred to as management and everything *good* as leadership – which will not help us learn anything about leadership.

There are countless executives who look to the future, act with foresight, innovate, and meet all the criteria applied to leaders – but are personally too modest or too smart to call themselves or have others call them leaders. It would feel presumptuous to them. They are content being called good managers.

Thus, we first need to distinguish between *bad* and *good* managers before we can reasonably ask what distinguishes leaders from *good* managers, and in what points a leader may be superior to a good manager.

Mystification by Attributing Characteristics

The most common mistake is the *mystification* and glorification of both true and perceived leaders. All others are – rightly or wrongly – vilified. This exaggerated elevation results from attributing properties to them which are considered to be particular leadership qualities and thus as the reason, cause or origin of leadership.

This is a grave misunderstanding and – for those having to make staffing decisions – a source of misjudgment. There are so many examples of people who excelled as leaders without having even one of the so-called leadership traits *that the whole characteristics theory becomes useless.*

Neither President Harry S. Truman nor General George C. Marshall[83] – both ranking highly among the true leaders of the 20th century – had any unusual characteristics. Truman is a particularly good example. What is essential about him is perhaps not even the fact that he was President of

---

83 Marshall was a Chief of Staff with the US Army from 1938 to 1945, as well as Secretary of State and Secretary of Defense later on.

the United States and in this function had to take a series of difficult and important decisions. The key point in explaining his leadership is that he did and became all these things *without* meeting even *one* of the prerequisites which are commonly considered important. Not many people have achieved so much in such a short time and from such a bad starting position as Truman did.

He did not have any striking qualities, let alone those constantly claimed in relevant literature. Based on Truman's personality structure, nobody would have expected him to have that kind of political success. Probably he would have flunked all "leadership tests". Truman had a few *principles* which helped him keep a cool head even in very difficult situations – in particular those where the burden of his duties nearly drove him to despair and there was nothing he desired more than being spared this difficult office. He often felt overwhelmed and challenged far beyond his abilities. He was anything but a "shining hero" – as opposed, for instance, to one of his "antagonists": General Douglas MacArthur.

And it was not due to his leadership qualities that Roosevelt made Truman Vice President but – quite to the contrary – due to his lack of them. After all that was known about Truman, he could never become a threat to Roosevelt, and apart from a few party-political compromises, that was the main reason for Roosevelt's offering him the Vice Presidency.

Truman's example also shows quite the importance of the particular *situation* as an element of leadership. It took the death of President Roosevelt, which came at the worst possible time on April 12, 1945, to make Truman one of the leaders of the 20th century. Without it, he would have remained a footnote of history.

Truman had a few *principles*, and they were actually of a kind that would disqualify him in the eyes of most leadership experts. In addition, it was the way he *acted* in the historically significant situation he was in which made him a leader. The essential points which can be generalized are described in the following section.

In truth, there are *no* commonalities in the *characteristics* of people typically considered to be leaders. Some are exceptionally bright, others rather mediocre. Some are "nice guys", easy-going and open-minded; others are rather inaccessible, reserved, and awkward, characterized by strict discipline and even asceticism. Some are daredevils and "macho" types, others are cultured people, gentle and reserved. Some love luxury and show, others cannot stand them. Some are rather impulsive and spontaneous; others tend to study everything thoroughly and have to go through periods of brooding and endure serious doubts before they reach a decision. Some seek contact with people and keep an open office or house, while others do not feel at ease in the company of others and prefer solitude and privacy.

It is very specific behaviors – in very specific situations – rather than characteristics which explain and constitute a person's leadership and have a certain effect: they create *following, credibility, and trust* – not cronyism.

Characteristics do not bear a causal relation to leadership. Getting to the bottom of the matter, one will usually find an error of a very specific kind. It is the false conclusion that what happened earlier has to be the cause and what happened later has to be the effect. As soon as leadership starts manifesting itself and a person starts having followers, he will naturally be the focus of interest of his immediate environment and, for as long as there have been mass media, especially the focus of interest of the media. At this point – usually no sooner – people will start noticing all kinds of qualities that this person actually has (sometimes they may be mere projections) but which no one has considered to be of note before.

It is then concluded that the leader must have achieved leadership *because of* these qualities. In the vast majority of cases, however, it is the other way round: these qualities are considered remarkable *because* the person achieved leadership. Leadership came first; only then – and because of it – were the person's qualities noticed. It is a classical fallacy which occurs time and again in connection with the scientific notion of causality. It has been studied rather well in the philosophy of science, which is why good scientists try to avoid it.

From Manager to Leader

The foundation of good management is *craftsmanship* – that is, *skills* that can be taught and learnt: observing a few *principles*, fulfilling a few *key tasks*, and mastering a few *tools*. Even *leaders* cannot do without the practical basis for right management, and no organization can function without it.

True leaders do *not stop* here, though; they go several steps further.

They master a few things particularly well – not necessarily because they come naturally to them (although this may occasionally be the case) but because they know, intuitively or consciously, that they only have a few means at their disposal to mobilize human strengths, so they concentrate on the essential things and work tirelessly and consistently to improve crucial *leadership skills*.

Note that I am speaking of *true* leaders, not of *great* ones. There are people considered "great" leaders who, upon closer inspection, cannot pass muster as true leaders. John F. Kennedy is one example.[84] Kennedy was a media event, the product of a public relations strategy, and after his death he was deliberately put on a pedestal by hired biographers. From an objective standpoint he did not achieve very much politically, and it would have remained that way if his term of office had been longer. Most of his important decisions were downright disasters. On the other hand, there are people whom nobody would consider to be "great" but who were certainly true leaders. Wars, natural disasters, accidents, and so on provide more than enough examples of people having shown true leadership, without having attracted any attention as "historically great leaders".

For the members of a supervisory body who have to make staffing decisions concerning top-level positions – which, as I have explained earlier, are rather critical – it is important to consider the following. My suggestion is *not* to absolutely insist on selecting people who are true leaders. It depends on the specific situation whether a position requires a leader or whether a good manager will do. It seems more important to me to look very closely whether a candidate for a top-level position clearly *fails to meet* the requirements described below. In that case there would be a considerable risk of the company being led astray rather than led forward, and sooner or later getting out of hand.

True Leaders Focus on the Task

The key questions they ask are not: *What do I want? What is convenient for me? etc.* – instead, they ask: *What needs to be done?* Immediate

---

84 I have to admit that I found this hard to accept. Kennedy was one of the heroes of my youth, and of most other people my age. He seemed to embody everything that was important to us.

returns usually do not matter to them. They do not pay much attention to the rewards, least of all monetary ones. They feel an obligation to do what needs to be done. This obligation can even reach the point of obsession, with all other things being blocked out. The driving force, however, is the *task* at hand, rather than the fulfillment of personal needs. Quite often they will put aside all personal needs and take on substantial sacrifices and renunciation – which often meets with incomprehension by those around them.

They are driven by these questions: *What can I do? Where and how can I bring about change, make a difference? What is right for this particular organization? What are the right goals and tasks for this company?* For them, all that counts is the performance and results achieved in these tasks.

They are not interested in the usual motivators. Their motivation (and their strength) results from the task and the achievements it entails. *They work for a cause.* A task well-solved is satisfaction enough to them.

True Leaders Force Themselves to Listen

The emphasis is on *forcing* because nobody will find that easy to do. Most leaders are impatient, and many are deeply convinced that they are doing the right thing. Yet they know how enormously important the information is which they can only obtain from *others*, in particular from the basis of their organization. Over and over again, they muster the will and the self-discipline to listen – not least because they know that otherwise they would lose their people's *trust*. They at least give the impression of being particularly interested in what others have to say, and really good leaders do not only give that impression – they *really are* interested.

That does not necessarily mean they listen for *long*. Usually they do not have much time. But even when they only take ten minutes, they will listen very attentively – noticeably to the other person – during that time.

True Leaders Tirelessly Work on Making Themselves Understood

They are aware of the fact that what is clear to *them*—their views, *their own* imagination—is *not evident* to others. This is why they *repeat* the messages they consider important, again and again, with patience and persistence, possibly even bordering on stubbornness. In their endeavor to make themselves understood, they simplify things and use the language of their target groups, as well as metaphors and analogies. Occasionally they oversimplify because they know that complicated things cannot be understood, and thus cannot become effective, or will even become counterproductive. To be understood, they use the best means of communication wherever possible: *they demonstrate how things are done.* They behave in the way they expect of others, as every leader has learned from experience that he can ultimately only lead *by personal example.* Leaders must painstakingly follow the rules they want to see implemented. They may take privileges in other areas, but they must observe the basic rules, as otherwise they will lose *credibility in their organization.* Once they violate this principle, it will be their leadership position will start eroding.

True Leaders Do without Alibis and Excuses

They are interested in results, and when they fail to achieve them they do not resort to lame excuses and justifications. This is a good point for establishing where persons in history have failed. Their leadership positions started showing the first cracks when they began to operate with alibis and excuses, or with scapegoats and conspiracy theories. Techniques like these may work for a while, but they carry the seed of failure and of a loss in credibility and in power of persuasion. In some situations it may take quite a while for the failure to become fully apparent, but it usually starts with the leader *no longer being authentic* and *honest.* Many kinds of political maneuvering may be tolerated or even admired as a sign of particular intelligence and smartness – but not fudging with regard to this aspect.

True Leaders Accept Their Own Meaninglessness in Comparison to the Task

Let me clearly emphasize this: in comparison to the *task* – not to other *people.* Leaders are well aware of their importance, and they let others feel it.

As much as, in one way or another, a *personality cult* may be associated with leaders and sometimes demanded and built up by those around them, even against their will – they themselves *subordinate* themselves *to the task*, which they always consider to be greater and more important than themselves. This is the *only* way of maintaining *objectiveness*, despite and particularly in view of the uniqueness of a leadership situation, to obtain a clear picture of the situation. They *accept* the task in all its significance, but they do not *identify* with it. The task always remains something they clearly separate from themselves as persons. This, too, is a point where many historical leaders have failed. Once the *"L' état c'est moi"* attitude took hold, a particularly *glamorous period for the* person in question may have set in, but in most cases this was also the *beginning of the end of leadership*.

There is something else which is even more important: by accepting their own insignificance in relation to the task, true leaders are able to muster the necessary bravery and moral courage when it matters most – when they have to choose between the task's significance and correct execution and their own careers. In case of doubt, they will sacrifice their careers for the cause. That is what gains them other people's respect, and it is a major source of their *power of persuasion*. Those around them see that they are not primarily interested in their own concerns but in the good of the cause – to such an extent that they risk their own personal failure to serve that cause. There is not much more a person can throw into the ring, and when he does, it is a very clear signal to others that he *means* what he says. He displays *personal integrity*.[85]

One of the best examples is General George Marshall's behavior toward President Roosevelt. One of the instances[86] in which Marshall defied the President almost to the limit of what was acceptable to him may serve to illustrate my point: A few weeks after having been appointed Chief of Staff of the United States Army, Marshall attended a meeting with the President as well as several other members of government and high-ranking military officers. Until then he had not met the President very often. Roosevelt, who had a soft spot for the Air Force but knew little to nothing about it,

85 See also my book *Managing, Performing, Living. Effective Management for a New Era*. Frankfurt am Main/New York, 2006, part II, chapter 5.
86 See Cray, Ed: *General of the Army. George C. Marshall, Soldier and Statesman*, New York/London, 1990.

laid out his ideas about its expansion. Marshall saw that Roosevelt's plans would lead straight to disaster. After the President had talked at length about the Air Force and its equipment – but, in Marshall's view, at a level of superficiality that was almost irresponsible – he turned to the meeting's participants and asked each for his opinion. Everyone agreed with the President and, with polite reserve, found a few nice words. Finally Roosevelt asked the Chief of Staff what he thought about his suggestions. With a sharp undertone in his voice, Marshall replied: *"Mr. President, I am sorry, but I don't agree with that at all."* Roosevelt stared at Marshall in silence – and abruptly ended the meeting. Marshall had obviously committed a fatal error by the way he interacted with the President – so fatal, indeed, that the then Treasury Secretary, Henry Morgenthau, who was also present at the meeting, in leaving said to Marshall: *"Well, it's been nice knowing you."* In his eyes, Marshall's career was over before it had started.

But this was exactly how General Marshall won the respect and trust not only of the President but of everyone else involved in the issues of warfare. This, among other things, was what made Marshall one of the best and most uncontested leaders of the 20th century. He had the courage to fight for the cause even if it could mean the end of his career – which he proved many times in the course of his life and which was one of his most outstanding character traits. It also speaks for Roosevelt's leadership qualities that he did not put an end to Marshall's career.

True Leaders Give their Best for the Organization, but Not Their Lives

They constantly strive for perfection and – I repeat – they give (almost) anything *for the cause*. They demand, both of themselves and of others, the *greatest performance* and the *highest standards* – they do not *offer* anything but *make demands*. They know it is the performance of the organization which creates pride, respect, and self-respect, and this is why they expect the most from people's performance. And although they occasionally have to demand others' lives – literally or in the figurative sense – in special situations, they do not give their own, unless they are *forced* to do so. So there is a difference between leaders and martyrs.

True Leaders Do Not Steal Their People's Achievements

Despite all their successes, and despite their deep belief that they can do many things better than others, true leaders do not take credit for other people's achievements. They think in terms of "we", not "I". They know what their people and their organization have accomplished, and they *acknowledge* it. Success in a *matter* is more important to them than *their* success as an individual.

True Leaders Are Not Afraid of Strong People

This applies with regard to both superiors and subordinates. True leaders know that it takes the *best people* to fulfill the great tasks of the organization, and they will do anything to attract, develop and deploy the best people. They may take harsh, possibly even brutal action against any attempt to question or undermine their *authority*, but they do not eliminate strong people merely because they fear for their own authority. Anyone who surrounds himself with weaklings, protégés and stooges, hermetically sealed off from any criticism, shows *sure signs* of *weak* leadership.[87] True and strong leaders are outright allergic to yes-men. They want honest and controversial opinions, even though it may happen that they respond with resentment and gruffness.

It is not as if leaders *like* to hear criticism. Rather the opposite, as is the case with most people. So they are likely to respond gruffly to criticism. However – and this is what matters –, while a *fake* leader ignores and usually suppresses it, a *true* leader – no matter what his emotional response may be – *takes notice* of it, which does not mean he will always accept it.

The episode I recounted above about the relationship between General Marshall and President Roosevelt vividly illustrates this point.

---

87 Some of the dramatic difficulties major corporations have found themselves in resulted from the failure of top executives in this point. Several times over the past years this has included a big name in the automotive industry. Although the public rarely becomes aware of such management deficiencies, they are the talk of the day in the company itself and among the immediate associates of the person concerned.

True Leaders Accept the Heterogeneity of People

Not only do they accept it, they turn it into an *opportunity*. They focus on what people are *capable of*, and are often tolerant of their weaknesses. They do not seek to be popular. The strengths it takes to cope with the task are almost the only thing that matters to them. Whatever they may be like in dealing with other people – humorous, easy-going and jovial or strict, prim, and unapproachable – these are not essential aspects but superficial ones. What matters is the task and the results achieved – and as tolerant as they may be with regard to people's different ways, they will be adamant when *performance, results*, and the associated *values* are at stake.

True Leaders Do Not Have to Be Inspiring Individuals

A consistent demand in literature and discussion is that leaders must be *inspiring* people, capable of instilling *enthusiasm* in others. In my opinion this is more than a fallacy – in truly critical leadership situations, enthusiasm is actually an *obstacle to true leadership*. Anyone demanding of leaders the ability to enthuse others is obviously thinking of *positive* and *easy* leadership situations. True leadership, however, is only necessary and called for when it comes to dealing with *difficult* situations calling for unpopular, tough decisions – decisions which demand serious sacrifices but are clearly right. Anything that people can *basically* be excited about does not require true leadership; usually, brilliant rhetoric will do. Leaders may have to take *tough* decisions and demand superhuman commitment of people. In situations like these, they need to be *convincing* – but enthusiasm would nearly always be counterproductive.

Typical cases in point are orders to retreat after lost combat, the troops having been decimated, or business situations in which tens of thousands of people have to be laid off. Only cynics and sadists could muster enthusiasm for such measures, or attempt to enthuse others about them. It is the most depressing things in an organization that require truly difficult leadership decisions. Nobody can take such decisions enthusiastically, and if he did, he would immediately lose the trust and loyalty of those around him. People would succumb to his factual power – but they would not follow his "leadership".

Churchill did not display any enthusiasm when, during the most critical phase of the Second World War from the British point of view, he had to demand the greatest sacrifices of the British people. But he managed to convince people of the need for this sacrifice. He appealed to their sense of duty, their endurance and their willingness to make a contribution, but there was nothing to be enthusiastic about in this situation, and nothing would have been more inappropriate than an attempt to create enthusiasm. There was an *obligation* to be fulfilled.

True Leaders Are Not Utopians

They may have a vision – or better still, a *mission* – but they are not out to create heaven on earth. Rather, they concentrate on avoiding hell. True leaders are *realists* with regard to *human nature* and they make an effort to learn from history. They know that, all the fascinating utopian philosophies notwithstanding, it is impossible to create the New Man – all that can be done is to alleviate the misery in the world, step by step and very moderately. In their public relations work, they might operate with a *touch of utopia*, as they know about people's fascination with such concepts. In their *actions*, however, they go by what they know about the risks of each intervention in a complex social structure, and about the unintentional side-effects of even the best-intentioned changes. They know it is *impossible* to make utopia come true.

True Leaders Are Neither Born Nor Made That Way

If they are neither born nor created as leaders, what are they? They are nearly always *self*-made, and the way to do that is always the same: There are *four* elements which are important: The *first* is the situation a person is in. It may be a historically important situation which will find its chroniclers later, or it may be an everyday situation that will find no mention in the history books. It is a matter of coincidence, for hardly anyone can choose the situation that provides a chance – or the burden – of displaying true leadership.

In this situation they recognize, *second*, the *crucial* task which is critical for *changing* the situation – whether it is the solution to a problem or the grasping of an opportunity. This is where the much-vaunted property of vision may be considered to apply; in the majority of cases, however, it is not a transcendent or creative spark that brings a vision to life, but simple yet *careful thinking through* the options and priorities.

Third, they uncompromisingly face up to this task. The situation and the task may be as significant historically as were Churchill's after years of a meaningless existence as a back-bencher, or it may be as mundane as that of a mother devotedly nursing her sick child, night by night, until the crisis has passed. In both cases we have all elements of true leadership. The value that historians attribute to each situation may differ. The *value attributed by people* is always the same, as *Viktor Frankl* has made clear.[88]

Fourth, they take *responsibility* for this crucial task. There is a well-known quote by Harry Truman: *"I am president now, and the buck stops here."* What we wanted to express was that it was up to *him* to complete the task and make the decision – he could not delegate this job to anyone.

Charisma

Last but not least, I will outline a few ideas on the subject of "charisma." The call for *charismatic leaders* in business and society is ubiquitous and marks one of the greatest weaknesses of current leadership zeitgeist.

Charisma is a *dangerous* subject. The 20th century was the century of charismatic leaders par excellence: *Hitler, Stalin*, and *Mao Zedong*. Should we not be wary of them? Should we not deal with the subject more prudently? Are 50 years of distance (less, in the case of Mao) enough to erase from memory all the horrors?

Charismatic leaders have regularly caused *disasters*. Only few of them were lucky enough to have a boss who *prevented the worst*. Field Marshal *Montgomery*, one of the most charismatic military leaders of World War II, is one example: his superior, Churchill, understood the effect he had on people and repeatedly prevented disasters. For instance, he never supported him *against Eisenhower*.

---

88 Frankl, Viktor: *Man's Search for Meaning and the Question of Meaning*, Washington, 1984.

Perhaps Churchill was aware of the evaluation which Montgomery, when he was as a young lieutenant in British India, had gotten from his superior, the gist of which was: "People will follow Montgomery wherever he will go; but I suspect it will be out of curiosity and not out of confidence."

Montgomery was a daredevil, a hero, who would attack at the head of his troops "with his sword drawn". A character like this has an impact on people, he intrigues them – and they will rally around that person. But they do so out of curiosity, not because they trust him. Leaders like that have a *crowd of followers* because they are where the action is. True leaders have a *following* because people have confidence in them.

I do not deny the *impact* of charisma on people, nor that there are persons who possess that kind of charisma. But the crucial thing is not *whether* or not we forge ahead but *where* to; not *whether* we are led but *where* we are being led. This is the point where so many misunderstandings occur. The impact that leaders have is important but it has to be controlled through the *kind of goals* set and through *accountability*. This is also why the considerations I put forward in the chapter on corporate governance, as well as the goals and parameters I describe, are so important.

Unlike Montgomery, some highly effective leaders of the 20th century had no charisma whatsoever. They include such famous names as Dwight D. Eisenhower, George C. Marshall, and Harry Truman in America or Konrad Adenauer and Kurt Schumacher in Germany. And in the 19th century there was probably hardly anyone with as little charisma as Florence Nightingale, Abraham Lincoln, or Henry Dunant. All these people are prime candidates for the accolade of true leadership, though in very different fields. They led by self-discipline and personal example, not with grand slogans and battle cries. *Their capital was not charisma but trust.*

Charismatic leaders are *dangerous* because they do not observe any rules; they are unpredictable; they believe they can control the universe, they pursue utopias; they think they are always right; they tend to get rigid and thus to be on the wrong track pretty soon. They are not *leaders* but *misleaders*.

It is quite possible that charismatic personalities can *also* be good leaders, but they are exposed to great dangers and temptations. *They are always a risk.*

Chapter 5

Power, Responsibility, and Liability

Top-level management positions always involve a wide range of powers. In large organizations, their power is multiplied by the resources available to them. Top management power is therefore often a subject of criticism, and at regular intervals it inspires all kinds of conspiracy theories. This power, however, is necessary for companies to accomplish something, which is why I will not make any suggestions here on how to limit the power of top management. Rather, my considerations refer to the *distribution* of *relative* power between the two top management bodies.

Power as such is *not* a problem. The problem is its *abuse*. This is why power has to be *controlled* and accounted for at all times. There are numerous ways of controlling power, as I hope to have shown before. But what about the *accountability* for it?

Responsibility and accountability are a matter of *ethics*. I am not referring to grand philosophical concepts but to something much simpler – a kind of everyday ethics. In essence, it means accepting responsibility for whatever one does or fails to do. There is hardly a management symposium or a speech held by top people without the responsibility of management being addressed – often in very grave words. But as important as the subject of responsibility may be, I prefer speaking of "liability". What are managers *liable* for, and in which way?

At one such symposium of senior managers, with two full days dedicated to the topic of management responsibility, I addressed the gathering: *"We have now spent two days talking about responsibility. But what are you actually liable for?"* Apart from a few irritated comments, the general response was uncomfortable silence. The conclusion then drawn from the ensuing discussion was: *"We are liable for our reputation in society."* Well, in view of the scope of top management power, I think this is not very much.[89]

---

89 The negative image in the media does not do justice to top management reality.

Duty of Care Is Not Enough

I am not talking about the liability for criminal acts which is anchored in the different legal systems, nor a violation of duty of care regulations. We have laws and enforcement authorities to take care of that. What I am referring to is a liability for the *quality of management*, for conscientiousness of action and correctness of decisions, for fulfilling the organization's business mission, for the productive use of resources, for innovation performance and the creation and maintenance of competitiveness – in short: for *fulfilling the entrepreneurial task*. It is certainly possible for someone to fulfill his *commercial diligence* duties, yet fail in his *entrepreneurial* role.

This issue casts the spotlight on the *entrepreneur*. In most companies today, entrepreneurial behavior is one of the key things demanded of people. Managers and employees are expected to become entrepreneurs, or if they cannot possibly be, at least to be "intrapreneurs". Numerous, often large-scale, training programs are dedicated to this purpose; evaluation and incentive systems are aligned with it. But will these actions create entrepreneurs?

Entrepreneurs and entrepreneurial behavior are often emphasized, praised, and rated much too highly. People usually have a particular *personality type* in mind: the creative, daring, visionary pioneer. There are people like that – but it is a mistake to generally view entrepreneurs as the "shining heroes" of business. There have been all kinds of personalities among the entrepreneurs, just as there are among people in general. In truth, there is no common feature in their personalities. Some correspond to the ideal type, others are far from it.

There is only *one* single element which entrepreneurs have had in common throughout history, and which actually *defined* them: it is the element of *liability*. An entrepreneur is a person liable for his own decisions, to an *unlimited extent, in solidarity with everything happening in his organization, regardless of fault or blame and with all his assets.* For many years, entrepreneurs and their families were even liable with their freedom and their lives. The consequence of their failures was not an escape from responsibility through the bankruptcy of a legal person, but debt bondage.

Now we shall not and cannot turn back the wheel of history. There are good reasons why the modern incorporated company with limited liability has emerged as a legal entity. However, as important and even indispensable it certainly is, its *consequence* is that the entrepreneur has been replaced by the manager. Managers are not liable; at least not in the same way. They may be particularly capable and bring plenty of expertise to the job; they may be high-ranking and earn an income which former or current entrepreneurs can only dream of. But they are still employees. Even the CEO of a global group is a salaried employee. He works with other people's money; the consequences of his decisions first and foremost affect other people's assets; all the more so as probably every top manager today has an employment contract ensuring him a most secure and comfortable existence as well as generous severance and retirement benefits.[90]

No doubt, being liable with one's social reputation, along with the risk of not being reappointed or even being dismissed, *does* have an effect. However, it is impossible under German law to replace a board member simply on grounds of his incompetence. Even a supervisory board member will hardly be removed for that reason. Rather, there will be an "amicable separation" in such cases, as mentioned before. And while the business community will know what is going on, making it difficult for the person concerned to obtain another, equivalent position, severance benefits often make the problem too easy to bear.

The most important point, however, is this: when tens of thousands of people are dismissed due to management failure, it will be difficult to explain to them why no one from the executive or supervisory boards has had to step aside, and it will be equally impossible to explain why, once a board member does have to resign, he is rewarded with a generous severance package. The issue here is not so much the money as what the gesture *signals* to people. Over and over again they will feel confirmed in their belief that it is always the "little people" who suffer, while the "big shots" get away with everything.

---

90 Under the influence of the shareholder value principle, this has partly changed. Variable income components prevail. Hence managers do bear a personal risk, yet they are still not liable for their actions. Moreover, the share of mismanagement due to purely monetary incentives has dramatically increased. Severance pay continues to be common practice.

The Issue of Liability in an Employee Organization

The emergence of the legal person has created what one could call the *employee organization* – an organization characterized by a *lack of liability*. It is still a relatively recent development. Although the predecessors of the entity with limited liability as an organizational form of business enterprises go back as far as the 17th century, it took another long while for the majority of people actually to work in corporations. Life took place in the family, on the farm, in small handicraft businesses. Today, nearly everybody is an employee of an organization. The resulting problem of a loss of liability, as well as the potential loss of responsibility associated with it, seems to have gone unnoticed by most.

Almost everything a manager needs for the job can be taught. Responsibility cannot. It can be demanded and appealed for. But ultimately it all boils down to a *decision* which everyone *personally* has to make, to take responsibility for one's actions. Contrary to the appearance created by the media, the majority of executives act in this way, freely taking all due responsibility in doing their jobs. Upon close inspection it turns out that it is all a matter of upbringing.

But there are also others who shirk their responsibility in the crucial moment, using all routes of escape that exist in every company, particularly the large ones. They act according to the motto: *I have made a mistake but I would be stupid to take responsibility for it.*

In view of the range of power associated with senior management positions, the question is whether it is enough to rely on those who freely assume responsibility, or whether many of them could also be strongly tempted to take an escape route when the crucial moment arises. One also has to ask whether liability should not be integrated in top management positions *constitutionally* and *unavoidably*, as difficult as this may seem.

I do not claim to be able to solve this problem, but I believe that in the long run society cannot function without responsibility. Here, the same point applies that I have made elsewhere in this book: current solutions, both for corporate supervision and for responsibility, will be viable as long everybody's standard of living improves from year to year and there is more and more wealth to distribute, so that social tensions can be alleviated by an increase in material wealth.

But what will happen when that is no longer possible, when many will be excluded from prosperity, perhaps even slip through the holes of a welfare net that can no longer be financed? Is it not likely that these people, provided there are enough of them, will then ask the question of responsibility in an entirely different way? Might they not forcibly demand that this liability be settled? And would it therefore not be a wise precaution to think about possible solutions to prevent such developments – which I consider anything but improbable – and to reduce potential exposure to them?

As difficult as it may be to solve the problem of how executives' responsibility and liability can be anchored constitutionally – if we dedicate to it just a fraction of the intelligence that has been invested in developing the welfare state, we will be able to find viable solutions. Incidentally, this is not only a business problem. Although we still know much too little about how to deal with this issue in a complex society, the task is clear: *Blocking any routes of escape from responsibility and liability for the leaders of societal organizations.*

As much as we have to respect people who take on responsibility *of their own free will*, our search must focus on *system design* solutions. Systems need to be designed in such a way that responsibility is built into them. Leaders should not be able to avoid responsibility; this should be the inalterable price for attaining a senior management position – as it always has been for entrepreneurs.

Every company can basically find its own solutions. A major share of their design and implementation will naturally be in the hands of the supervisory body. For reasons of equality of competitive conditions, it may be concluded that certain matters should also be ruled by legal provisions.

Groundbreaking Examples for Liability Regulation

Some examples of company-specific regulations do exist. They concern those companies where executive board members are expected to be personally liable partners, and anyone refusing to accept this liability cannot become a member of the board.

Another model concerns instances in which top managers receive part of their income in the form of company shares or options (with shares being preferable from the point of view of those concerned) – but only if their sale is subject to considerable waiting periods. Preferably, permission to sell papers of this kind should only be given several years after the person owning them leaves the company – that is, only after the effects of their decisions have started showing in the company's financial results. The risk associated with this solution is that successors, in turn, may take different and wrong decisions. Another risk is that the stock market development, irrespective of the company's own performance, negatively affects all stock prices, as is the case in bear markets. As everyone knows, the high tide lifts all vessels, including the scrap ones, while the falling tide takes all of them back down – even the best ones. However, subsequent corrections to option prices must, of course, be excluded.

Another solution could be to make retirement and severance packages conditional not on past but on future business success. For instance, half of the pension due to a top manager could be subject to renegotiation, of which the first could take place, say, three years after his retirement from active service and the second perhaps five years later; alternatively it could simply be tied to the cash flows achieved by then.

Solutions of this kind force managers, *first*, to focus on the future; *second*, to apply a longer-term approach; and *third*, to be liable for their entrepreneurial action with their own money. The aim of such solutions is not to enable a claim for damages on the company's part. The amounts involved would generally be too small for that. Rather, the intended aim is to ensure absolute *diligence* in the execution of managers' tasks, as well as the *quality* of their decisions. These suggestions aim at closing the loop between decisions and their effects and consequences for the decision-maker's property and income. A person will take decisions differently if his own money is at stake and any lack of diligence directly affects his financial situation.

I have often witnessed how top managers and their staff take decisions of key significance for the company's success with remarkable superficiality – too often, indeed, for me not to take these issues very seriously. I have even experienced cases – though rarely – where board members said, right in front of their staff, that they would never have agreed to a certain decision if their own money or business had been at stake. This can hardly be considered a role model for good management.

Some may object to my suggestions, arguing that they make it more difficult to find a sufficient number of capable people. This does not necessarily have to be a disadvantage, for a top manager unwilling to take these risks – which are accompanied by considerable opportunities – is likely not to be the best for the company. Perhaps he does not believe in his own capabilities; in any case he is not prepared – for whatever reasons – to back his belief with liable assets. In that case, the question is whether he should be given responsibility for other people's resources and for the people themselves.

The regulations described above would have a positive effect on the selection mechanisms for leaders, as well as on their personal ambitions. If potential and would-be leaders were aware that a managerial post would inevitably involve a considerable degree of responsibility and liability, many would refrain from aiming at such positions, which would not be a bad thing for society. Others would get better prepared and educated, and deal with the requirements of a management position more thoroughly.

Yet another counterargument is that the dynamics of a business would be reduced because the executive body, under conditions of liability, would no longer be willing to take any risks with innovations and investments. This seems plausible at first. On the other hand, there are enough examples among fully liable entrepreneurs of risk-taking and innovativeness.

A society which fails to resolve the questions of control of power, responsibility, and liability, or does so poorly, will run into considerable difficulties before long with regard to the quality, effectiveness, and credibility of its leaders. These difficulties can go to the very roots of a free and lawful society, to the point where a relapse into forms of society believed long gone – such as the anarchic or totalitarian kind – cannot be ruled out, as the examples of the formerly communist countries or the corrupt societies of Latin America, Asia, and Africa show.

Chapter 6

Selecting Candidates and Filling Top Positions

Both the overall management of a company and the way in which the two top-level bodies function – that is the basic proposition of this book – have to be governed *constitutionally*. It must not be left to the discretion of those involved to decide what the tasks are and how they are to be executed. In the final analysis, however, the work has to be done by people. Selecting them is therefore absolutely critical, however well thought-out the corporate bylaws may be. They have to be brought to life on a daily basis, otherwise they will become a worthless piece of paper; they have to be interpreted, applied to the specific situation, and, above all, implemented.

Four Risks in Top-Level Personnel Decisions

Filling key positions in an organization, in particular those of the executive body, requires maximum care – a point that hardly needs stressing. In practice, however, this care is often lacking. Although it is difficult to say from an outside perspective how the filling of positions is prepared and executed in detail, the results give cause for doubt.

Quite a few of the personnel decisions made since the mid-1990s with regard to top-level business positions in the German-speaking world were *wrong* – and could have been recognized as such beforehand –; others turned out to be wrong in retrospect, and a sizable share at least warrants some skepticism. Instructive examples also exist in politics. One of the main reasons for the partly disastrous policies of John F. Kennedy was his alarming lack of diligence when filling government positions. "Sloppy" is a rather mild expression when comparing his approach to the conscientiousness with which Truman made his decisions. The former Federal Chancellor of Austria, Bruno Kreisky, may have been a great statesman and expert on foreign policy; the vast majority of his personnel decisions, however, were downright disasters.

The quality of personnel selection for the executive body lies wholly and solely in the hands of the supervisory body. It has unlimited powers in this respect and bears full responsibility. But the *impact* of the supervisory board's personnel decisions goes far beyond the executive body. Its members and the way in which they are selected determine how *all other* personnel decisions in the company are made.

Personnel decisions are *an organization's ultimate means of control.*[91] Everything stands or falls with them. This is why senior, competent managers dedicate a major share of their time to staffing issues – not only when they are directly responsible for the HR department. Alfred P. Sloan, who was at the helm of General Motors for 36 years, dedicated up to half of his time to personnel decisions, and he got personally involved even in those concerning relatively low hierarchical levels.[92]

Staffing decisions and everything that pertains to them – selection, promotion, transfer, demotion, and dismissal – determine, first, the *performance capacity* of an organization. All other resources – machines, money, computers, etc. – have their significance, but the key factor driving performance is *people.*[93]

Second, staffing decisions are the true linchpin of *corporate culture.* No matter what programs the organization may carry out to foster and change its culture – if there are discrepancies between these programs and the personnel decisions taken, people will go by the latter. If the two elements contradict each other, even the best and greatest programs will evaporate in thin air, and may even be perceived as a higher form of cynicism. Staffing decisions are the *main source* of frustration, of inward and outward resignation, of agony, bitterness, and cynicism.

---

91 This is how Peter F. Drucker put it several times in his publications, as well as in personal talks.

92 From a "motley bunch" of bankrupt pioneer enterprises, Alfred P. Sloan turned General Motors into the largest manufacturer and also one of the most profitable companies worldwide in his time. It was not without reason that Drucker referred to him as *"The professional"*. See also Drucker, Peter F.: *Adventures of a Bystander*, New York, pp. 256 et seq.

93 In pure knowledge organizations, and increasingly in the knowledge functions of the industry sector, it is exclusively people.

Third, personnel decisions involve the *greatest risk* because they are *difficult to rectify* and therefore have a *long-term impact*. That is particularly true for decisions regarding the company's top, as well as key positions in divisions and subsidiaries. Also, personnel decisions send the *strongest signals* because they are visible to everyone. They cannot be kept confidential. Many other decisions are not really of much interest to, or understood by, the bulk of the workforce. Bad decisions regarding other matters can often be concealed, if necessary. Failed investment decisions or innovation projects are rarely of interest to all employees. They may attract attention while they are ongoing but are gradually forgotten. Not so with staffing decisions. They are of interest to workers, media, and the public, and when they are wrong everyone will be reminded of them on a day-to-day basis.

Fourth, whoever fails here will run the risk of losing his organization's *respect* – apart from the problems he creates for himself. How often can a supervisory board make mistakes in filling top executive positions, let alone that of a CEO, before everyone starts doubting its competence? How often can the executive board afford to make the wrong choices when staffing management positions in divisions and subsidiaries?

Yet I do not know of any useful studies focusing on the quality and success of staffing decisions. It seems we are largely dealing with *uncharted territory* here. Based on many years' experience and discussions with executives at all levels I daresay, however, that no more than a third of all personnel decisions are good decisions overall – that is to say, of such high quality that even after years people say, *"this is or was the right person for this position."* Another third is good enough to live with; the last third are downright wrong. There is no other field in which success rates – or rather, failure rates – like these would be tolerated.

In this context, it is striking that there are people with an excellent track record in this respect, and who – although or perhaps because they had to make a lot of personnel decisions – have only made very few bad ones in their lifetime. We can learn from them.

Examples include Alfred P. Sloan and General George C. Marshall, and in Germany, Hermann Joseph Abs, the long-time CEO of Deutsche Bank.

When Marshall took office on September 1, 1939, the US Army was approximately 200,000 strong and its officer corps was hopelessly aged. At the end of the Second World War, the country's armed forces boasted about 10 million people and the best management elite that has ever existed in America – before or since. Most personnel decisions, down to the level of division commander, were either taken by Marshall himself or he had a significant say in them. In Germany's post-war business sector, not many top-level positions were filled without Hermann Joseph Abs being involved at some point. In addition to his achievements as a banker, this was another major contribution of his to the success of post-war reconstruction.

When hearing about examples like these, most people's spontaneous response is that these were particularly good *judges of character*. This is a popular myth and a delusion. The reasons for good personnel decisions do not lie in good judgment but in the disciplined application of a series of *principles* as well as a simple *method* – or in other words, in the way in which these people approached their decisions in personnel matters.

Below I discuss the key aspects of this, not only with reference to candidates for the executive body but in a more *general* sense, referring to the whole company and all management levels – and fully aware that only the executive body is a *direct* responsibility of corporate supervision. The comprehensive perspective, however, is justified due to the indirect and transferred effects; it is even necessary because the overall quality of personnel decisions, whether good or bad, has its origins in the supervisory body.

Seven Principles for Good Personnel Decisions

1. The *first* principle is that nobody is a judge of character. Stated clearly, this principle evokes surprise and resistance, which is all the more reason to take this maxim very seriously. Of course there are people with better insight into people's personalities than others – usually because they have interacted with others more and had to make or participate in more personnel decisions. But precisely these people whom one would believe to have considerable judgment capabilities make a point of adhering to this principle. They do have good judgment but they *do not rely on it*. It is a sign of their very competence that *because of* their experience they know how misleading first impressions and intuition can be. The risk involved in staffing decisions is too big to base these decisions on *perceived* certainty.

2. The *second* principle refers to how mistakes in personnel decisions are dealt with. Not many people can claim never to have made a poor personnel decision. What matters more, however, is how one reacts when

a mistake becomes evident. An obvious and frequent reaction is to blame the other person – the person one has selected and who is now failing. Experienced people repress that impulse. They act according to the motto, *"I have made a bad decision – now I have to correct it."*

This is why the famous Peter Principle, about everybody being promoted to the level of his incompetence, is unacceptable. In fact, it is only a convenient justification for a lack of diligence in personnel decision. For every failed individual in a top-level position there has to someone else who put him there, and that person – not the one who was promoted – has to take responsibility.

3. In the lives of top managers there will always be situations in which they have to make *fast* decisions. This should not be the rule but it is necessary sometimes. Personnel decisions – and this is the *third* principle – must *never* be made in a rush. Quick personnel decisions nearly almost are *bad* personnel decisions. Due to the reasons for the significance of such decisions, their duration, their prejudicial and signal effect, staffing decisions – in particular for senior positions – must be taken with all the care, diligence, and thoroughness that imaginable. This will take up some time, so one will have to make the time.

4. The *fourth* principle is never to entrust a person that is new to the organization with a critical task that is equally new to the organization. New and critical tasks may only be given to people whom the decision-maker knows and whom he can judge. People he does not know yet must be given other assignments which the organization is familiar with.

A breach of this rule – which occurs remarkably often – means facing up to an equation with two unknowns, and thus taking on incalculable risks. One unknown is enough. If the task is new, at least the person who has to solve should be known. The decision-maker can estimate what that person's reactions and behavior in critical situations will be; he knows what he can and cannot expect of him; he is familiar with his strengths and weaknesses. On the other hand, if the person is new to the organization, nothing is known about him despite all the analyses and clarifications done beforehand. But if at least the task is known, others may be able to help in critical instances.

In most cases it is possible to adhere to this principle. It hits a brick wall, however, when top positions must be filled with candidates from *outside* the company. This is usually one of the riskiest situations of all, which should be avoided as far as possible.

5. The *fifth* principle is closely linked to the fourth. Really difficult positions should be filled with the best people. At first glance this is so obvious that it does not seem worth mentioning. Reality teaches us otherwise, though. In many corporations the best people are found in the headquarters, instead of where results have to be produced, and working in established home markets rather than new emerging markets.

This point is most evident when looking at globalization efforts. As a general rule, the people heading local organizations in other countries were not sent there based on their capabilities and experience but because they volunteered. Volunteering, however – as much as it ought to be valued –, is not the same as competence. Many operations in Asia have failed or had limited success because management did not have the courage or strength to entrust the best people with this difficult task. Those who have taken it on – for whatever reasons – are confronted with the best people the target countries have to offer, be they customers, politicians, or competitors. Even if these counterparts are business partners, it is not advisable to have them work with second or third-rate managers, as they may perceive this to be an offense.

6. The *sixth* principle is to grant people the right to be managed competently. When someone is put in charge of other people, their *fate* will be in his hands. Poor, incompetent, or corrupt management has caused more harm than natural disasters or diseases. So the *highest* standards are just good enough when it comes to putting people in charge of others.

"A soldier has a right to competent leadership" was an old adage even back in Julius Caesar's time, and for all we know he took it to heart. But to this date, two thousand years later, this right has yet to be included in the Charter of Human Rights – which is remarkable in a world where 95 percent of all people have a boss.

7. In general, but especially when it comes to filling senior positions, there is the tendency to fall into a *trap* – that of the universal genius. People go looking for the "accomplished personality", the "multi-talent", the "all-rounder" and "generalist". That is understandable and almost inevitable due to the variety of tasks at the top level. It is also a mistake – and a trap. The *seventh* principle therefore is: *There are no universal geniuses.* They are fiction – a myth. They can be *described* but not *found.*[94]

---

94 This subject is dealt with in detail in my book *Managing, Performing, Living. Effective Managment for a New Era.* Frankfurt am Main/New York, 2006.

Human beings have strengths and weaknesses. The greater their strengths, the greater and more serious their weaknesses will usually be. There are certainly people who have more experience or more capabilities than others. And they may be better suited for certain positions than others. But even they have their fortes and their shortcomings.

Having accepted that fact, some people fall into *another* trap, which is the opposite one: They select the candidates with the *least shortcomings* – the "well-rounded personality". While the former mistake results in a quest for the *impossible*, the latter leads straight into *mediocrity*. The secret of every successful organization does not lie in its "universal geniuses", nor in its "well-rounded personalities". It lies in people with *extraordinary strengths* – with exactly the strengths that the organization, in its specific situation, needs to be successful. Unfortunately, they always occur in conjunction with considerable weaknesses. For many managers, this principle is remarkably difficult to follow. They find it hard to accept and adhere to.

Methodology of Personnel Selection

So the key to good personnel decisions is not excellent judgment, nor does it lie in psychological tests, in reports from graphologists, or indeed the services of astrologers and clairvoyants, to whom recourse is made more often than one would think. Nor is it in assessment centers, which cannot be used for top-level positions anyhow.

Of course, professional assessment methods can and should be used wherever possible; they do have significance. They cannot, however, replace a personnel decision as such. Their main value is in recognizing and weeding out *unsuitable* candidates quickly, but they usually do not help to find the *suitable* ones. To do so, a method is required – basically a simple sequence of steps which one should follow systematically and carefully; the more so, the more important the vacant position is.

The steps described below are appropriate for filling positions with either *internal* or external *candidates*. In terms of methodology, I suggest *not drawing a fundamental distinction* between the two. However, when positions are filled with people from the organization, their *state of information* will be better. They will also be *better* known, and this knowledge will be more *reliable*. Some of the steps I am suggesting will therefore be simpler and easier in this case, but not basically different. As for the fundamental question as to whether candidates for key positions should rather be recruited inside or outside the organization, I will deal with it at a later point.

1. Think Through the Assignment

The first step is to thoroughly and diligently think through the task associated with the position in question. This is something *much more comprehensive* and *entirely different* from drawing up the usual job profile. For it is these profiles which – in particular when outsourced to executive search firms – lead into the "universal genius" trap.

The key question should not be: What are the requirements of this position? But, rather differently: What are the specific tasks to be faced in this position in the foreseeable future? Or: What exactly is the assignment that this person will first and foremost have to fulfill?

This relates to an aspect which is usually neglected: There is a difference between "position" and "assignment". It is not that difficult to describe the position of a general manager, an executive board member, or a CEO in *general* terms. Any lawyer can take from his word-processing system a pre-formulated model contract comprising the key elements. As a consequence, such contracts may differ greatly with regard to *terms and conditions* or *severance regulations* but not in the description of tasks, which is why they are quite vague in this respect.

So this first step must focus on capturing very precisely the *task* to be done, *not* the job requirements. The position may be called "Managing Director" or "CEO". But will the assignment be to continue managing a prospering business? Or to manage a turnaround? Will the business grow under its own steam, or will a targeted acquisition strategy have to be pursued? Will there be innovation surges to be managed? Will there be strategic alliances? Does the business face profound restructuring?

Depending on the answers to these questions, the company will need very different strengths in its top-level positions, and a very different combination of strengths in each of them. It is almost impossible for one person to be equally suited to all situations. People who are good at managing "business as usual" will probably fail in a period of massive restructuring; managers of acquisitions and managers of alliances are two different breeds.

The ideal would be to be able to exchange at least some of the people in key positions depending on the situation. In reality this will hardly be possible, so one will always have to accept compromises. But the possibilities associated with each replacement can and should be exploited. It is a window of opportunity.

As a note in passing, military organizations are much more flexible in this regard than are business ones. They are certain to use a different division commander depending on whether a division is to be set up and trained, led into battle, or to be reestablished after a defeat. Centuries of experience and many bad decisions are good teachers. The major advantage of an army, and what enables it to make these decisions, is a pool of equally trained people who are known to have learnt their trade. On this basis, specific and situation-related strengths can be used. Business organizations do not or barely have this advantage.

2. See Several Candidates

The emphasis is on "several". This headline may sound trivial. It seems to be an obvious thing to evaluate *several* people before a decision is taken. Not so in real life, though. While this step is usually made when positions have to be filled from outside the organization, it is much rarer when candidates are recruited internally – although it is just as important then.

Crown princes and favorite candidates are put in place early on, which, while not actually *constituting* the decision, will certainly *prejudice* it. The result will be an early fixation on someone who, for instance, has worked with the incumbent for many years or served as his deputy. Or a preference for someone who has recently made particular achievements which one has heard about. Conversely, someone may immediately be out of the running because he has just suffered a setback. All of these are impulse actions, not decisions.

There must be at least *three* or, better even, *five* serious candidates. This criterion is very *demanding* when top positions are to be filled. It is not easy, neither in business nor, for instance, in politics to find three to five people equally suited for a position.

3. Think Carefully About Appropriate Criteria for Assessing Candidates

To do this, the results of the first step must be available. What *specific strengths* does the key task require in terms of professional expertise, experience, and personality? Here, it is particularly important not to look for a candidate that is "good all around" but for what the person can bring *specifically* to the task at hand. The attention must be on the candidates' strengths. What specific capabilities does each of them have with regard to this task? Of course, if any weaknesses are detected – which, incidentally, are much easier than to find strengths – they will naturally lower someone's chances of being selected. But it is the strengths that have to make the difference.

How can one recognize a person's strengths? This is always a difficult thing. Someone's strengths are most easily found in a résumé, but only if one pays attention to something that is almost never mentioned: the *result* so far achieved in a person's career. Based on my own experiences, I find it remarkable that CVs almost exclusively contain a list of *positions* – often impressive and glamorous ones. They do *not* indicate what people achieved there, what results they delivered, what the position was like before and after their term of office. Yet the results someone has achieved in his past career are the element most important for his assessment. In the case of an internal promotion this is not a problem. The person's achievements will be known. With candidates coming from outside, it is not that easy.

Another aspect to be considered is a person's *effectiveness* with regard to his working approach. Even the best talent, the greatest intelligence and the most outstanding skills are worthless if not used. It is not easy to find out how effective a person is. Among other things, one will have to look for things they may seem banal at first and which will probably not be addressed in the first interview. But they have to be kept in mind.

Further important aspects are these: How has this person previously dealt with *mistakes* he committed? Did he face up to them and correct them, or did he try to shirk responsibility? Are there any signs of someone being *afraid of strong people*? That is a clear signal of a lack of leadership. How did the candidate himself go about *clarifying* his new tasks? Of course, many more things will have to be examined. There are checklists for this. Test results can also be useful here.

But the most meaningful pieces of information when assessing a candidate include the so-called *critical incidents*, which I will come back to later.

4. Never Take a Personnel Decision Alone

Personnel decisions for top positions should be reviewed and screened by *several* people. The decision-maker will need other people's opinions, in particular those of people who have worked with one or several of the candidates before.

This fourth step is the phase in which one goes on to obtain *references* – and *not* from the sources which the candidate volunteered. No one in his right mind will provide negative references. But that is no reason to base a decision on the information provided voluntarily. Rather, one will need the opinions of people *not* mentioned by the candidate. These people must be sought – which is the more important, the higher up and more significant the position is. This step has to be formally built into the decision process.

I recommend requesting the references for key positions personally, rather than have them requested. Also, it does not suffice to talk with people who "know" the candidate. Knowing him will not serve the purpose. They should be referees who have *worked* with the candidate before – former colleagues and bosses, former staff, former secretaries or assistants. There are people who, when important personnel decisions are up, go on retreat for several days to solve this task and do not rest until they have found out everything about a person. They use all their contacts to this end.

Having done that, one should discuss all the information at hand with a few trusted others. Perhaps one will have to take the ultimate decision alone then, but other people's opinions should at least be considered.

After a thorough and conscientious application of these four steps, a decision can be made. Or, to be more precise, it must be made now, for there is little more to do. Of course there will still be many "blank spots on the map" of the candidate. It will *never* be possible to know everything one would like to know, and there will never be enough information for what should be a rational decision in theory. On the other hand, within the time usually available for such matters one will usually not be able to gain more information.

After the decision has been taken, many believe the job is done. People truly experienced in these matters, however, take two additional steps which require quite some tact and sensitivity. They are at least as important as the first four steps for successfully reaching a good decision.

5. Ensure the Candidate Truly Understands the Task

It goes without saying that in the interviews with all candidates the position in question and the tasks involved have to be discussed in detail. If candidates are at all competent, they will attach maximum importance to achieving clarity on this point – and if they don't, they should be sorted out. In most cases, however, much has been kept very general. Now it has to be put in specific terms by clarifying the mutual expectations.

There are two points here which are particularly important: The first is to call the newly appointed manager's attention to one condition for his future success which many, even in senior positions, are not aware of: *The same thing that has won him the new position will be an impediment rather than an asset in this new position.*

Let us assume that a marketing manager has been appointed to head a subsidiary company. He was selected because of his particular experience and success in marketing. As head of a subsidiary, however, his role is quite different, for he now has an integrated, entrepreneurial assignment to fulfill. In this example, his marketing skills will not exactly hamper him, but if he continues to behave like a marketing expert he will fail in his new role or enjoy moderate success at best.

The *second* point is to make it very clear to the person promoted how he should behave during the first 100 days in his new position. The worst thing that could happen is for the new incumbent to start his job on January 2, and on January 3 to tell the assembled workforce "what's what." It would be a surefire way – both for the incumbent and for those who appointed him – to lose every ounce of credibility in one fell swoop and prove to everyone that an idiot has been put in the boss's seat. Apart from a downright crisis situation, the first 100 days are a period of learning and getting familiarizing oneself with everything.

This is not one of the more pleasant tasks of the supervisory board, as far as top-level positions are concerned. A certain amount of diplomacy will be needed. It would, however, be a serious mistake not to point out these things to someone before he starts his job, and instead to rely on everything being obvious and clear. If an incumbent nevertheless acts in the manner described, this raises the unpleasant question as to whether it would not be better to quickly have him replaced. That is a difficult thing, and not easy to communicate both inside and outside the organization. However, if it is not done solely for reasons of legal form and appearance, it may well be that the consequences will be all the more disastrous.

6. The Hundred-Day Report

As a final step, executives who are experienced in personnel selection ask the new incumbent to submit a report after the first ninety to one-hundred days. The question he will need to answer is: *After having studied and trained for your new assignment for three months, what do you feel you have to do now in order to be truly successful?*

At this point, the last uncertainties regarding mutual expectations have to be eliminated. It must be known how the new incumbent views the situation, where he wants to set his priorities, how he defines his key contribution, and so on. Perhaps there will be a consensus, perhaps not. Whatever the case may be, one has to be aware of it, and the other person needs to know.

With regard to the "report" mentioned here, it would be preferable to have it in writing; however, this may not always be possible for psychological reasons – although my suggestion is not to give exaggerated consideration to the psychology of senior and top-level executives. They can be expected to have some endurance and be reasonably robust, which should be one of the points considered in the selection process. If it still seems inappropriate to demand a report in the stricter sense, it must *de facto* be obtained by other means, through conversations serving the same purpose.

Succession Decisions at the Top

As already discussed, *all* personnel decisions are important and difficult. The principles and methodology described here are basically valid for all decisions regarding the selection of people. Depending on the kind of position to be filled, they will have to be applied in different ways. For senior and top-level positions, they need to be applied with utmost care and thoroughness, and for the decision on the successor to the top position a few additional aspects should be considered:

This is the *most difficult* decision, and it is the most difficult to correct in case it turns out to be wrong. The only test for success at the top is ... success at the top. There is hardly an appropriate way to prepare for it. Even if someone has occupied very important positions elsewhere and perhaps worked closely with top managers, he will still always have been in rank and file. Particular scrupulousness is therefore required in selecting a person who will be in the *top* executive position of an organization for the *very first* time in his life.

First, it has to be ensured that one is not looking for or getting a mere copy of the man previously at the top. The temptation is great if the top executive stepping down was particularly effective. It makes no sense for a candidate, however, to try to imitate someone else, and it makes even less sense for those having to take that decision. Nobody can permanently imitate someone else and get away with it. The new incumbent has to solve the task in *his own* way – he *should* be different.

Second, one has to be very careful with the long-time assistants or deputies of top managers. While they have the advantage of being very familiar with the situation, the company and the situation in the executive suite, they have helped *prepare* many decisions but never had to *take* a final decision themselves, let alone take *responsibility* for it. Therefore it is important that they have proved their worth in a series of other positions that involved responsibility for decisions and results.

Third, one has to be careful with "anointed crown princes." Very often, they are people who have so far managed to stay out of the line of fire. Maybe they have cleverly avoided doing anything at all, and thus also avoided making mistakes, being judged, and facing up to the realities. In the eyes of the workforce they will never be credible, unless they prove their worth at a later point. People in this category include the protégés of previous top mangers and, in family-run businesses, the sons and daughters of successful entrepreneurs. Selecting a "crown prince" as successor does not serve the interests of the business, nor of the person concerned.

The relatively easiest and safest option seems to be to put someone into the top executive position who has had a comparable position in another organization. That, however, means that, *first*, this person cannot have sufficient knowledge of the company he has to lead; *second*, there may be a competition close that is in the way; *third*, this may – quite dangerously – send the signal that nobody in the organization is considered capable enough for the position.

So if the members of a supervisory body frequently have to appoint a first-timer to the top position, they will have no choice but to keep that person in their sights for quite a while. They may also have to provide plenty of guidance. In addition, it is advisable to make all necessary contractual arrangements to be able to correct the decision should it turn out to be wrong.

One final rule is: The previous incumbent should not be involved in the decision regarding his own succession. Of course he will be heard, and his assessment of a candidate will carry some weight. But he should have no vote in the decision itself. I consider this point to be particularly important when a former chairman of the executive board becomes a member of the supervisory board and, in this function, is also involved in the succession decision. He should voluntarily refrain. After all, no pope has ever been involved in the decision as to who should succeed him, and if there should ever be an age limit for popes, the church should be expected to abide by this rule.

Personnel Decision Outside the Executive Body

To what extent should the supervisory body be involved in key personnel decision below the executive body level, for instance when filling management positions in subsidiaries, foreign country organizations, major divisions, perhaps even critical projects, special assignments, and the like? This is a delicate issue in many ways, for which there may not be a conclusive answer, perhaps not even a single right one.

Decisions for the levels below the executive body should not be *taken* (in the narrower sense) by the supervisory board; but I do tend to think that it should be involved in their preparation by assessing the quality, care, and diligence of the decision process and by controlling it if necessary. It is possible and necessary to make the filling of key positions in a company a process requiring the supervisory body's approval. The law does not rule it out.

A possible objection could be that the executive body will thus be given a means of escape from responsibility. However, this would be true of all matters requiring supervisory board approval, so the argument is invalid. Another argument could be that these things will be very time-consuming for some or all of the supervisory body members, in particular the chairman. Not only do I consider this argument irrelevant – in accordance with the basic tenor of the view outlined here –, I also think that the time spent on personnel issues is perhaps the most important and best-invested resource of the supervisory body. If the decision process is organized accordingly and decisions are prepared appropriately, the time required will remain within acceptable limits, provided one is basically willing to give the supervisory body an active and central role.

Recruitment From Inside or Outside?

Should the executive body and, in a broader sense, the key positions of an institution be filled with people from inside or outside the organization? The answer is: For most organizations, a *mix* will be the best solution for obvious reasons. On the other hand, one should not overlook the fact that in permanently *successful* institutions it is unthinkable to appoint external people to top executive positions, as long as an extended – if possible life-long – tenure within the organization is the only way to obtain a key position.

Even for organizations that basically want or have to be open to appointing people from outside, the emphasis must be on internal recruitment for *substantive* and *practical* reasons. Recruiting more than one fifth, at most a quarter, of key people from outside should normally be neither necessary nor desirable. Radical cures and the infusion of "new blood" are certainly not recommended. If they are necessary, then both the executive and the supervisory body have long neglected important governance tasks. Perhaps this can be corrected by taking a drastic measure; it will, however, always be a consequence of earlier failure and quite risky. One should not be misled by the successful cases occasionally publicized, and which are very rare anyway.

As pointed out above, one of the most important tasks of top management is to develop and retain human resources. The only way to reduce the risk inherent in key personnel decisions to a tolerable level is to prepare a sufficient number of people for senior and top-level management tasks, and to do this in good time – that is, over several years. People have to be educated, shaped, tested, and coached for such tasks.

A trial period of less than five years is too risky in my opinion. Seven to ten years should be enough to get to know a person – provided it is done deliberately and systematically – to the point where a sound decision can be taken even for senior and top-level positions. I am aware that this is in contrast to the current practice of taking short-term and short-lived personnel decisions, particularly in major corporations. I consider this practice to be misguided and wrong. It will pose major problems for the economy in the years to come.[95]

What is a "sufficient number"? You can never have enough candidates for key positions. In my view, the number to be aimed for should be roughly one third larger than the number of positions to be filled.

The suggestions I am making here may seem demanding, even bordering on the impossible. On the other hand, this is about the definitely most important tasks of personnel and management development. It is indispensable for employees considered to be basically capable of filing key and top positions in the institution not only to go through appropriate training, education, and development processes but also to be systematically *monitored* and *evaluated*. The former is usually done today in major business organizations; the latter is far from being common practice. Nor is it covered by staff appraisals and evaluations, which are often treated as a routine and an insignificant ritual.

If you examine more closely what people did who had to make numerous staffing decisions and were quite successful with them, you will often find that they kept a "little black book" in which they noted all their observations. In most cases, the truly critical information was not found in the official files, but in what they had collected over the years. Over and over again they took the time to watch people and test them with increasingly demanding tasks. They also noted seemingly irrelevant things, in case they would need them at some point, and paid particular attention to three things: to the *results* a person delivered in the course of his life, to the way that person dealt with his *mistakes*, and to the so-called *criti-*

---

95 Ever since this book was first published, there have been plenty of cases of misguided personnel decisions for top positions.

cal incidents. The latter are occurrences and behaviors which, in and by themselves, may not really be that relevant, but which, in the combined effect and over time, provide a basic pattern of what can probably be understood to be a person's personality and character. Examples of critical incidents include an overly "liberal" attitude toward the truth, blaming mistakes on others but taking all the credit for achievements, shirking responsibility wherever possible, always seeing people's weaknesses but never their strengths, and so on.

A policy corresponding to the views outlined here will be bound to have side effects, which may not be desirable but will be inevitable. Due to recruitment from outside and the spare capacity of one third, some good people may also be lost – those who did not succeed in getting promoted for mere quantitative reasons, although they were appropriately qualified. One has to stand firm here and make it clear from the outset to everyone involved in the preparations for senior positions that there are no guarantees for careers, but a fair and equal chance for everybody meeting the qualification criteria.

It is particularly important not to permit any systematic disadvantage for certain groups of people, but to ensure that it is performance and results that matter. Some of the most unfortunate developments in business and society have been caused by the fact that certain groups were excluded systematically, irrespective of performance and objective qualifications. Even today such things do exist. There are companies where key positions are open to university graduates only, or to those who have graduated in a certain subject or studied at certain institutions, or to the members of a certain ethnic group, a sex, a political party, and so on, will sooner or later show signs of mediocrity or inbreeding. They cease to be attractive to good people, instead attracting those whose only qualification is being part of a certain privileged group.[96] The result is a systematic negative selection which, once it shows its detrimental effects on the organization and its results, it is difficult to correct.

---

96 State-owned organizations regularly belong to this category.

Epilog

The organized society consisting of numerous, very different organizations, is a rather recent phenomenon. Its beginnings go back less than 150 years, and the phase of its strongest quantitative growth, as well as of its most intense qualitative development, occurred after the Second World War. Thus, today's organizations look back at roughly sixty years of evolution, which is not very much.

The political theories on which today's form of democracy is based have not taken this fact into account. They were not able to because they go back at least 200 years. Social theories, too, have largely ignored this evolution. Even our legal systems stem from a time when we had a different societal structure and different institutions.

The decision and power centers of today's society – and this will *a fortiori* also apply for the society of the future – shape, steer, and control themselves. They have more resources and, above all, more information and intelligence at their disposal than ever before, and in part more than the authorities and institutions which were supposed to determine and control their design and direction, but which have largely become obsolete.

In principle, self-organization and self-control of societal organizations are not only right but, for reasons of complexity, even the only way possible. It is paradoxical and dangerous, however, that there are no useful foundations, no theory, and only a very limited degree of experience to date. Even the business sector, whose degree of organization is still low in absolute terms but very sophisticated when compared to other sectors of society, is faced with a considerable need for change, as I hope to have shown here. The considerations on corporate governance outlined in this book are basically, in an appropriately adapted form, applicable to all types of organizations in all sectors – in education and healthcare, in the charities as well as in the arts and media; for private non-profit organizations and, to a considerable extent, for public administration, at least the non-statutory sector. Not only *corporate* but *organizational* governance in general will be important.

While economic value-added is generated by business organizations, it its still, and to an increasing extent, utilized by the countless organizations of other kinds. It will be interesting to determine how and where this utilization takes place. But this is only the economic view. The more comprehensive question regarding society as a whole, the question as to what constitutes a functioning, healthy society, its leadership, its elites, goals, results, and values, will be much more important. I hope I have left no doubt about that in this book. The old answers have served us well until now, but they are not going to be very helpful in shaping a future that will look quite different. Shaping, managing, and supervising not only businesses, but all kinds of organizations, will play a crucial role in determining what this future will look like.

Appearance and Reality[97]

Uncertainty in the stock markets is growing; and so – though still only small – is the number of people who are slowly beginning to doubt whether it is true what they have been told over the past few years, and have been happy to believe, about the world economy in general and above all that of the US – and whether the economic situation is really so good.

Back in the first Letter for the year 2000 I pointed out that although there is a lot of talk about the so-called New Economy, the arguments supporting it are very flimsy. Even flimsier are the figures that can be put forward to demonstrate what it has actually accomplished. Dramatic proof is now being seen on the stock exchanges of just how little there is to the majority of New Economy firms. Disappointed and angry people have set up websites where the debacle that is taking place is clearly and precisely documented in numbers and reports. In fact, however, the problem is far from being exclusively or principally a problem of the New Economy. The so-called American economic miracle is really only a phony miracle, as can clearly be seen if one bothers to check the figures. Never before have I seen a case where there was such a vast difference between the reality and what the media made of it.

First, however, I will briefly summarize what the usual view is of the American economy: Having struggled through three years of recession in the early 1990s, the US economy began the longest upsurge there has even been in history. In the eight boom years that followed, around 17 million new jobs were created. This brought unemployment down to its lowest level in 30 years. Hand in hand with this went the most vigorous growth in the economy and the greatest growth in profits since

---

97 This is a slightly revised version of a *M.o.M.*® *Malik on Management* Letter first published in December 2000.

the Second World War. Although the economy was running flat out, inflation dropped and went down to its lowest level since the sixties. There was a marked rise in productivity in the old industries thanks to massive restructuring efforts. What is more, America took over the lead in the new high-tech and communications industries, where the highest growth rates of all were seen.

All these achievements led to a steady upward movement on the stock market and to share prices reaching new record levels year after year. The tremendous rises in the price of shares were seen not as an indication of a speculative bubble but as a result of a fundamental change in the economy from an Old Economy to a New Economy, a change fuelled chiefly by investments in entirely new areas for which people had high hopes; above all information technology but also the life sciences. The productivity increases of a kind never seen before have been particularly impressive, along with the continuing restructuring of companies – including companies in the Old Economy sector – combined with small stockholdings due to successful just-in-time management, and also the successes there have been in battling with the budget deficit and getting public finances back to a healthy state. Fundamentally, the US economy is therefore considered to be so sound and productive that though there may be certain slowdowns in growth and, in line with these, certain adjustments to share prices on the stock exchanges, there cannot be any major upsets to the financial system and certainly not a crash on the stock exchange.

That is how America's current situation is being described virtually everywhere in the media. If, however, as mentioned, one gets to the bottom of the figures and looks into the constantly repeated buzzword of "New Paradigm", the picture that is revealed is entirely different.

Growth

As can be seen from the illustrations below, if a long-term comparison is made, the US growth rates are far less impressive than they are generally depicted as being. The 1990s were outstanding neither in terms of increase of the gross domestic product nor in terms of growth in industrial production. There was also nothing very remarkable about the picture shown by the indicator of new orders for durable goods.

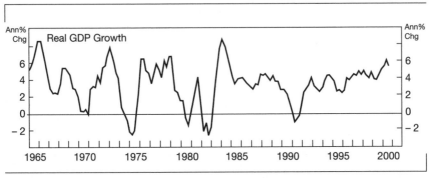

Figure 1 (Source: The Bank Credit Analyst, November 2000)

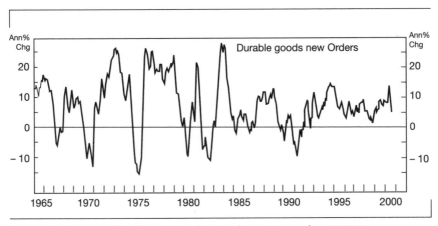

Figure 2 (Source: The Bank Credit Analyst, November 2000)

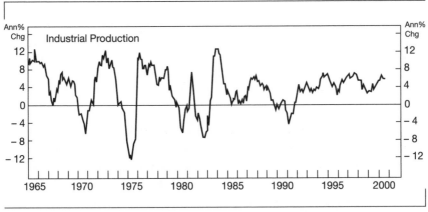

Figure 3 (Source: The Bank Credit Analyst, November 2000)

Even from these long-term periodical statistics it can be seen that what has been happening in America is far from being an economic miracle. The miracle is rather that it could ever have been viewed or misinterpreted as one.

The illustrations shown above still do not show the whole picture, however. A realistic picture of the growth in the American economy cannot be obtained until two further points are appreciated and the appropriate corrections made.

The *first* correction relates to the financial sector. As I have explained on various occasions in my *Malik on Management* Newsletter, the United States does not have just *one* gross domestic product, but *several* of them. At fairly long intervals I have published constantly updated versions of Figure 4 seen below:

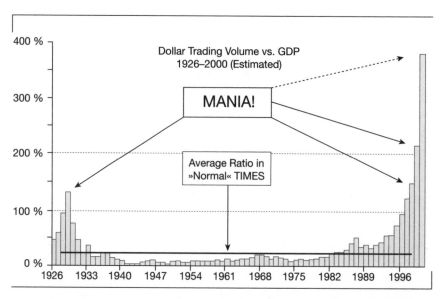

Figure 4 (Source: HD Brous & Co., Crosscurrents, November 2000)

The graph shows the share trading volume as a percentage of the gross domestic product. In plain language, what it says is that, as I have already mentioned, America has not just one gross domestic product, i.e. the one made up of real goods and services, but another three on top of that are the result of share trading. For every dollar that is spent on real goods, cars, shoes, computers and so on, about three dollars are spent on shares.

Each transaction causes fees and commissions to be paid and these become part of the gross domestic product as income in the financial sector. This would be a good thing if it were a normal phenomenon, or in other words something that, by and large, could be assumed to last.

If, however, the picture is considered over a *long* period, there is clear evidence that it is actually an exceptional phenomenon. The last peak corresponded to the bubble of speculation in shares in the nineteen-twenties. It is difficult to think that now, as the true nature of the stock exchange is beginning to be revealed, trading volumes of this size can be maintained. What is more likely is that there is a massive correction in store for the whole of Wall Street and the finance industry, and not just in the US Over the past few years, the majority of banks have been making their profits not from banking business in the classic sense but from business on the stock exchange. This will be difficult to maintain on the scale that has been seen to date; and of the million or so people who are employed in this sector in the US, there will be many who find that their services are no longer required.

The second correction that has to be made relates to the computer sector and to the dubious "creative" way in which investments in information technology are calculated in American statistics. Since 1995, investments in computer equipment have been displayed in the national accounts not simply by stating purchase prices, but – in an attempt to compensate for the dramatic price drop in this sector – by adjusting these expenses for the power of the computers. So in all this time there has been a falsification of the gross domestic product and its growth.

One economist said that this was equivalent to not calculating car sales simply from the prices of the cars but also multiplying the prices by engine power. An example should help to illustrate this further: Between 1998 and 1999, net investments in computers rose from 90 to 97 billion dollars, which would represent a modest 1.3 % contribution to the overall growth in the gross domestic product. However, as computer investments were dramatically boosted by applying a dubious multiplier intended to reflect computing power, a growth of around 7 billion dollars swelled to a massive 150 billion. As a result, the share of computer investment in the growth of the overall gross domestic product went up from 1.3 % to around 49 %. For the first half of 1999 this effect was even more marked. In this case the computer industry would have been responsible for around 90 % of growth to the gross domestic product.

If, however, this multiplier inflating the computer industry's contribution is disregarded, then what is left is a *modest* 2.5 % overall growth. So the question is, how could it be that the computer industry, with a contribution of not much more than 1 % to total employment and with continually falling prices, could be used as evidence of a growth boom? The answer is simple: it is a sheer statistical illusion – but one that is attributable not to an arithmetic error but to a "paradigmatically" new vision of the economy. Or to put it in simpler terms: *they deliberately work themselves out to be richer than they are.*

The same, by the way, is true of the computer industry's contribution to the *rise in productivity*. In a speech he made in 1997 in Frankfurt, *Alan Greenspan* described the figures, which had been established by his own experts, as unaccountable and implausible, and expressed the view that it was possible they had not been gathered correctly.

Profits

Until a short time ago there was a stream of enthusiastic, not to say rhapsodic, commentaries dealing with the enormous *profit-making power* of the American economy. If, however, the figures are considered more closely, this is another case where an entirely different picture emerges. All in all, the growth in profits in the *non-financial sector* in the 1990s was fairly modest. There were earlier decades in which the growth in profits was appreciably higher. This is clear even from the straightforward *official* data.

However, the point where it gets interesting is the moment you take a closer look at the sources of the profits. What then becomes clear is the full extent of the impudence, but also the naïveté which characterizes so much of the coverage of the US economy. The bulk of the profits are actually attributable to extraordinary effects and *creative accounting* rather than actual *operative performance*, something that will also be seen when the subject of productivity is considered later on.

The *temptation* to make profits look as good as possible and to juggle with the figures has probably never been as great as in the past few years. It is clear that the companies themselves and their managers have a vital interest in putting the best possible face on things. It is a question of their personal income, their opportunities for promotion, their prestige and their standing in the community. This interest is exactly the same as that of the entire finance industry of which they are part, and it also lines up with the interests of a good proportion of the media, such as TV stations like CNBC in the US and N-TV in Germany, as well as magazines such as *Business Week, Fortune, WirtschaftsWoche*, and so on.

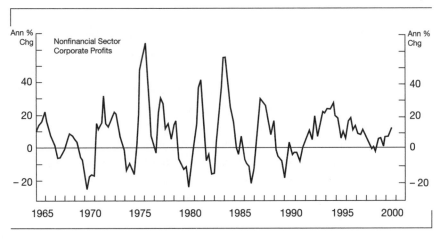

Figure 5 (Source: The Bank Credit Analyst, November 2000)

As long as it was possible to cause rises in share prices by reeling off figures, it was also in the interests of the players on the stock exchange, chief among them the institutional investors. At some time, though, the true facts inevitably emerge.

A crucial factor in the profits that were shown was the stock options that, to an increasingly large extent, were being used to pay managers and employees, particularly in the so-called New Economy companies. In this way, labor costs were kept at an unusually low level, boosting profit. This works as long as share prices are rising, because staff can overcompensate for their poor pay with the paper profits on their options. They feel that they are the ones who are profiting; everyone is an entrepreneur and capitalism is making everybody rich. That indeed was what they were promised. However, when share prices no longer rise but start *falling*, it is the employees who find they have been taken for a ride. In the long run they will refuse to stand for it or will have to be better paid. So, either the workforce leaves or the profits disappear. It was not for nothing that we heard about Amazon employees threatening to strike.

A second factor is companies' *repurchasing of their own shares*. The market and the analysts focus, above all, on *profit per share*. The repurchase of own shares reduces the number of shares in circulation and thus increases the arithmetic profit per share. IBM provides one of the most striking examples. The company bought back around 5 million of its own shares in 1995 and around 6 million in 1996. This helped to achieve an increase in share price of 30 % in 1996. The circulating equity was around 22 thousand million dollars in 1996, 40 % less than in 1990. At bottom, this is nothing but the use of a leverage effect to make the profit per share look better.

A third factor was the fact that the majority of companies obtained *financial earnings* from stock exchange dealings. It did not escape the heads of the finance departments that for a certain period it was easier to make a profit on share transactions than it was on real business. Some time ago even the *Wall Street Journal* featured an article on the fact that firms like Intel and Microsoft were obtaining a considerable proportion of their profits from options on their own shares. This of course has nothing to do with the real *performance* of a company.

Productivity

The popular view is that one of the mainstays of the success of the American economy is the enormous *rise in productivity* that has been made possible and caused, firstly, by fundamental *restructuring*, but secondly, and chiefly, by *information technology* in its role as a key technology. One of the cornerstones of the New Economy philosophy is that economic activity *generally* changes from the bottom up and leads to new types of company and business models – and for this very reason to dramatically improved productivity.

The trouble is that so far it has been difficult or impossible to find in the figures any evidence of the rise in productivity that is constantly being claimed. The more plausible it sounds that information technology is helping to make everything run faster, easier, cheaper and hence more productively, the more stubbornly does this phenomenon refuse to be quantified.

There are two things that can be seen from the following graph: firstly that there have been enormous *fluctuations* in the improvements in productivity since 1960, and secondly that the long-term trend has been for the improvements to *fall*. There is also a *third* thing that can be seen: that, contrary to prevailing opinion, the 1990s were *no* exception to this rule.

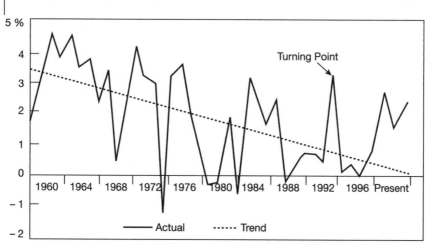

The chart shows annual change in output per hour in the business sector and the trend of the same series, estimated by fitting a linear time trend to the data.

Source: Ecomomic Indicators

Figure 6: Productivity Growth in the USA

Despite the restructuring operations (some of them drastic) that took place, and despite all the investment made in information technology, growth in productivity in the 1990s was only around 2.5 % per year. In the 1960s the average growth in productivity was 4.4 %, in the seventies it was 3.2 % and even in the eighties it was still 2.8 %.

The *true* growth in productivity was confined to the *computer* industry. Here there were in fact two-figure improvements. However, the proportional contribution that the entire industry made to the gross domestic product was so *small* that, all in all, it did not have any significant effect.

What can be seen very clearly here is a phenomenon that has been central to the discourse of the past few years since people began to talk of a New Economy: a part of reality, often only a *small detail*, has been singled out and *blown up* to the point of dominating everything else. This is one of the worst possible mistakes when carrying out an analysis because it is dangerously misleading. It causes one to lose sight of the whole or deliberately to blot it out, so that the detail appears all the larger and clearer. It means that one loses sight of the context – and it is only in context that figures can be interpreted in a reasonable way.

The best analyses of this issue were provided by Professor *Robert Gordon* of Northwestern University. These studies are far from being easy reading, but the conclusions they reach are clear and, more than anything else, refute all the idle chatter there has been about the New Economy, because they start out from the very point at which it ought to be evident what is new about the New Economy: from the enormous productivity increases that have been reported.

Debt

So what it was that actually drove the financial sector in the second half of the nineties and triggered the dizzying lights on the stock exchanges, was neither a real *rise in productivity*, nor real profits, nor real growth. It was just the *illusions* that determined what so-called investors did.

I emphasize this point because it is likely to constitute the crucial *potential risk* for the future. The awakening from those illusions will be rude and shocking to many people because they will be forced to recognize that there was nothing there to provide any firm basis, no solid foundation, but simply an economy showing very normal, not to say moderate performance, contrasted with a collective erroneous belief held for many years that this time everything was different and new and better – and that things would go on like that for ever.

Now it is true that people can fall prey to illusions, but of course that *alone* is not sufficient to drive stock market prices to record heights. Yet there must have been a real factor that was able to produce the greatest bull market in a hundred years. The factors on which public attention was *concentrated* may have been unreal, but what was perfectly real were the driving forces that were *actually* at work: *debts*.

A first factor was *private debt*. There are two main aspects to this: the massive *dis-saving* that US citizens have been indulging in for some years, with a negative savings ratio of about 5 %, and at the same time a build-up of real *property debts* which were mainly due to the Fed's low-interest policy. Due to the cuts in interest rates, 1.8 trillion dollars flowed into the mortgage market, two thirds of which served only to re-finance earlier mortgages.

A particularly important and problematic role in all this was played by the so-called GSEs, the *government sponsored enterprises*, the former government agencies Fannie Mae, Freddie Mac and the Federal Home Loan Bank System. This is not the place to look at the operation of these organizations in detail. Suffice it to say that for every dollar that was spent on building homes, another ten dollars of mortgage debts that made their way, via the GSEs mentioned, onto the capital market and basically onto the stock-market. To put it plainly: people in the US first ran through their savings and then mortgaged their homes up to the hilt to buy shares, confident that there was going to be an everlasting bull market.

The second aspect of America's total indebtedness is *corporate debts*. In the days when the stock exchanges were flying high and there was a steady series of IPOs with shares priced at fantastical levels, only a few people bothered to look at the *debit side* of the balance sheets. Particularly to maintain the prices of the shares issued and thus, as described above, to look after their own stock options and to make the profit figures look good, companies bought up their own shares; and since they could no longer pay for them with their earnings from stock issues they had to borrow money to finance them. Added to this were the parts of acquisitions and takeovers that could not be financed with companies' own shares by way of an exchange of shares but for which, once again, loans were needed. In certain sectors, this led to a process of massive *debt contraction and over-indebtedness*. One such case was the case in the telecoms sector, where the current figures tell a clear story:

In the case of *Deutsche Telekom* turnover is 35.5 billion Euros, profit 1.5 billion, but debt is 62 billion Euros. In the case of *AT&T* the figures are as follows: turnover 62.4 billion Euros, profit 5.5 billion, debt 72 billion. And for *British Telecom* the picture is only slightly better: turnover 36.5 billion Euros, profit 3.4 billion, debt 32 billion. This means that many banks are running a risk, too.

The firms mentioned – and many others that find themselves in a similar position – are now looking to reduce their indebtedness by selling shares in subsidiaries and divisions and floating them on the stock exchange. However, now that the technology-related stocks and shares are in difficulties and the stock exchanges are beginning to spread fear rather than greed, it is difficult to believe that their efforts will meet with much success.

The third main factor contributing to US public debt is its *trade deficit*, which has reached the highest levels in history and for the time being shows no sign of steadying or declining. Other factors contributing to indebtedness are *derivatives* and *margin debts*, both of which are at the highest levels in their history. America's indebtedness has assumed *new guises*. Up until a short time ago it was formed by public debts, but now it is private individuals, companies and foreign trade. Just for the record, even the situation relating to the *national budget* is by no means as reassuring as it is always claimed to be. What is known as *gross public debt* is continuing to rise. In 1999, the net figure (i.e. after repayment of old debts) for public indebtedness was around 521 thousand million dollars. The apparent removal of the public deficit, too, was achieved mainly by tricks of accounting and airbrushed figures, not by any real and substantive action being taken. All in all, the picture that emerges on the debt front in the US is that for every additional dollar of gross domestic product around three dollars of new debt have been incurred.

Germany – Healthier than People Think[98]

The forthcoming elections to the German Bundestag (the federal parliament) are provoking a general debate on the state of the country, and particularly that of the German economy. What has struck me in many discussions is that Germany is in a better state than many people are willing to admit or are capable of appreciating.

There have been times when Germany tended to overestimate itself; today the opposite is true. A good deal of the criticism being leveled at politics and the way things are in the country is justified. There is a lot that needs to be changed. However, this is true not just of Germany but of virtually every country. It is simply that in Germany the debate is conducted more vehemently, more searchingly, and even, sometimes, more doggedly than elsewhere. That does not mean that the debate ought not to take place. It might, after all, have the effect of stopping things from becoming any worse, which would itself be a success.

Complaining about "the state of affairs" is, more than elsewhere, a sort of national pastime among German entrepreneurs and managers. In their heart of hearts they all know that it is one of their duties as

---

98 This chapter is an almost unchanged version of my *M.o.M.*® *Malik on Management Letter* dated August 2002, an abridged version of which was also published in the *Frankfurter Allgemeine Zeitung*, a national German daily. It explains how the German economy is underestimated while the US economy is overestimated. I have neither played down the existing weaknesses and problems of Germany, as some critics claimed in 2002, nor am I doing so now. Still, there can be no doubt regarding Germany's subsequent achievements, and after almost five years of continuous growth its strength is visible to anyone. Of course, this does not suffice to guarantee a prosperous future. By contrast, America's weaknesses had long been visible, even though few people were able to see them.

entrepreneurs, albeit an unpleasant one, to be successful *in spite of* the circumstances. And they have repeatedly managed to be. For decades now, the German economy has again and again shown that, even under *difficult* conditions (often created by politicians), it can be competitive. To some degree, over the past fifty years it has undergone a *continuous fitness training* course under "special load" conditions, first in the form of the reconstruction problems after the war, then in the form of adverse exchange rates because the Bundesbank was making the Deutschmark a hard currency, then due to high wages and the cost of the welfare state, then because of the belligerent unions or the burden of Reunification, and finally because of European integration, for which Germany has had to foot much of the bill while other nations have reaped the benefit.

Owing to these circumstances, people time and again had to look for the opportunities hidden in the problems, and indeed have found them. They have also discovered that, in essence and when considered over fairly long periods, their economy has been *more productive* and *more capable of solving problems* than that of *any* other country.

Misleading Comparisons

Justified though the criticism leveled at politics may be, the evident obsession with it involves a risk: another danger – one that is *intrinsic* to the economy and possibly *greater* and one that has hardly been debated as yet – that is in danger of being ignored. I am talking about what I, somewhat provocatively, call the *Americanization* of the German economy and German corporate management

It is the adoption of supposed formulas for success of American origin in the fields of economic policy and management. Chief among these is that theory of corporate governance which focuses on shareholder value, with all the *disastrous* consequences this inevitably has: concentration on the short-term, purely monetary thinking, dependence on stock exchanges and stock exchange pundits, personality cult, susceptibility to corruption up to the point of white-collar crime, hostility to investment and innovation, and the assets-eroding strategies of profit maximization and what is referred to as value creation. This can all be seen in the USA today and cases of it are increasingly becoming a matter for investigation by US prosecuting attorneys.

The obsession with misguided comparisons results in German *strengths* being overlooked or disparaged and hence being left unexploited. It also means that companies are entering into a competitive struggle that they will find difficult or impossible to survive, not just because it is governed by the *rules* made by others but also because it has to be fought with the opponents' *weapons*.

Contrary to common opinion, the adoption of American ways of thinking and methods is to only a small extent imposed by market forces; to a greater degree, it is happening voluntarily in the conviction that it provides the key to success.

The main argument driving Americanization is the apparently outstanding success that the American economy has been having over the past ten years, which is unanimously felt to have been far beyond anything that could be compared with existing standards, together with the conviction that this success was caused precisely by the very ways of thinking and methods that corporate governance proposed. Both these things, the supposed success of the US economy and the presumed reasons for it, are based on misjudgments of a magnitude seldom encountered anywhere else. There is no reason for either admiration or imitation.

I cannot summarize the position any better than I did in the analysis I made of the US economy in December 2000 and I will therefore, if I may, repeat what I said then: *Having struggled through three years of recession in the early 1990s, the US economy began the longest upsurge there has even been in history. In the eight boom years that followed, around 17 million new jobs were created. This brought unemployment down to its lowest level in 30 years. Hand in hand with this went the most vigorous growth in the economy and the greatest growth in profits since the Second World War. Although the economy was running flat out, inflation dropped and went down to its lowest level since the sixties. There was a marked rise in productivity in the old industries thanks to massive restructuring efforts. What is more, America took over the lead in the new high-tech and communications industries, where the highest growth rates of all were seen.*

All these achievements led to a steady upward movement on the stock market and to share prices reaching new record levels year after year. The tremendous rises in the price of shares were seen not as an indication of a speculative bubble but as a result of a fundamental change in the economy from an Old Economy to a New Economy, a change fuelled chiefly by investments in entirely new areas for which people had high hopes; above all information technology, but also the life sciences. The productivity increases of a kind never seen before have been particularly impressive, along with the continuing restructuring of companies – including companies in the Old Economy sector – combined with small stockholdings due to successful just-in-time management, and also the successes there have been in battling with the budget deficit and getting public finances back to a healthy state.

The US economy was therefore considered to be basically so sound and productive that though there might be certain slow-downs in growth and, in line with these, certain adjustments of share prices on the stock exchanges, there could not be any major disruptions to the financial system and certainly not a sharp drop, let alone a crash, on the stock exchange. If the worst came to the worst, or so people continued to think until well into 2001, there would be a "soft landing" and a steadying at a high level, a pause before further and lasting upward movements. In principle, people mistakenly imagined that there was no longer any such thing as the economic cycle. Still typical of the prevailing view is what MIT economist R. Dornbusch said in June 1998 in the *Wall Street Journal*: "*The US economy likely will not see a recession for years to come. We don't want one, we don't need one, and, as we have the tools to keep the current expansion going, we won't have one. This expansion will run forever.*"

America apparently had the strongest economy in the world and in history; all the other economies were far outclassed and there was no end in sight. It was, therefore, no wonder that the logical conclusion, which was as natural as it was convincing, should be drawn: *Do what America does and you will be as successful as America.* There is only one flaw in this conclusion: *it is wrong!*

Deceptive Appearances

The so-called American economic miracle was a *phony miracle*. It never happened. It was a *media event* and that was it. What actually happened was the *opposite* of a miracle, namely an inexorable slide into disaster, as can now be seen.

There was no extraordinary growth or high profits, no rise in productivity or any readjustment of the public accounts. It was not a miracle of economics but of disinformation, comparable in nature to that in the 1920s. What the New Era was in the first twenty years of the twentieth century, the New Economy was in the last twenty. Lazy journalists could copy their headlines straight from the old volumes of the *Wall Street Journal* or the *New York Times*.

Even in their published form, American *growth rates* were in no way higher than they had been in earlier periods, as any long-term comparison with the era since the Second World War will show. There had repeatedly been growth rates of the kind recorded in the nineties, both in the USA and elsewhere.

Yet even these figures, which are actually not particularly impressive, require massive *correction* if the aim is to get at the true facts. Once this is done, the outcome is that in non-monetary terms there was more or less *zero growth* in the American real economy in the 1990s, due amongst other things to the greatest *lack of investment* since the Second World War.

Only in two areas was there any growth: firstly, in the *financial sector*, though in a form which, as was apparent from early on, could not be maintained. At the same time, this growth led to a massive *misallocation* of resources. The result that this in turn is now having is that all the financial institutions require drastic restructuring, a process that will not be completed for a long time yet.

Secondly, there was also growth in the field of *computers* and the associated peripherals and software. However, in the first place, this sector is far less important than it is made out to be in the media, given the less than 10 % contribution it makes to the national product, and, in the second place, there was also the fact that this growth was massively inflated by the statistical effect of so-called "hedonic price indexing", which in some years boosted it by a factor as great as 20.

There is no other country in the world where statistics of this kind are applied in this way. The result is that the USA publishes statistics that paint a rosy picture of itself, whereas other countries give figures that are a true reflection of reality – hardly a good basis on which to make comparisons. The authorities responsible have now begun to make *retrospec-*

tive downward corrections to the figures, though nobody is taking any notice of these, of course.

The consideration that led to hedonic price indexing was, it is true, *statistically* valid, but it was an atrocious piece of *economic* thinking. Prices in the computer sector are continually falling, but the power and performance of computers are constantly getting better, so people imagine that the contribution the sector is making is not being correctly expressed if, as is usual in economics, it is factored into the national product at selling prices. It was thought that it should be corrected upwards by a factor that expressed the power of the computers. The result was as follows: from 1995 to 2000 investment in computers in the US economy in fact rose from around 23 billion dollars to 87 billion dollars. However, the trick of hedonic price indexing turned the quite modest 23 billion dollars into a fabulous 240 billion dollars – but only in statistical terms, because this did not produce a single extra dollar of factor income.

If Germany had calculated like this, then IT investments over the last ten years or so would have grown not by the 6 % actually shown but by a tremendous 27.5 %. At a single stroke, it would have marked the change from a developing country in IT terms to one that was the mega-super high-tech leader, and it would never have occurred to anybody to think of Germany as technologically inferior to the USA.

Another statistical effect that gave the illusion of a boom in growth and investment resulted from the decision to stop treating computer software as an operating cost and instead to capitalize it and treat it as an investment. From 1995 to 2000, this produced the mathematical effect of 110 billion dollars' worth of growth. Nobody in Germany has ever come up with such an absurd idea.

If the rates of growth are cleansed of these effects, then, as mentioned above, the result in the non-monetary economy is zero growth. It is only on this basis that useful comparisons can be made between Germany and the USA and, in this way, Germany shows up as a good deal better than the USA, and in important respects considerably ahead of it.

Nor was there ever any productivity miracle, except in the small sector of computer *manufacture*. Professor Robert Gordon of Northwestern University has been one of the few clear-sighted analysts of the published figures for productivity. As he has shown, there was not then and is not now any quantitative evidence to support the claims that were made for a general rise in productivity. In the main, the supposed advances in productivity are attributable to the national product being shown at too high a figure – due to hedonic price indexing.

Not only is there no significant growth in productivity to be recorded but also – and this is far more serious – the statistical illusion of a *boom in investment*, with its effect on the stock exchange of raising share prices, concealed the fact that in reality there is the exact *opposite*, namely a marked *lack of investment*. Net fixed business investments have fallen to their lowest level in the postwar era. This is the main reason for the *implosion of profits* that became apparent in the USA in 2001 but had started well before that.

The seemingly fantastic American *profits* that were shown were mainly due to creative accounting, massaging of the balance sheets and artful disinformation rather than to any real economic output. They arose *first* from the questionable practice of not showing stock options in the accounts, combined, on the other hand, with the resulting tax benefits being shown on the income side. *Second*, they arose from expenditure on software being capitalized instead of being written off at once; *third*, they arose from the artificially low *salaries* that the stock options produced; *fourth*, they arose from the sometimes cavalier way that *goodwill* was treated, being far too high and, in fact, simply reflecting enormously inflated and, in some cases, absolutely insane purchase prices but representing bogus assets that were totally unproductive; and, *fifth*, they arose from maneuvers on the financial markets, including *share buyback programs*.

It has now emerged that many companies were "shaping" their profits to a more than creative degree and beyond the limits of what is legally permissible by, amongst other things, the remarkable way in which leasing deals are treated in their accounts. As well as other tricks, the NASDAQ 100 companies, for example, reported *profits* of 18 billion dollars to the public for 2001 whereas the same companies had to report a *loss* of 82 billion dollars to the SEC Securities and Exchange Commission, the regulator of the US securities markets. The whole world believes the figures it sees in the media, but nobody bothers to look at the SEC files.

To make the profit-per-share figures look more attractive, companies were buying back their own shares with their own shares. But this could not be done by paying with one's own shares, as was practiced with mergers and acquisition. Hence, buying back the shares now called for *real* money, so companies put themselves in debt in order to be able to keep on satisfying the expectations they had themselves created on the stock exchanges. Today, *US corporate debt* is at an all-time high of 156 % of the national product and is thus almost 50 % higher than it was 10 years ago.

Despite what was claimed and what the media propagated all over the world, the *stock market boom* was not based on real value-added but, as any bull market of this magnitude must be, on *greed* and *debt*, and in this case on the perfectly organized, systematic *misinformation* of the public by the companies, working in conjunction with the Wall Street industry.

Hence, the so-called New Paradigms have in no way led, as has been claimed, to the economy becoming transparent, but to the *opposite*. Under pressure – produced by the companies themselves – from ever greater expectations on the stock exchanges, new, so-called *pro-forma profit figures* were constantly published. Their only purpose was to factor out, on very flimsy grounds, items on the expenditure side.

All of this was not only covered up by acquiescent auditors, corrupt analysts and stock exchange pundits, but driven by devices that were always risky – a fact which has now, as everyone knows, become the subject of investigations by the US Attorney General's Office and the Securities and Exchange Commission; even the President can no longer ignore it because there is the risk of politically damaging indignation among the American people. As a result of the euphoria in connection with the stock market, the savings and pensions of two generations of Americans have been "invested" in risky stock market securities. In 2001 alone, around 5 trillions dollars were lost, or around half the national product. It is quite possible that, for the first time in the history of the USA, this will create a serious social problem. Back in 1997, in the first edition of my book on effective corporate governance[99] (*Wirksame Unternehmensaufsicht*), I drew attention to the advent of a new hostility to business, for it was obvious that the true enemies of capitalism were not its declared opponents, but its strongest proponents.

In addition to corporate debt, another component of the US economic miracle is the exorbitant *indebtedness* of all the other sectors of the American economy and particularly of *consumers*. The savings ratio, which at the beginning of the nineties was still about 8 %, had dropped to less than zero by the end of the decade.

---

99 The third edition of this book, entitled *Effective Top Management,* was published by Wiley in 2006.

Nor was there ever any such thing as the much-lauded American *budget miracle*. The indebtedness of America's public sector continues to rise and is higher now than it was at any previous time. Like company profits, the surpluses shown by the federal budget, for which the US have been admired all over the world since 1998, are the result of *accounting tricks* and did not arise from any real achievement. Since 1998, the reality has been not a total surplus of 710 billion dollars but, in fact, deficits amounting all in all to 1,644 billion dollars, or, in other words, an overall difference in the negative direction of 2,365 billion. And that is without two other factors that have not been mentioned yet, namely the *debts of the federal states and the municipalities as well as the foreign trade deficit*.

In 2001, national income rose by around 178 billion dollars. Debts on the other hand increased by a total of more than 2 trillion, of which 1.1 trillion was in the non-financial sector. Debts are thus rising *ten times* faster than the national product.

The horrendous increase in credit is going into *three areas* which generate no national product and no productive investments: into *imports*, into largely unproductive *expansion strategies* taking the form of mergers and acquisitions, which are not productive net investments, and into *financial speculation*.

Most American figures for the economy over the last five years have been *incorrect* or incorrectly *interpreted* and were *propagated* by the media with increasing effectiveness. This steered people's actions in the wrong direction, which in turn led to a massive *misallocation* of resources. Now that the illusion of a steady upward trend in economic activity has had to be abandoned and the first slumps on the financial markets have had to be coped with, this is leading to a need for massive corrections, a process which will take time and claim victims.

There is, therefore, no reason to take America as the yardstick by which to ascertain Germany's weaknesses. In the light of the facts, it is remarkable how admiring, almost worshipping, even seasoned entrepreneurs and managers have been in taking the US economic miracle as a standard for comparison in order to show Germany's plight in as dramatic a light as possible. Equally remarkable, and in fact dangerous, is the naïveté with which American management, American education and training, and American management philosophy are being imitated by managers and recommended by – once again American – consultants in the belief that they were the cause of an economic miracle.

Advantages Despite Negative Developments

The German economy, like the economies of many other countries, is marked by the aberrations resulting from the illusion of a never-ending boom, although to a far *smaller* degree than the American economy. As mentioned above, much of the damage is due to the uncritical adoption of American management practices and particularly of the corporate governance theory, with its orientation towards shareholder value.

The damage and weaknesses that have arisen in the economy are at least as severe as the disadvantages that have been caused by errors or omissions in German politics, and they should be discussed and criticized just as thoroughly. Changes can be made much more quickly here than in politics, and the effects will be felt much sooner.

Quite justifiably, the policy currently being pursued is viewed as flawed by the business sector. It does, however, have the approval and support if not of a majority then at least of a large part of the population. With the business sector it is a different story: in the event of economic aberrations, there are never majorities or even significant minorities but, quite to the contrary, even demonstrations of militant opposition.

The *social climate* in Germany is marked by a new belligerence on the part of the workforce; this is a signal that has to be taken seriously. The unions may be basing their demands on misapprehensions and incorrect arguments, but they will certainly have all the emotions on their side when people realize that the same CEOs who were talking so big up until recently were really only concerned with their personal gain and not, as was their duty, with the fate of the company. When managers' bad decisions lead to tremendous financial losses, dismissals, decisions on the fate of German employees being taken by corporations based abroad, multinationals not paying any taxes, and when managers, regardless of their horrendous mistakes, leaving the company unscathed or even with a golden handshake, then there will hardly be a way of restoring the corporate world's credibility.

In a *media-informed society*, any undesirable development in the business sector can be seen and felt by everybody. It does matter much to public perception that these problems occur with just a few people and only in certain parts of the sector, above all in certain major corporations, whereas the segment of *small and medium-sized businesses* – which is much *larger* in terms of value-added and employment – has been affected much less or not at all by the aberrations and excesses of the boom years.

Small and medium-sized companies have had almost no media exposure over the past few years. Media reports focused on the "powerful groups" and on corporate CEO's with their "airs and graces" on the one hand and on the New Economy firms on the other. Neither of these is as representative as the attention they received would suggest. Yet, because they did attract attention, they were considered to be representative.

So, even though the consequences of mistaken corporate management need to be taken seriously in Germany, too, the German economy is nevertheless in a state which not only bears comparison with the USA but is even healthier in essential aspects. If there have been any economic miracles, then one of them has certainly taken place within the German *automobile industry*. In the early 1990s, a majority of German carmakers were in a bad, sometimes even terrible state. Japanese manufacturers seemed to be unstoppable in penetrating the markets worldwide, and, depending on the category of vehicle, were on a par (or close) in terms of quality and engineering; in terms of costs they were clearly superior. They were putting the fear of God into US and European car makers. VW was deep in the red, its productivity between 25 and 30 percent lower than that of the competition. Daimler-Benz had, in a matter of ten years, been pushed into an unspeakable policy of diversification by its CEO, Edzard Reuter; and Porsche, with its obsolete models and out-of-date production facilities, was facing demise.

Ten years or so later, Germany has the *best* automotive industry worldwide. Japan has suffered as severe a setback as the United States, the Scandinavians have sold out, the Italians, premium brands aside, are leading a marginal existence, and where the French are headed is yet to be seen. Remarkably, there has been no Americanization of management at the German car manufacturers (with one exception). Criticism by stock market analysts is a nuisance to them but of no significance, and they pursue long-term strategies placing an emphasis on sustainable innovation. Occasional risks of being taken over by foreign groups are taken seriously, but the response is different and more astute than that of, for instance, the telecommunications sector has been. Something similar has been accomplished in the European *aircraft industry,* under the strong guidance of German players. The overwhelmingly dominant position the US still had ten years ago has been almost totally reversed by the success of Airbus. It is all the more to the credit of the industry that it is capable of containing its internal power struggles. And there are many other industries, such as mechanical engineering and parts of the pharmaceutical industry, in which Germany's accomplishments are quite respectable.

It is quite likely that over the next few years the German automobile industry, just like its counterparts elsewhere, will also face problems, that it will also have to report poor results and extensive layoffs. However, it will face the problems of the world economy from a position of *strength*, and any problems will not alter the fact that major achievements have been made, that the weakness of Japan and America was cleverly taken advantage of, and that the very thing was done that, in strategic terms, is the only possible way to success: *attacking the weaknesses of one's competitors with one's own strengths*. This is the exact opposite of what companies that are Americanizing themselves do – which is to confront the US businesses with poor imitations of that model. Imitation can only work if the imitation is better than the original. Up until ten years ago the Japanese proved this. Germans, however, will never be able to be better Americans than the Americans are themselves. They can only be better Germans – and the outcome will be even greater success.

Exploiting Strengths

The patient is not Germany, but the world economy – and clearly Germany is not going to be spared the malaise. Due to mismanagement resulting from flawed theories of American origin of the 1990s and the misallocation of resources based on it, the American economy, as well as those of most other countries, is in a state that makes a swift and lasting recovery unlikely.

The widespread belief that the economic problems in the US are a short-term phenomenon, a so-called "V-shaped" recession, is likely to be proved wrong for structural reasons. It was the same with the economies of other countries which, for a time, were euphorically and indiscriminately praised and made out to be new paradises. The Asian Tigers and most of the Latin American states find themselves in bad and partly desperate states. One can only guess what things are really like in India and China; there is not much we can really know because the figures are notoriously unreliable.

The belief in the natural and universal superiority of American management practices is just as naïve as was the belief in Japanese superiority, which prevailed from the mid-1980s to the early 1990s. The US economy has strengths which the European economies lack, but it also has its weaknesses. It should be emulated in the areas where its strengths lie. Contrary to popular opinion, corporate governance in particular and management in general are *not* among them. Experienced people realized this from the start and acted accordingly.

For the reasons outlined above, there is not much of a point in complaining about German politics. Entrepreneurs and managers have to accept the fact that a fundamental reorientation is needed. They need to forget about the high-flying ideas of the 1990s and prepare for rather wintry times. A tough, customer-oriented business strategy, uncompromising improvements in productivity, professional innovation management, rigorous elimination of all illusions, boasting, and big-talking in all parts of the company, a sober examination of pompous e-concepts, renewed emphasis on performance and responsibility at all levels – these are likely to be the most important reference points for companies in the next few years. Bluffers and frauds should not get a chance. They had them – and plenty of them – in the nineties. What can and must be demanded again now is real substance.

Competent managers are immune to fads and their thinking is independent of the zeitgeist. They are masters of the craft of management. They set the standards for a new humility and sobriety which can trigger people's willingness to perform – which will be required for this reorientation – much more effectively than the visions and illusions that led to false hopes and expectations.

In many ways, the German economy is better equipped to face this situation than most others. And the demands that will have to be met correspond to traditional German strengths – strengths that can be used immediately, without further ado, rather than having to be built and developed over many years.

German businesses are more familiar with *customer value* and *quality* than most others are. They hold strong *market positions* in important areas; in some cases they are market leaders. There still are *small and medium-sized businesses* which are good or even excellent, and where not the investor mentality but the *entrepreneurial* element prevails. Germans are good at thinking and acting with a focus on the *long term*, at putting up with hard times and at making sacrifices if need be. In Germany there are still plenty of *performance reserves,* which can be tapped if people are given a reason to perform.

Politics can provide people with reasons for making this contribution; but first and foremost these reasons have to be provided by the corporate world, by the bosses at all levels with whom people interact on a daily basis. To achieve this, what matters most is the *example set at the top.*

Bibliography

Albach, Horst: "Shareholder Value und Unternehmenswert"; in: *Zeitschrift für Betriebswirtschaft*; Vol. 71 (2001), pp. 643–674.

Beer, Stafford: *Brain of the Firm – The Managerial Cybernetics of Organization*, 2nd edition, London, 1981.

Idem: *The Heart of Enterprise*, London, 1979.

Bleicher, Knut: *Der Aufsichtsrat im Wandel*, Gütersloh, 1987.

Buzzell, Robert D./Gale, Bradley T.: *The PIMS Principles. Linking Strategy to Performance*, New York, 1987.

Carlsson, Sune: *Executive Behavior*, Stockholm, 1952.

Chussil, Mark/Roberts, Keith: *The meaning and value of customer value*, Online Sheet 02/2007, Malik Management Zentrum St. Gallen, www.mzsg.ch.

Cray, Ed: *General of the Army. George C. Marshall, Soldier and Statesman*, New York/London, 1990.

Drucker, Peter F.: *The Unseen Revolution*, London, 1976.

Idem: *Adventures of a Bystander*, New York, 1979.

Idem: *Managing for the Future*, London, 1992.

Idem: *Post-Capitalist Society*, London, 1993.

Idem: *Management. Tasks, Responsibility, Practices*, London, 1973.

Frankl, Viktor E.: *Man's Search for Meaning*, Washington, 1984.

Gale, Bradley T.: *Managing Customer Value*, New York, 1994.

Gälweiler, Aloys: *Strategische Unternehmensführung*, 2nd edition, Auflage, Frankfurt/New York 1990.

Glaus, Bruno U.: *Unternehmungsüberwachung durch schweizerische Verwaltungsräte*, Bern, 1990.

von Hayek, Friedrich: *The Constitution of Liberty*, Chicago/London, 1960.

Idem: *Law, Legislation and Liberty*, 3 volumes, 1973–1979.

Heinsohn, Gunnar: *Privateigentum, Patriarchat, Geldwirtschaft. Eine sozialtheoretische Rekonstruktion zur Antike*, Frankfurt, 1984.

Heinsohn, Gunnar/Steiger, Otto: *Property, Interest, and Money. Unsolved Puzzles in Economics*, Hamburg, 1996.

Hilb, Martin: *New Corporate Governance. Successful Board Management Tools*, 3rd edition, Berlin, 2008.

Hoffmann-Becking, Michael (ed.): *Münchener Handbuch des Gesellschaftsrechts*, Volume 4: *Aktiengesellschaft*, Munich, 1988.

Jürgensen, H.: *Die Bundesrepublik Deutschland zwischen Wiedervereinigung und Binnenmarkt '93. Wirtschaftsperspektiven für die neunziger Jahre*, Hamburg 1991.

Malik, Fredmund: *Managing, Performing, Living. Effective Management for a New Era*. Frankfurt am Main/New York, 2006.

Idem: *Uncluttered Management Thinking. 46 Concepts for Masterful Management*. Frankfurt/New York, 2011.

Idem: *Management. The Essence of the Craft*. Frankfurt/New York, 2007.

Idem: *Strategie des Managements komplexer Systeme, Ein Beitrag zur Management-Kybernetik evolutionärer Systeme*, 10th amended edition, Berne/Stuttgart/Vienna, 2008.

Idem: *Systemisches Management, Evolution, Selbstorganisation*, Berne/Stuttgart/Vienna, 1993, 2nd edition, 2000.

Idem: *Corporate Policy and Governance. How Organizations Self-Organize*. Frankfurt/New York, 2011.

Malik, Fredmund/Stelter, Daniel: *Krisengefahren in der Weltwirtschaft*, Zürich, 1990.

Martin, Paul C./Lüftl, Walter: *Der Kapitalismus. Ein System, das funktioniert*, Munich, 1986.

NACD – *Report of the NACD Blue Ribbon Commission on Director Professionalism*, Washington 1996.

NACD – *Report on Director Professionalism*, Washington 1996.

Rappaport, Alfred: *Creating Shareholder Value*, revised edition, New York, 1998.

Siegwart, Hans: *Der Cash-Flow als finanz- und ertragswirtschaftliche Lenkungsgröße*, 3rd revised and amended edition, Stuttgart/Zurich, 1994.

Vester, Frederic: *Die Kunst, vernetzt zu denken*, 7th edition, Munich 2001.

Wunderer, Felix R.: *Der Verwaltungsrats-Präsident*, Zurich, 1995.

Index

Buzzell, Robert D. 30, 36

Cadbury Commission 48
Calvin, John 248
candidates 42, 84, 196, 233, 252,
    269–286
capitalism 103, 136, 140, 241, 295,
    308
– corporate capitalism (owner model)
    61 f., 136–138
– corporate capitalism II (corporate
    model) 145–148
– shareholder capitalism 62, 136, 142
– stakeholder capitalism 62, 136
Carnegies, the 136
cash flow 64, 130, 159–161, 163, 177,
    267
Central Performance Controls (CPCs)
    147, 149–162
CEO 22, 39, 41–43, 79, 97, 173, 182 f.,
    230 f., 237, 264, 271, 276, 310 f.
charisma 93, 258–261
Charter of Human Rights 274
China 10, 70, 118, 312
Churchill, Winston 123, 247 f., 259–
    261
Chussil, Mark 30
CNBC 69, 295
commodity market 115
communism 100, 103, 129, 268
competition 41, 63, 117, 161, 166, 176,
    193 f., 222, 228, 311
competitiveness 30, 32, 56, 64 f., 80,
    124 f., 127, 224 f., 243, 263, 302
complex systems 26, 31, 49 f., 136, 171
complexity 24–26, 33, 50, 83, 96 f.,
    105, 121, 156, 171, 202–204, 287
compromise 26, 30, 193, 229, 277
computer industry 158, 293 f., 297, 303
conglomerates 85, 93
consulting 23, 26, 35, 38, 59, 66, 97,
    190, 192, 220–222, 229 f., 309

Coop 47
Cordiner, Ralph 139
corporate culture 26, 39, 42, 93, 159,
    163, 175, 178, 189, 214, 223, 229,
    270
corporate governance
– code 25, 29–50, 173, 176, 184–185,
    192, 194, 201, 240
– history of 34–38, 135–48
– interdisciplinary nature of 85
– single-tier system 35, 51, 173, 181,
    191
– two-tier structure 25, 35, 51, 173,
    181, 218
– wrong 23, 26, 29, 34, 43, 50
corporate policy 26, 31, 39, 50, 85,
    174 f., 180
corporate strategy 31, 36, 39, 60, 63,
    94, 121, 174, 189, 222
corporate structure 39, 42, 121, 224 f.
corruption 34, 176, 192, 214, 216, 274,
    302, 308
creative accounting 60, 66, 71, 294,
    300, 307, 309
credibility 9, 30, 33, 55, 98, 121, 123,
    128, 143, 158, 180 f., 190, 195,
    203 f., 206, 224, 233, 251, 254, 268,
    280, 282, 310
crisis management 31, 226 f.
critical incidents 98, 279, 285 f.
crown princes 277, 282
currency market 115
customer value 30, 32, 45, 62, 64, 88,
    96, 133, 145 f., 151, 313
cybernetics 26, 36, 48, 167, 178, 211
Czech Republic 101

Daimler-Benz/ DaimlerChrysler 42, 59,
    179, 311
de Gaulle, Charles 248
debt 61, 70 f., 104, 106 f., 113–115,
    298–300, 307–309

Fannie Mae 299
fear of strong people 257, 278 f.
Federal Home Loan Bank System 299
Federal Reserve 68
financial bubble 56, 61, 102, 114, 290, 293, 304
financial markets
– collapse of 60 f., 114 f., 144
financial planning 40, 42
financial reporting 42
follow-up 205 f.
Ford 111, 136
France 103, 137 f., 311
Frankl, Viktor 260
Freddie Mac 299
free enterprise 54, 62, 130
French Revolution 103
Fugger group 90
functionality 31, 85, 171, 177, 185, 187 f., 216–218, 227, 230, 238 f.

Gale, Bradley T. 30, 36, 150
Gälweiler, Aloys 60
Gates, Bill 137
General Electric 110, 139, 142, 154
General Motors 111, 270
Germany, 101, 119, 246, 301–314
– automobile industry 311
– economic strengths 47, 133 f., 136–138, 154, 311–314
– executive body 21, 76, 179 f.
– health of economy 241 f.
– legal situation 21, 35, 76, 79, 81, 173, 179 f.
– post-war economy 272
– reunification 302
– social climate 310
– supervisory body 21, 76, 79 f., 179 f., 183–185, 196, 201, 203, 208
– terminology of corporate structure 22
Glaus, Bruno U. 184, 201, 203

globalization 10, 47, 53, 68, 118, 129, 274
Gordon, Robert 71, 298, 306
government sponsored enterprises (GSEs) 299
greed 65 f., 69, 141, 240, 300, 308
Greenspan, Alan 294
gross domestic product (GDP) 105, 110, 290–294, 297, 300
– falsification of 293
– of the USA 291–294
– several GDPs 292–294
growth, 88, 100, 287, 290–309
– size vs. strength 85, 91 f., 146 f.
– trend 297–298
– of US economy 71, 290–298, 303–309

Haniel 47
Hausbank system 137
health of companies 149–167
healthcare system 113, 127 f., 287
hedonic price indexing 71, 305–307
Heinsohn, G. 115
heterogeneity 258
high-tech companies 68, 95 f., 109 f., 290, 303, 306
Hilb, Martin 52
Hitler, Adolf 248, 260
Hoffmann-Becking, Michael 180–182, 196, 201, 208
holding period 44
hostile takeovers 139–141
human resources 126, 135, 177, 220, 222–225, 229, 284
hundred-day report 280 f.

IBM 296
illusions 36, 54, 60, 66 f., 72, 92, 104, 242, 294, 298, 306 f., 310, 313
imports 309
India 70, 109, 261, 312

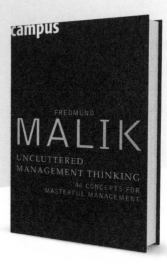